¡Plantemos!

A New Dawn for Hispanic Church Planting in the USA

Hernando Sáenz   **Anna Portillo**, Editor

Copyright © 2022

Cover art: Debbie Sáenz
debbiesaenz.com

All rights reserved.
Published independently through Kindle Direct Publishing.
ISBN: 9798849283487

For questions, comments, and more information, contact us at:
hsaenz@pcanet.org

All Scripture quoted is ESV, unless otherwise noted.
Imprint: Independently published.

TABLE OF CONTENTS

Preface..iii

Acknowledgment & Contributors..v

Foreward..vii

Introduction to the Church Planting Timeline..1

PART 1: PREPARATION STAGE..3

    Chapter 1: *Counting the Cost*..5

    Chapter 2: *Spying Out the Land*..15

    Chapter 3: *Creating a Plan*..16

    Chapter 4: *Stepping Out in Faith*..69

    Chapter 5: *Learning by Example*..75

PART 2: PLANTING THE CHURCH..107

    Chapter 6: *The Evangelism Stage*..109

    Chapter 7: *The Discipleship Stage*...117

    Chapter 8: *The Worship Stage*...123

    Chapter 9: *The Leadership Stage*..135

    Chapter 10: *The Church Formation Stage*......................................145

    Chapter 11: *The Reproduction Stage*..155

PART 3: PRACTICAL MATTERS..161

    Chapter 12: *Practical Steps for the Mother Church's Growth*..........163

    Chapter 13: *Recruiting and Raising Up Hispanic Church Planters*...169

    Chapter 14: *Practical Ways to Support the Church Planter*............175

Chapter 15: *Practical Considerations Regarding the Ordination of Spanish-Dominant Pastors*..181

Chapter 16: *Realistic Budgets and additional funding Strategies for Hispanic Church Planting*..189

CONCLUSION..199

APPENDICES..201

Appendix A: *Preparation Ministry Ideas*..................................203

Appendix B: *Tools for the Demographic Study*..........................205

Appendix C: *Networking, Outreach, and Evangelism Ideas*..........207

Appendix D: *Church Planting Proposal Outline*........................209

Appendix E: *Assessment Center Categories and Questions*............211

Definitions of Key Terms..215

Resources..217

Notes..221

PREFACE

¡Plantemos! is packed with everything you need to navigate the extreme complexity of Hispanic church planting in the USA. Through arresting vignettes, step-by-step instructions, contextualized church planting principles and timelines, we will equip you for planting among the largest minority in the USA: Hispanics.

It's high time for a tool like *¡Plantemos!* In 1998, driven by love for Hispanics and a passion to equip pastors for effective ministry among them, Dr. David Moran wrote his "Manual for Church Planting Among Hispanic Americans." Demand from the field for more information motivated Dr. Moran to revise and expand his manual in 2003. Since then, church leaders from many denominations have benefited enormously from his insights. However, the urgent need for a new type of church planting resource – one with up-to-date case studies, written from a Hispanic perspective, with plenty of *Sabor Latino* (Latin flavor) – was obvious and galvanized us into action.

Our passion with *¡Plantemos!* is to accelerate your ability to reach, equip and mobilize Hispanics for the gospel. As soon as you turn the first page, you'll know this is not your typical simplistic church planting book. The parade of insights from practitioners and creative ideas will warm your heart, educate, and inspire you.

The three-fold aims of this book are bold and exciting. First, it will help church planters and their sending organizations apply the principles of the seven stages of church planting to measure their progress and to persevere in exciting church-planting adventures. Second, we desire that it will equip church planters to write well thought-through and compelling church planting proposals. Third, we believe the principles in this book are transferable to other cultures and may help create church-planting movements in them.

We all want God to get the glory and see the Kingdom of His Son grow beyond our wildest imagination!

– Rev. Hernando Sáenz
MNA Hispanic Ministries Coordinator

ACKNOWLEDGEMENT & CONTRIBUTORS

Church planting is the best of times and the worst of times! It is one of the most challenging ministries anyone can attempt. Failure is common and discouragement lurks at the door. Yet those who succeed declare how incredibly rewarding it is.

¡*Plantemos!* is earthy and compelling, rather than academic and theoretical, thanks to a distinguished list of contributors. The contributions from so many – from new and experienced; from first-, second-, and third-generation Hispanic leaders and church planters; from small towns and big cities spanning our country from the West Coast to the East Coast – are the strength of the book.

One clear compelling voice was needed to coalesce the many contributions into a coherent project. Through prayer, God granted a gifted editor who brought it all together: Anna Portillo (M.Div., MABS).

Anna's editing work in ¡*Plantemos!* is what the soccer world calls a *golazo* – a goal so beautiful and skillful that it thrills the team's supporters and awes the opposition. Her editing skills and love for Hispanics shines through on every page. Incredibly, she edited ¡*Plantemos!* after giving birth to twins at the beginning of 2022, plus raising two toddlers, supporting her husband in his church plant, and getting COVID. ¡*Plantemos!* would not be what it is without each contributor, but we are especially grateful for Anna's labor of love.

Our prayer is that this book may help churches and organizations send and support church planters like never before and make church planters feel equipped and confident in their calling.

Project Manager:

    Hernando Sáenz, *MNA Hispanic Ministries Coordinator, Atlanta, GA*

Editor:

    Anna Portillo, *Charlotte, NC*

Thank-you to these contributors:

    Aldo León, *Senior Pastor, Pinelands Presbyterian Church, Cutler Bay, FL*

    Jahaziel Cantú, *Church Planter, Iglesia el Buen Pastor, Dallas, TX*

    José Portillo, *Church Planter, Vive Charlotte Church, Charlotte, NC*

Thank you to these PCA leaders for their stories and insights:

Alejandro Cid, *Pastor, Rey de Gloria, Miami, FL*

Alejandro Villasana, *Senior Pastor, Christos Community Church, Norcross, GA*

Dr. Brad Taylor, *Global Missionary, World Reach, Birmingham, AL*

Dr. David Moran, *Executive Director of Clase Internacional de Teología Aplicada, Miami, FL*

Denine Blevins, *Executive Director, Parakaleo, Huntsville, AL*

Elías Gamaliel Pozos, *Church Planter, The Crossing Church, McAllen, TX*

Israel Ruiz, *Associate Pastor City Church Wilmington, Wilmington, DE*

Jorge Trujillo, *Pastor, Park Rd. Hispanic Ministry, Park Rd. Presbyterian Church, Hollywood, FL*

Josiah Katumu, *Senior Pastor, New City Eastlake, East Lake, TN*

Juan Arjona, *Senior Pastor, Misión Vida Nueva, Escondido, CA*

Manuel Padilla, *Missionary, Equipping Leaders International, El Paso, TX*

Ómar Ortiz, *Lead Pastor, Harbor City Church, San Diego, CA*

Pablo Toledo, *Spanish Pastor, First Presbyterian Church, Coral Springs, FL*

Pablo Torres, *Church Planter, La Viña Presbyterian Church, Orlando, FL*

Ronnie García, *Senior Pastor, Denver Presbyterian Church, Denver, CO*

Salatiel Chuc, *Spanish Pastor, Carolina Presbyterian church, Locust, NC*

Víctor Martínez, *Associate Pastor, Redeemer Presbyterian Church, San Antonio, TX*

William Castro, *Church Planter, Emmanuel Upstate, Greenville SC*

FORWARD:

En un cerrar de ojos (In the blink of an eye)

Unless you are actively and consistently taking the time to see how our nation is changing all around us, or unless perhaps you have noticed the demographic changes occurring *poco a poco* at the elementary- and middle-school levels, you may not have realized how, *en un cerrar de ojos* – in the blink of an eye – God has been changing the demographic make-up of our nation. Over the past several decades, and increasingly so, God has been drawing people from each of the 21 Spanish-speaking countries around the world into our midst. And this reality does not even mention the Hispanic native people who have been here even before the nation's formation.

Following the current trends, by 2050, the Hispanic community will reach over 110 million residents in the United States, thus allowing the US to continue holding the tile of the second largest Spanish-speaking nation in the world, following Mexico. The implications of this reality for the American church are that the ministry opportunities within this rapidly-expanding context are both endless and immediate, as the Lord draws the diversity of Spanish-speaking nations right into our own cities and neighborhoods. Such opportunities should be exciting, and compel us as Christians to engage our newest neighbors.

> ***Hispanic vs. Latino?**
>
> Historically, "Hispanic" refers to people from Spanish-speaking Latin-America, while "Latino" refers to those from any of the Latin-American countries, regardless of language. In spite of these different origins, these terms tend to be used interchangeably today to describe individuals with Latin-American ancestry in the United States. Studies have shown that U.S. Hispanics/Latinos are equally divided on preference for terminology, with a slightly higher preference for "Latino" as a racial identification. Therefore, this book will use the terms interchangeably, as they are used throughout the United States today.[1]

At the same time, it is important to recognize that ministry to this new demographic brings with it a layer of complexity. In seeking to engage the Hispanic community, we must see that it is not one, monolithic group, all best served through the same methodology. Rather, we must also recognize a new, emerging generation of

American citizens – the sons and daughters of these immigrants – that is rapidly growing in turn. These second-generation Latino-Americans* are growing up and finding their feet in the United States, but facing the stark reality that America has not learned to see them for who they are. They are not immigrants, but rather (like most Americans) the sons and daughters of immigrants. Many of them have never personally experienced the countries their parents left, yet they find themselves not quite at home in their own country where they are often still viewed as foreigners.

Thus any church planting work and movement towards the Hispanic community will have to account for the complexities of engaging at least two groups of individuals: a young immigrant people, who are still working their emigration losses, and simultaneously dealing with the challenges of assimilation and language; while at the same time accounting for their sons and daughters, who are growing as new American citizens, and seeking to find their identities as Hispanic-Americans. Therefore the work of church planting in this context cannot merely copy church planting among majority-culture Americans. In fact, it will not even look the same from one Hispanic context to the next; what works in one city among one group of Hispanic immigrants and Latino-Americans may not work in the next, where the countries of origin, or even generational break-down differs.

Rather, churches and planters seeking to reach this community need to develop a flexible, contextualized approach to reaching this growing harvest field with the Good News of Jesus, one that will bridge generational, linguistic, and cultural differences. The work ahead is great, but the Lord is One who delights to draw people from every nation and complex history into a people of the Kingdom, and members of the same Body.

This work seeks to aid in giving a useful, panoramic view of what it takes and will take to engage, train, multiply, empower, resource, and deploy workers to a field that is ready for the harvest.

– José Portillo

Church Planter and Pastor of Vive Charlotte Church (a small church with a great heart for this work.)

INTRODUCTION TO THE CHURCH PLANTING TIMELINE

There are many misconceptions in the world of church planting, especially here in the United States. Yet it seems that many of the apparent disagreements actually come down to the different seasons for planting, watering and harvesting, rather than different strategies for church planting.

After decades of working with Hispanic pastors, training new leaders, mentoring pastors and church planters, one thing has become extremely clear: for a multiplicity of reasons (which this book will address), the church planting metrics or church health metrics normally used in majority-culture denominations do not seem to apply amongst majority first-generation immigrant pastors and church members. It may be helpful to consider the lack of transferability by considering an analogy to the different stages of harvesting.

In the American majority-culture context, church planting largely has become associated with the idea that a church planter is someone who comes with an empty wheelbarrow or basket to a fertile ground where there are a variety of trees with fruit ready for the picking. In this scenario, the planter enters the orchard, quickly finds fruit to fill his basket, and a new church emerges. Most timelines and metrics among majority-culture denominations are designed to fit this ideal.

However, planting a church amongst the Hispanic community looks different. This is not to suggest that the overall process of growth is different. Rather, the church planting ecosystem of this community is at a different stage: the fruit is not yet ready for picking. Thus a church planter for the diversity of the Hispanic community cannot simply come with a basket ready to collect a congregation; instead, he must come with a handful of seeds, ready to plant trees that eventually will lead to a harvest. The process is more arduous; it requires more time and effort; yet with the proper watering, fertilizing, and patience, the harvest will come!

Church planting in the Latino context is not primarily about the discovery of new systems and metrics, but a rediscovery that the church planting ecosystem is younger and less developed, and that a church planter will need to do the work of setting the ecosystem into motion for the next church plants to have an easier process. In other words, the biggest needs in church planting within the Hispanic community become time and commitment.

Thus new metrics, new timelines, and new expectations have to be part of planning, supporting and engaging in this much-needed work. The chart on the following page offers a visualization of what years of examination and research have thus far shown, and it is the timeline this book will use and recommend as a starting point for Hispanic church planting in the United States.

Part 1 of *¡Plantemos!* will take a detailed look at the Preparation Stage (see the Church Planting Timeline), as this stage requires gaining awareness of the different challenges of reaching the growing Latino community in the United States. Part 2 will then examine the following six stages of church planting in turn, while Part 3 will narrow in on some practical ways churches and planters may put these stages into action within their particular contexts and fields of ministry. Readers should use this chart as a reference to keep in mind how each stage builds upon the next, while also keeping in mind that there may be some fluidity, depending on how a prospective church plant finds its particular ecosystem.

CHURCH PLANTING TIMELINE

Preparation Stage	Evangelism Stage	Discipleship Stage	Worship Stage	Leadership Stage	Church Formation Stage	Reproduction Stage
Time TBD	*Year 1*	*Years 2-3*	*Years 4-5*	*Years 5-8*	*Years 7-10*	*Ongoing*
Count the cost	Prayer support					
Spy out the land	Relationship building with non-believers					
Create a plan	Deliberate outreach and evangelism					
Step out in faith		Intentional discipleship				
			Develop church ministries	Church ministries		
				Launch weekly worship	Worshiping community	
					Train leaders	
					Ordain officers	
						Multiply

PART 1:

THE PREPARATION STAGE

"But seek the welfare of the city where I have sent you into exile, and pray to the LORD on its behalf, for in its welfare you will find your welfare." – Jeremiah 29:7

"The harvest is plentiful, but the laborers are few; therefore pray earnestly to the Lord of the harvest to send out laborers into his harvest." – Matthew 9:37b-38

"For we are his workmanship, created in Christ Jesus for good works, which God prepared beforehand, that we should walk in them." – Ephesians 2:10

CHAPTER 1:

COUNTING THE COST

"For which of you, desiring to build a tower, does not first sit down and count the cost, whether he has enough to complete it? ²⁹ Otherwise, when he has laid a foundation and is not able to finish, all who see it begin to mock him, ³⁰ saying, 'This man began to build and was not able to finish.'"
— Luke 14:28-30

Church planting in the Hispanic context: it sounds exciting; it sounds bold; and, when considering the rapidly growing Hispanic and Spanish-speaking population in the United States, it sounds necessary for the growth of the church! The temptation among eager church planters and churches desirous of reaching this community may be to go into this field or to send someone without the proper preparation, or without first taking into consideration some of the cultural complexities that are necessarily involved in planting within this context.

Perhaps Aristotle put it well in his *Nicomachean Ethics* when he remarked that, "one swallow does not a summer make…similarly one day or brief time of happiness does not make a person entirely happy."[2] Reworded in the context of Hispanic church planting, the adage might read, "one Spanish-speaking Christian man does not a church planter make; similarly, one year of surplus budget does not make a happily committed church ready for the hard work of planting a church amongst the Hispanic community." While the work is indeed exciting, it comes with many challenges unique to this community that both church planters and churches must take into consideration. In other words, they must begin the work of preparation by counting the cost!

Jesus' call to his disciples to "count the cost" in Luke 14 is, at first glance, quite sobering. "If anyone comes to me and does not hate his own father and mother and wife and children and brothers and sisters, yes, and even his own life," Jesus says, "he cannot be my disciple" (14:26). Following Jesus and His call requires sacrifice – for both church planter, and mother church. Yet it also requires wisdom. The sad reality is, many churches and pastors have sought to plant churches among the

Hispanic community with good intentions; but in the absence of considering the cost, far too many of these efforts have failed. (See *Chapter 5: Learning by Example* for many real-life case studies of Hispanic church plants: both ones that have walked the hard road to planting, and others that have had to close their doors.) Planters have begun to build, but have been unable to finish (cf. vv.29-30). This chapter seeks to build on the experiences and wisdom of ministry workers within the Hispanic church planting context, and offers rubrics by which churches and planters may assess whether they indeed are in a healthy place to go forward with beginning a new work.

The Mother Church Counts the Cost

One of the first steps in beginning a new work is for the mother church (or, in some cases, this might be a sending agency, collection of churches, or Presbytery) to assess its own readiness to support a new church plant and church planter within the Hispanic community. Referring back to the quote from Aristotle, while eagerness is good and necessary, it is not enough. Even finding an able-bodied planter should not be the starting point. Rather, the mother church needs to take time and put forth concerted effort to prayerfully consider its own health, understanding of the work to which it is feeling called, and awareness of the needs of the community which it is desirous to serve. A sending church must truly ask itself, *¿vale la pena?* (Is it worth it?)

> *¿Vale la pena?* Literally, "Is it worth it?", a common Spanish phrase used to determine whether the potential results of an action are worth the cost involved to get there.

Self-assessment

Perhaps the first step in assessing readiness is for the mother church to stop and seriously consider its own successes and failures in ministry. A simple cop-out to ministry is to agree to sponsor work somewhere else that a church (or individual) is unable or unwilling to do among their own sheep. Thus it can often happen that churches seek to initiate ministry in the Hispanic context without evaluating their previous and present ability to engage their own congregation and community.

Yet such a pursuit, when a church is not already meeting the needs within its immediate context, is detrimental both to the mother church, and to the church planter. For the mother church, it can add undue stress, as congregants and staff are called to care for another ministry when they themselves are not receiving adequate care. This, in turn, can lead to a lack of vibrant support of the new work. The engagement of a second context should go hand-in-hand with a church that is effectively caring for its own sheep. Thus, the leaders in a mother church must begin their church planting efforts within the Hispanic context with self-examination: ensuring that they know what it means and are able to engage with and effectively minister first to their own sheep. The desire to pursue Hispanic ministry should come from a sincere overflowing of joy and eagerness from seeing fruit among their own flock.

Prayer

Once the mother church has conducted an honest and thorough health assessment of its own congregation and determined its readiness in this category, the next step is to commit to prayer. Extraordinary and pervasive prayer is at the core of every advancement of the gospel, and this is no less true within challenging church planting contexts, where experience might dictate that efforts may fail. Even Jesus, as One with the Father, prayed for His work and ministry, and especially for His sheep, entrusting His ministry to God (cf. John 17:1-26). Knowing His impending death, He prayed, "Holy Father, keep them in your name… Sanctify them in the truth…" (vv.11, 17).

> *"I do not ask for these only, but also for those who will believe in me through their word, 21 that they may all be one, just as you, Father, are in me, and I in you, that they also may be in us, so that the world may believe that you have sent me."*
>
> – John 17:20-21

If a mother church is desirous of planting in the Hispanic context, its leaders must be willing to engage not simply in casual prayer, but, following the Lord Jesus, in intentional and kingdom-focused prayer. Indeed, Jesus prayed not simply for the sheep already in His fold, "but also for those who will believe in me through their word" so that the truth of Jesus might go into the world (John 17:20-21). As leaders engage in such kingdom prayer, they should also involve the prayers of the congregation. No amount of prayer is too much; rather, the danger is attempting to begin without prayer, or without enough prayer, and instead relying on human efforts and wisdom.

Some ways to encourage prayer among church members, while testifying to the necessity of prayer for the new work and setting the tone for the mission ahead, would be for the mother church to hold various prayer events. These might be events such as concerts of prayer, prayer vigils, days of fasting and prayer, prayer in small groups, prayer in the worship service, and prayer walks. The church should pray for the community, the planter, the team, the resources, etc., and particularly for God's plans to come to fruition. This commitment should continue through the entire planting process. Such prayer not only speaks to the congregation of the importance of the church plant, and of God's work in the mission, but will provide much encouragement to the eventual church planter, and whatever team he may have, knowing that they are not alone in the work, but carried along by the prayers of the saints (cf. Rev. 8:4).

Only once a mother church is able to care for its own, and also has a robust commitment to pray for the new work, should they look towards the next phases of counting the cost in planting a Hispanic church.

The Mother Church Commits to Growth

There is a certain humility in learning; humility in admitting that, no matter how educated or successful a person or church may seem, there is still a need to sit and learn from others with different knowledge and different experiences. Such humility is crucial for a mother church desirous of reaching a context other than its own. And acquiring the knowledge necessary is costly; it requires time, effort, and especially ears to hear! In order to successfully call and support a Hispanic church planter, the sending church must be able to evaluate both its own preparedness for this kind of work as well as the particular suitability of the prospective planter. This requires a commitment to growth and learning in a number of areas.

To evaluate its own preparedness to send out a Hispanic planter, a mother church's leadership must do the important work of honestly assessing their current cultural awareness, and then commit to growing in their ability to understand and adapt to cultural differences. The temptation most individuals face is to overestimate their ability to do this. Yet when a majority culture church fails to properly account for the inevitable cultural differences that it will confront in sponsoring a minority culture work, the results are usually tragic. It is far too easy for supporting churches to process prospective planters through the lens of their majority-culture context experiences; however, this attitude prohibits them from discerning whether the prospective planter and his vision for planting in the Hispanic context may be a good fit. Unfortunately, there are many stories of both churches and pastors that have been wounded in this process when decisions happen too hastily and without proper cultural awareness. As a result, sending churches decide that this kind of work is too costly and therefore turn towards other, simpler ministry fronts. Meanwhile, the

Hispanic planters are left as collateral damage: disenfranchised, hurting, and unsupported.

Thus, it is crucial that a mother church commits to equipping itself to discern the Hispanic context fluently in order to be effective in supporting and guiding the planter, and to also be able to understand the planter's reasons for various philosophical mechanics. If sending churches do not seek to become culturally intelligent in the Hispanic context, they will struggle to understand the planter, while also proving ineffective in admonishing and directing him in his efforts. This commitment to growth is imperative for beginning the next step of counting the cost in calling and supporting a Hispanic leader and church planting pastor. Churches must pause here and earnestly ask themselves: are we ready? Are we committed? Are we growing? Are we willing to be humble and learn? Is our congregation growing and ready? And by God's grace, this humility, prayer, and commitment to growth will go a long way in supporting and encouraging the planter and his congregation.

Admittedly, the process of learning a new context is costly; however, a church that earnestly desires to reach the Hispanic community will consider the effort required for growth to be a worthwhile Kingdom commitment. Chapter 12 of this book will detail many practical ways in which mother churches and their leadership can become more culturally equipped and effective for Hispanic church planting. Yet prior to considering the details, count the cost, commit to prayer, abound in the work of the Lord, and know that in Christ, the labor is not in vain! (I Corinthians 15:58).

> *"Therefore, my beloved brothers, be steadfast, immovable, always abounding in the work of the Lord, knowing that in the Lord your labor is not in vain."*
>
> – I Corinthians 15:58

Counting the Cost in Finding a Church Planter

At this point, the question for sending churches to ask is whether or not they are willing to take the time to do the legwork involved in looking for the right candidate for their prospective church plant. Consider the Lord's words to Samuel, when He told Samuel to anoint King Saul's successor. Samuel was ready to anoint Jesse's eldest son, Eliab; yet God let all seven of Jesse's older sons pass by Samuel, before bringing the youngest, and seemingly most unexpected candidate, David. The Lord told Samuel: "Do not look on his appearance or on the height of his stature, because

I have rejected him. For the LORD sees not as man sees: man looks on the outward appearance, but the LORD looks on the heart" (I Samuel 16:7). Surely Samuel must have wondered who the Lord had in mind, as God quietly told him "no" to seven seemingly able-bodied men.

Similarly, finding a qualified church planter is not easy, and a mother church must also consider this aspect when seeking to plant within the Hispanic community. The temptation (and what happens far too frequently) is for sending churches, in their excitement, to see only Eliab: that is, to settle for the first Spanish-speaking pastor they can find, assuming that language skills will ensure this individual's success in their church planting efforts. Yet this is simply not the case, and mother churches must ask themselves whether they are willing and ready to both learn what is needed within their particular target group, and then look long and hard to find the right fit.

Certainly, just as not every majority-culture pastor is qualified or able to successfully plant a church, mother churches must keep in mind that not every Spanish-speaking pastor is cut out for church planting. Sadly, overly-eager churches who fail to spend time searching and instead send unqualified and unprepared individuals into the field do a great disservice to the cause of Hispanic church planting. In fact, the results can be even catastrophic on multiple levels: they can be catastrophic for the individual and his family, who may have scars for the rest of their lives, feeling they have failed the church, their community, and even God. They can be catastrophic for the sending agency which, after investing time, energy, and resources to plant the church, feels disillusioned as to whether such efforts are worthwhile. And on a larger scale, they can be catastrophic for the Presbytery and regional churches, who see the failure of one project, become disappointed, and begin to feel pessimism towards future Hispanic works.

How then does a mother church begin to look for a qualified leader for a prospective Hispanic church plant? In evaluating the preparedness of a planter, sending churches should firstly research and consult those who have particular and practical experience in this area. While the real-life examples of both successful and non-successful Hispanic church plants throughout this book provide excellent resources, conversations with those who have first-hand experience prove invaluable and will assist churches in becoming equipped to discern the suitability and viability of the prospective planter. Such individuals will be able to help them consider both the needs of their context, but also the particular gifts and life-experiences of various candidates who may or may not be appropriate to that context.

Chapter 13 of this book discusses in further detail some very useful and practical considerations in both raising up and calling the right planter. For now, however, sending church leadership should pause and pray, and sincerely ask whether they are willing and ready to hear the Lord's voice and wisdom – and even pass over several seemingly attractive candidates, even if the process is lengthy, in order to find the right fit for their context. Indeed, choosing the right candidate is crucial to being able to support this individual in the long road toward church planting that will follow.

Committing to Support the Church Planter

Just as learning the context and finding the right candidate for that context involves much time and effort, the road to church planting within the Hispanic context is also distinctly long and hard, particularly within the confessional Presbyterian context. When compared with majority-culture models, growth, discipleship, and financial stability will often be significantly slower, for a multiplicity of reasons (see Chapter 10: *The Church Formation Stage*). This means that a planter likely will experience financial challenges, along with seasons of loneliness and emotional discouragement. Hence it is imperative for the supporting church to have a relational commitment to the planter that has a longer trajectory than the typical Presbyterian model. The traditional timeline of 3-5 years is insufficient for the demands and needs of Reformed church planting in the Hispanic context. Sending churches must count the cost here as well: are they ready and willing to commit to supporting the right church planter – financially, but also emotionally and spiritually – for the long haul?

The relational component of the supporting church is also vital. In the Hispanic context, the relational component of investment is just as important as any other element of investment. This means that holistic commitment to the planter personally, emotionally, and ministerially, is essential in a mother church's plan for ongoing support. It also necessitates that the sending church plan for a long-term investment of regular and robust communication and interaction in a formal and informal manner, not allowing the planter to flounder without the intentional, brotherly support and encouragement of the Body of Christ through the hard beginning stages. Is the sending church not only willing to make such a commitment, but also equipped with the right people and resources? A sending church that desires the Hispanic planter to flourish must be willing and able to commit to walking hand-in-hand with the church planting pastor for the many years his journey may take.

It may be helpful at this point to look at a real-life example of Hispanic church-planting which, sadly, did not have a fruitful outcome, but that helps to point out the need for truly counting the cost. Many of the specific details of this example have been removed to protect the individuals and churches involved. (See *Chapter 5: Learning By Example* for further cold case examples, and to understand the methodology followed in presenting these stories.)

Cold Case Example: A Small City Church Plant

In a small-sized town, a church began to notice the needs for ministry among the large Hispanic population. So they excitedly started an outreach ministry to this community, and their efforts proved fruitful. In fact, they were fruitful to such an extent that the Session saw the need to search for and call a Hispanic pastor. The target group was primarily first-generation Spanish-speaking individuals. Although the church-planting pastor was new to the area when called, he came with the advantage of being both bilingual and bicultural, thus with the capacity to communicate with his target audience and the mother church. Upon his arrival, he was able to begin evangelizing and to start Bible studies. These measures eventually resulted in being able to launch a Spanish-language worship service.

> **Cold Case: Small City Church Plant**
>
> ***Population between:*** 50,000-99,999
> ***Population Breakdown:***
> Hispanic: 41%
> White: 39%
> African American: 15%
> ***Ministry Methodology:*** Integrated

While the mother church fully funded their Hispanic congregation and pastor, they remained fairly segregated through the two separate worship services. Moreover, although the Hispanic pastor attended Session meetings and had individual meetings with the Senior Pastor on occasion, he was not actually a part of the Session. As often happens with churches with dual services and integrated methodology, while the first-generation Hispanics faithfully attended the Spanish-speaking services, their children and youth were attracted to the English ministries of the church, where, unlike their parents, language barriers did not hinder their participation.

As time passed, the two congregations began to move increasingly more in their own directions: the Hispanic congregation struggled to grow, due to constant turnover (which can be common among transitional, immigrant populations), meaning also that giving was minimal. Meanwhile, the English-language congregation was growing steadily, to a point that they were outgrowing their own space. They also went through a leadership transition at this time, and with the growing space concerns, the mother church began eyeing the space the Hispanic congregants were using. The Session, eager to meet the needs of their growing congregation, decided to transition back from dual services to a single, English-only service, in order to use the entirety of the space. While they did provide simultaneous translation, the change was too much for the Spanish-speaking congregants and pastor, who felt that they had been overlooked and not heard in the decision.

As he was not a member of the Session, the Hispanic pastor did not have a voice in the matter and was unable to advocate for his congregation. He resigned, feeling disgruntled and hurt. The mother church was unable to retain the Spanish-speaking congregants through this switch, and they dispersed into other local bodies where they could worship in their heart language.

The outcome of this Hispanic church planting example is sad and even frustrating; yet understanding the complexities at play that led to the fallout can provide some valuable insights. A mother church must indeed count the cost and be willing to go the distance when planting a Hispanic work! While mothering a majority-culture church plant might be equated to investing in one's college-age child to help them get established, mothering a Hispanic church involves raising the child all the way from the cradle to adulthood. Is the mother church truly ready to make such an investment? ¿Vale la pena? Sadly, in the case of this example, the answer was no.

Moreover, as they count the cost, the mother church must ask whether they can commit to ministry within the Latino context as a core value, or whether it simply falls into a special interest. The former looks like walking through thick and thin, while the latter will peter out when something else (like financial difficulties, the mother church's own growing congregation, or another special-interest ministry) arises. Regardless of leadership, which will inevitably transition as a church grows and matures, a church's commitment to a cross-cultural ministry must remain a non-negotiable value. Does the sending church truly have at its core a heart for Latino ministry? Can it make this commitment? (See Appendix A)

Indeed, as both this example and this chapter have demonstrated, counting the cost of church planting in a Hispanic context is multifaceted and complex. However, it is necessary not simply for the health of the church plant and community, but also the church planter, mother church, and even future Hispanic works. A mother church that commits without understanding the cost will do a disservice to future Hispanic leaders and the Hispanic church planting front. As Jesus explains in His parable, "For which of you, desiring to build a tower, does not first sit down and count the cost, whether he has enough to complete it? [29] Otherwise, when he has laid a foundation and is not able to finish, all who see it begin to mock him, [30] saying, 'This man began to build and was not able to finish'" (Luke 14:28-30). The cost may be great; yet what a privilege to be a part of bringing the truth of God's Kingdom to bear in a growing context that is ripe for harvest!

CHAPTER 2:

SPYING OUT THE LAND

"Moses sent them to spy out the land of Canaan and said to them, 'Go up into the Negeb and go up into the hill country, [18] and see what the land is, and whether the people who dwell in it are strong or weak, whether they are few or many, [19] and whether the land that they dwell in is good or bad, and whether the cities that they dwell in are camps or strongholds, [20] and whether the land is rich or poor, and whether there are trees in it or not. Be of good courage and bring some of the fruit of the land.'..." – Numbers 13:17-20a

The Latino population in the United States is growing exponentially; nevertheless, as alluded to previously, that growth looks anything other than a monolithic culture. Peoples from twenty-one different Spanish-speaking nations bring distinct histories and cultures. Divergent areas of resettlement within the United States also offer extremely different difficulties, experiences, and opportunities for immigrants and their children. Indeed, the stories and experiences are as numerous as the people. While it is imperative that a mother church not begin a work without first counting the cost and learning something of the complexities of planting within the Hispanic context, it is also imperative that a planter wishing to reach the Latino community understand the unique challenges and specifics of his target demographic.

Perhaps this concept of learning something of a demographic before engaging it sounds familiar – and it should! This is, in fact, what the Lord instructed His people to do regarding the land of Canaan prior to their conquering it. The Lord God commanded Moses to "Send men to spy out the land of Canaan, which I am giving to the people of Israel" (Numbers 13:1). Interestingly, God did not command men to go into the land to see whether it was the right land; He had already promised that Canaan was the land He was giving to the people of Israel! Rather, Moses sends them to spy out what it is they can anticipate upon their arrival in a land already promised to them. They are spy out information regarding the inhabitants of the land, their living situations, and the fruitfulness of the land itself (13:17-20). In other words, they are to go and conduct a demographic and ethnographic study in order to be better prepared for the task ahead. The Lord had already entrusted them with His vision, but they needed to be equipped.

Church planting in a new context is no different. The land is foreign, and while it indeed may be the place that the Lord has chosen for a new ministry (through the mother church, church planter, or other means), it is still prudent and necessary for the planter to learn as much as possible regarding the people whom he desires to reach: the circumstances, challenges, and possibilities that dictate how they conduct their daily lives. Such knowledge will help the planter not only in his own preparation for ministry, but will also enable the sending church to have a better grasp on what kind of support will be beneficial.

Preparing for a Demographic Study

As alluded to previously, there are many variables regarding the demographic make-up of a target area that will help to inform a church planter about the work ahead, and dictate what sort of approach to church planting he may need. Studying the demographic will also help him to determine what sort of financial support may be necessary, and for how long he may need it.

Yet in most cases, a mother church should conduct a basic demographic study even prior to calling the church planter. The purpose should be to confirm that the changes or opportunities they have perceived in the target area are correct and demonstrate a growing reality. Sending churches must consider whether the expected opportunity indeed exists, and ensure they can set appropriate goals for the planter. By being too hasty or not sending out their own spies, a church could pull the trigger with the wrong information at hand, or with the wrong expectations.

Once a sending church has done the legwork and called a planter, the planter must then perform his own demographic study, focused in discovering firsthand and in detail his immediate context. While some of this study is necessary prior to accepting the call, in order to assess whether he feels called to the particular context, the majority of the work must take place once the planter has moved to the target area. This is again the preparation stage of Hispanic church planting, and it involves the planter truly knowing, loving, and caring for those whom the Lord is entrusting to him. Without proper study and understanding of his area, the planter will not know whether he lives in the most strategic place, or where he should invest the majority of his energies and resources as he begins to make a presence in the community. This stage of study may take time, and may involve much work and creativity on the part of the planter in becoming well-versed in his target area. At the beginning stages for both he and his sending church, it is helpful to make one more observation from the example of the spies in Canaan.

When Moses sent spies into the Promised Land, of the twelve who went and saw the same good "land of milk and honey" that the Lord had chosen for them, only Joshua and Caleb were able to see past the obstacle of the inhabitants, trusting that "If the Lord delights in us, He will bring us into this land and give it to us…" (Numbers 14:8). The remaining ten spies saw the inhabitants as too fierce to contend with, and became discouraged, discouraging the people of God as well. Conversely, Joshua saw the hand of the Lord and His presence in facing the inhabitants, and encouraged the people to not fear (14:9). Thus the Lord did not allow the ten spies to enter the land of Promise, but used Joshua and Caleb to lead the people. Their example serves as a word of caution in demographic studies: if either the mother church or prospective planter is discouraged by what they find as they spy out the land, regardless of the possibilities, they may not be the appropriate sending church or planter for a particular area. The right sending church and the right planter will see the obstacles, but also see the possibilities of harvest, and trust that the hand of the Lord will make the work flourish.

> *"If the LORD delights in us, he will bring us into this land and give it to us, a land that flows with milk and honey. ⁹Only do not rebel against the LORD. And do not fear the people of the land, for they are bread for us. Their protection is removed from them, and the LORD is with us; do not fear them."*
>
> – Numbers 14:8-9

Conducting a Demographic Study

Once a basic study of the land encourages both the mother church and planter that this is indeed the Lord's work for them, a planter can begin to work more in depth. What then should a planter intend to accomplish as he seeks to conduct his demographic study?

First of all, a sending church should see this work on the part of the planter as an invitation for them to come to know, love, and develop a heart for the needs of their communities and target areas. This work is multifaceted. In practical ways, a planter should first assess whether people are moving away from or coming into the city, and what types of individuals are leaving or coming. This answer can be quickly obtained through a census report or a demographic study platform, and will help the planter develop a basic mental framework of the types of individuals he may encounter.

However, such a study is only the very beginning and elementary. More importantly, this most basic idea of who is coming and leaving actually invites the planter to enter into his community at God's speed. That is, the act of literally walking one's target area and community allows the planter to slow down and learn his demographic at the speed of Jesus' ministry. This means not simply reading a statistic and calling the work finished, but rather committing to a process of walking the neighborhoods over and over and over and over again. It looks like the planter faithfully and prayerfully walking the prospective *vecindarios* and allowing the Lord to open his eyes to see the land He has shown for the new work to inhabit. It looks like taking the time to meet individuals and learn about the community from their eyes and experiences. It looks like the planter making himself known and available, so that those statistics become more than interesting numbers on paper; so that encounters with strangers change to encounters with acquaintances, then with neighbors, then as friends, who are invited to become disciples of Jesus Christ. For even the work of learning a demographic first-hand is an opportunity to begin sowing gospel seeds!

> ***vecindarios:*** more than simply a neighborhood, *vecindarios* represent the joining of many dwelling near one another into one, connected group. They may represent a large group of neighbors in the same building, neighborhood, or area of town.

By walking at God's speed, the planter can begin to understand the mashup of cultures God has drawn near to his community. He will begin to see the places and individuals with obvious needs (i.e., poor, under-resourced communities), and/or those with an obvious lack of needs (displayed in manicured communities or gentrifying neighborhoods). By noticing stores and restaurants for different ethnicities (or a lack thereof), he will understand something of both the socioeconomic and also ethnic make-up of different pockets of the community. Slowly, by walking in neighborhoods, entering restaurants, parks, and *tiendas,* helpful conversations and dialogues will begin to take place.

> ***tienda:*** Literally a shop or a store, but tends to bear a more significant meaning within the Hispanic context of a community-based local shop or general store.

Through these conversations, the planter will learn about the stories of individuals' lives, which will include their countries of origin, family dynamics (along with familial structures), and livelihoods. By interacting, he will also glean useful information regarding language preferences and struggles, levels of assimilation among immigrants, and levels of education. As interactions move from the superficial stranger-encounter level into trust built on presence, he will become privy to some of the struggles of the stories of the community: whether they are cultural, socioeconomic, familial, emotional, or other. Individuals will begin to share their religious backgrounds, leanings, and fears. Indeed, as the church planter commits himself to the ministry of being present and listening, he will do much to develop the picture of his demographic, while simultaneously becoming a stable, present, and trusted member of the community.

This firsthand spying out of the land, slowly adding in more details to create a full-orbed picture is invaluable when it comes to church planting in a Latino context. The church planter will begin understanding both needs for gospel ministry, as well as obstacles he will need to think, work, and pray through in order to see traction in church planting. For example, if he discovers a large population of first-generation Spanish-speaking individuals, he may need to consider Spanish services, while a larger second- and third-generation population may mean he begins to think about English or multi-language ministry. Through walking his new community, the church planter will discover things that are impossible to learn simply through statistics. He will see the religious foundations individuals possess, and how much reeducation, reformation, or rediscovery they will need to be exposed to in casting a vision for church planting.

Conducting a Geographic Study

Spending time in the community with anyone who will open their doors is of the utmost importance. Yet through these interactions, a church planter can learn more even than stories, that will also be helpful for thinking through strategies for church planting. Moses instructed the spies to learn about the land of Canaan itself, to "see what the land is... whether the land is rich or poor, and whether there are trees in it or not" (Numbers 13:18, 20). It was important for the Israelites to know what they could expect about the way of life that the fruitfulness of the land would dictate: was there land for livestock? For farming? Were there already trees yielding fruit and shade, or would they need to come prepared with all their provisions, and equipped to endure the scorching sun?

Similarly, the church planter must understand not just the people, but the land itself that dictates some of the ways in which the people live. Regardless of whether the church plant will take place in Spanish, English, or a mix of English and Spanish, the planter should seek to spend quality time learning all he can about the geographic make-up of his target area. This means not only his own observations as he walks and drives the *vecindarios,* but especially interviewing and talking to people in English, Spanish, or other languages as he is able. One might be amazed at how much a person can glean from a neighbor who has been present for a decade or two, or even more. Such individuals, regardless of race or social status, will be able to explain housing and traffic patterns (and their challenges); they can talk about the churches already present in the community, and the observed work they are or are not accomplishing; and address the achievements or problems of the community's educational opportunities. These individuals may be privy to understanding the history of the community, how it has changed or is changing, and even some of the man-made or natural obstacles that may deter certain people from interacting with others.

Besides this valuable experiential knowledge, an involved neighbor-friend will also provide the best help in discovering what other organizations or churches are doing to connect with the community, and which organizations have a good reputation in helping, and which ones do not, and why or why not. Moreover, these neighbors are individuals who have a sense of who is actually living in the community as home owners, renters or investors. They may be able to help connect the planter to other neighbors and even community leaders, who will only help to grow this understanding.

Conducting an Ethnographic Study

In a similar vein to learning the geography and patterns that influence living in the target area, a church planter should also make sure to conduct an ethnographic (or qualitative) study of his new community. Once again, such knowledge happens best in relationship: through intentionally walking the community, getting to know individuals, neighbors, parents, and community leaders, and developing trust with them such that they are able to share the struggles and strengths of the community.

Certainly there is overlap here in demographic and geographic information, but an ethnographic study probes further to learn the heart of the community. One invaluable resource may be for a church planter to connect with other pastors across denominational divides to learn about how ministry looks and has looked within the particular context. The planter may also seek to know what other churches have attempted to plant in his target area, and what made them either fail or succeed. He may learn from parents and involved citizens about the history and racial tensions of his community that must necessarily inform how he plans to reach a minority culture. He may try and connect with the community activists and leaders, to learn their thoughts regarding the area, and their agendas.

Finally, only relational knowledge will help a church planter understand the deepest needs and desires of his community: their hopes, aspirations, and pleasures, but also their greatest fears, and the longings of their souls. Only intentional listening and caring for a once-unfamiliar community will allow the church planter to discover his pastoral heart as he listens to individuals' beliefs, doubts, and intellectual questions, and finds out what it is that they consider to be good news. Only as he begins to discover these things can he truly understand where the gospel is needed, and how he may begin to prayerfully approach the work of church planting in this area.

It is only through this sort of premeditated, prayerful walking, faithful conversations and interactions, supplemented with other resources, that the church planter will be able to have an accurate, tangible demographic study that communicates the stories, the real needs, and the great opportunities for the gospel to be poured out into his target area. These studies will prepare both his head and his heart for the next stage of preparation for planting within the Hispanic context, as he thinks through a plan for ministry. (For a more comprehensive list of resources and ideas for learning the make-up of a community, see Appendix B.) They will help him become excited for the work, and begin praying for the vision that the Lord has in store for reaching this community with the good news of Jesus.

CHAPTER 3:

CREATING A PLAN

"Then I arose in the night, I and a few men with me. And I told no one what my God had put into my heart to do for Jerusalem. ...I went out by night ...and I inspected the walls of Jerusalem that were broken down and its gates that had been destroyed by fire. ... [17] Then I said to [the officials], 'You see the trouble we are in, how Jerusalem lies in ruins with its gates burned. Come, let us build the wall of Jerusalem, that we may no longer suffer derision.' [18] And I told them of the hand of my God that had been upon me for good, and also of the words that the king had spoken to me. And they said, 'Let us rise up and build.' So they strengthened their hands for the good work." – Nehemiah 2:12-18

Nehemiah's example should be foundational when it comes to the work of church planting, particularly in a new and challenging context. Nehemiah heard tell of the pitiful condition of the walls of Jerusalem, since the city was lying in ruins after the Babylonian exile, and his heart went out to the remnant who was living there (Nehemiah 1:1-3). Nehemiah responded to this heart-calling from the Lord in his life, and left his home (Susa, in the Persian empire), his work (cupbearer to King Artaxerxes), to serve in a challenging context where he would serve a hurting people, and where there would be many who would oppose his work. This calling, not unlike church planting in the Hispanic context, looks difficult, and perhaps even doomed to failure. Yet Nehemiah's approach is one that the church must emulate, as it revolves around practical ways of seeking wisdom from the Lord, and acting in faith.

Nehemiah, upon hearing the news and feeling called, devoted time to prayer, seeking wisdom from the Lord (counting the cost!), and then even boldly requesting the help, blessing, and resources of his employer and captor, King Artaxerxes (1:1-2:8). And once he arrived in Jerusalem, he went to spy out the land for himself, in order to prepare himself for the work and challenges that would present themselves (2:8-16). At this point, informed and ready, Nehemiah committed to a plan of rebuilding, a plan that he was able to share with his followers, and which he had also committed into the hands of the Lord: "Then I said to them… 'Come, let us build the wall of Jerusalem…' And I told them of the hand of my God that had been upon me for good…" (2:17-18).

So must be the work of the church planter within the Hispanic context. After counting the cost and spying out the land, the planter is ready for the difficult yet exciting task of creating and committing to a plan for reaching his *comunidad* (i.e., his demographic). The process of creating a plan is multifaceted, and will require much effort and constant committing to the Lord's wisdom. This chapter will help the planter to prayerfully consider which church planting models, methodologies, and strategies may best fit his target group, as he determines values, mission, vision, and comes up with a church planting proposal. Even Nehemiah's plan was subject to alterations as opposition arose and he saw the need for different strategies (e.g., Nehemiah 4:10-23); yet the plan for rebuilding continued, always committed in prayer to the hands of the Lord. Church planters and their mother churches must keep these truths forefront as they plan and prepare for starting a new church.

> ***comunidad:*** literally, "community," but within the Hispanic context, the significance is more than simply a neighborhood and its surroundings, but a tightly-knit group of neighbors sharing life with one another.

Primary Methodologies for Hispanic Church Planting

Church planting in any context can be complex and even volatile. Yet as this book has already demonstrated and will continue to make clear, linguistic, cultural, generational, educational, economic, and religious issues can make Hispanic church planting (or planting within a minority context) even more difficult. While there are many ways to plant a church, Hispanic church planting methodologies typically fall

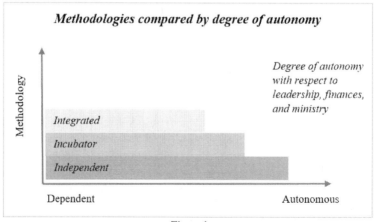

Figure 1

into three major categories, each with their unique strengths and weaknesses: 1) Integrated, 2) Incubator and 3) Independent. Figure 1 provides a preview of how these primary methodologies compare with one another, with respect to dependency upon the mother church and their own autonomy. A church planter should consider each of these methodologies with his demographic in mind, in order to choose which one may work best for both he and the mother church. This chapter will examine each of these methodologies, along with their strengths and weaknesses, in turn, before then discussing a number of other smaller categories.

Integrated Methodology

Integrated methodology (see Figure 2) is a flexible approach to church planting that occurs when an established church reaches cross-culturally to add another congregation. This new congregation may grow on the campus of the mother church, or off-site, and allows for both congregations to be involved with one another, to the degree that the mother church enables this.

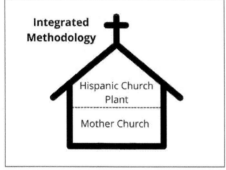

Figure 2

Integrated methodology has many positive aspects. Firstly, in a church planting context that is notoriously difficult to fund, the integrated approach is the least expensive way to start a new work, as the budget falls under the sending church, and the congregations have the opportunity to share both space and leadership. Additionally, it cuts both time and expenses with respect to administrative work.

Yet aside from a purely financial and administrative perspective, integrated methodology offers value to church members and the community as well. As the mother church begins to reach the diversity of the Latino community, done well, this can become a witness to the community of the unity the gospel brings in the midst of diversity. Moreover, because of the overlapping of staffing, space, and vision, members of the established church have an excellent opportunity to help in reaching the nations at their doorstep, while simultaneously growing their own vision for gospel unity. It may help to open their eyes to the richness of the diversity that surrounds them, providing the opportunity to be stretched in loving others with whom they might not otherwise interact.

Finally, integrated methodology can also be of assistance to the church planter, who has access to resources he would not otherwise have through other methodologies. For example, he may be able to minister immediately to the children, youth, and young adults of the families he is reaching in ways he could not as a solo church planter, by plugging them into the ministries of the established church. Thus it can provide encouragement to both him and others as he feels the support of the established church body.

Because of these many positive aspects, the PCA has used this methodology widely to reach Hispanics. Yet integrated methodology does not come without some potential drawbacks as well.

Some of these negatives include the tensions between majority and minority culture working together without proper respect or understanding. For example, even as noted in Chapter 1: *Counting the Cost*, majority-culture leaders may not always understand the complexities and struggles of the Spanish-language congregation, thus leading them to unintentionally make poor decisions on their behalf. And similarly, if the majority-culture leadership does not intentionally invite its minority leader into meaningful leadership roles, and take the time to truly listen to and understand his perspective, they may become quite paternalistic. Additionally, integrational methodology can hinder minority leadership development if the mother church does not ensure that rising leaders from the minority congregation are allowed to step into leadership roles.

Members of the established church may also respond in some negative ways to integrated methodology. If they do not embrace the direction of the mother church in bringing in a new culture and are not open to the changes this necessitates, they may complain and even leave. On the other hand, minority-culture congregants may feel hindered in expressing themselves at different events in their own culture, if the majority culture does not understand them and begins making wrong assumptions.

Logistically, integrated methodology can also present some challenges. Due to the mother church congregation already being established in services and events, the Hispanic congregation may find the facility to be available only at odd hours on Sundays or other days, thus making it more difficult to accommodate needs for worshiping and meeting together regularly. Moreover, the mother church may struggle to hire bilingual staff, if needed, to accommodate their Spanish-language members.

Churches looking to use integrated methodology to reach the Hispanic community must examine both these positive and negative aspects, and ask themselves whether they are able and willing to combat the challenges in order for integration to be successful. For some, it may work well, while for others it may not. First Presbyterian Church of Coral Springs, FL, provides an example of successful integrated methodology in beginning a new Hispanic work. (See *Chapter 5: Learning by Example*, for more real-life examples of integrated methodology at play.)

First Presbyterian Church, Coral Springs, FL Case Study

First Presbyterian Church, of Coral Springs, Florida, began as a Hispanic congregation of its mother church in 2012. After sensing a need and opportunity for ministry within the community, the mother church had taken action by launching an English as a Second Language (ESL) ministry, that subsequently had grown to roughly 300 students per week. The Session, encouraged by the success of the ministry, began to pray for a Spanish-speaking pastor who might be able to lead an effort to use the ESL ministry as a launching point for a congregation targeting first-generation Spanish-speaking Latinos. After prayer and searching, in 2012, the Session found and called a bilingual, bicultural pastor to join their Session and begin the work.

> **First Presbyterian Church, Coral Springs, FL**
> **Zip Code:** 33065
> **Population according to 2020 Census:** 134,394
> Hispanic: 29%
> White: 41%
> African American: 22%
> **Ministry Methodology:** Integrated

This church planter, himself an immigrant from Guatemala, had natural affinity to his target group but also the added advantage of conducting life in the Coral Springs area for 20 years prior to this calling. Ready for the challenge, the pastor came to truly engage as he saw opportunity. When the ESL students would have their breaks in class each week, he would begin preaching the gospel to them, making connections, and then following up with the students tirelessly throughout the week. The fruits of this effort allowed him to begin a Bible study with some of the interested students which took place on Sundays at the church, prior to the English worship service. Through the deliberate time and location for the study, he was able to encourage some of these Bible study attenders to stay for Sunday service; meanwhile, his continued efforts to evangelize within his context provided the opportunity to start another Bible Study.

At the same time, the church planter was constantly looking for other ways to interact with his demographic and create connections. This led to instituting summer soccer camps for the children of ESL students. Through his faithfulness, and the Lord working through his efforts, the pastor and his Session witnessed the exciting reality of people coming to faith. In fact, there were enough conversions that the church felt compelled to offer simultaneous translation during their Sunday worship to help these new believers be able to hear the gospel in their native language.

Spanish-speaking attendance at the English service continued to grow, and in order to better meet their needs, the Session made the prayerful decision to initiate a separate, Spanish-language worship service on Sundays in the church's chapel. The difficulty with two separate services is that it is easy for a congregation to become divided simply by language preference. Thus, in order to maintain a sense of unity, they chose to continue joining together several times throughout the year, while also ensuring that the Hispanic pastor would preach from time-to-time in the English services, and remain active in the Session.

For the mother church, the use of integrated methodology has allowed them to see and remain active in the ministry of the Hispanic congregation, while benefiting from the voice of the Hispanic pastor within their Session and as a preaching pastor. In using this methodology, they have chosen to keep all expenses within one budget, although a part of the Hispanic pastor's salary does come from the mission budget. For First Presbyterian Church, a vision to reach the Spanish-speaking community through hard, faithful, efforts, has yielded the Lord's harvest.

The church planter has also remained faithful in his ministry, constantly doing the work of training new converts, and continuing to plant seeds of the gospel. He has also remained intentional with his discipleship efforts among his flock, and consistently calls and follows up with both members and visitors.

The reality for the Hispanic congregation of First Presbyterian Church at this time is that COVID has severely affected church membership (as it has in so many churches). The congregation has shrunk to an average of 50 people per Sunday service, while ESL class attendance has also dropped to around 200 students per week. Nevertheless, both mother church and church planter have remained faithful, and it is encouraging to see the fruits of their labor in the work to which the Lord has called them.

First Presbyterian Church represent one example in which an integrated methodology can prove effective given the right context in Hispanic church planting. Through their work and outreach in the community prior to calling a Hispanic pastor, they learned to love their Hispanic neighbors and were committed to the involvement that successful integrated methodology necessitates. They have proved intentional in dealing with potential difficulties, and have remained focus and faithful. Yet there are other methodologies that may work better for different contexts.

Incubator Methodology

Incubator methodology (see Figure 3) allows the Latino church planter to start his work within the general confines of the sending church with the idea that, over time, his ministry will achieve holistic autonomy. Compared with integrated methodology, this process is more gradual and intimate, and can be a more prolonged process overall. Yet following this methodology, a mother church's intent from the beginning is to send the new group out once it has reached sufficient maturity. This strategy can easily become part of the sending church's DNA, such that they may choose to repeat it time and time again. Indeed, many churches have tried incubator methodology, and it has generally proved effective as there are many positive to this approach.

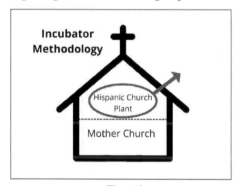

Figure 3

For the sending church, incubator methodology can be functional and attractive as the initial ingrown process means a significant reduction in financial costs. The fact that the plant begins within the mother church means that providing funding for things such as rent and equipment is not immediately necessary.

For the church plant itself, a reduction of cost permits the church plant to be able to follow a more leisurely timeline, which in turn allows for the vital process of unhurried, organic growth. While other methodologies can prematurely force particularization, the ability to walk at a slower pace allows the church plant to mature and become healthy enough for longevity and self-sustainability before being let loose.

This slower pace also can be a source of encouragement to the Hispanic church planter, as he will be able to invest more in ministry itself, rather than needing to focus on size, costs, and the demands of developing infrastructure and finding facilities. It also gives him a better opportunity to have accountability and receive better and more robust relational support, due to the mother church's close proximity in the beginning stages. Moreover, the use of the building can be beneficial within the Hispanic context, since traditional-looking worship spaces are often important and provide both the church planter as well as the church plant with an aesthetic of credibility and stability that an alternate meeting location might not afford.

Finally, members of both the mother church and the church plant can benefit from incubator methodology. Seeing a new work developing over a period of time in their midst can be a practical way for sending church members to know, understand, support, and even join the new work as they feel called. For both parties, this involvement can begin to break down some of the cultural prejudices and barriers that may have existed previously. It may encourage both congregations that ministry to different contexts need not be exclusive.

At the same time, incubator methodology may also present with some negative aspects of which both the mother church and the church planter should be aware. For the Hispanic church planter, there may be challenges in trying to reach a context apart from and lesser known to the mother church. Developing a church plant from within the confines of the sending church can inhibit his ability to form his church's unique identity, and the Hispanic plant runs the risk of becoming simply a Spanish-speaking ministry of the majority-culture church. On the other hand, the church planter may become comfortable with the heavy influence of the mother church, and he may struggle to move away from co-dependency.

Moreover, if members from the mother church are attracted to the Hispanic work and joining the efforts, the planter may become tempted to think less missionally regarding his target community, as he sees church plant membership growing through transfer. The church plant at this point may become focused less on being an actual Hispanic church plant reaching a needy community, and essentially become little more than an alternative worship space and environment for those more comfortable with or intrigued by the Latino context.

Lastly, the mother church and church planter must also consider carefully whether the location of the mother church in relation to the location of the target community may hinder growth. For example, the church planter may struggle to bring the Hispanic community to worship in the physical church building if it is situated too far from their *vecindarios*, or if it is located in an area of the city of which Latinos may have a negative perception.

While incubator methodology is generally viable, it does need some qualifiers. To prevent a prolonged co-dependency, the sending church must work closely with the church planter to develop a viable timeline for autonomy. Furthermore, incubator methodology demands that the sending church have a strong, clear identity and vibrance to ensure the Hispanic church plant does not quickly escalade into a conflict of interests when majority-culture members are attracted to the work. New City East Lake provides an example of a church plant that has successfully worked through this methodology.

New City East Lake, Chattanooga, TN Case Study

The congregation of **New City East Lake** (NCEL), in Chattanooga, TN, began as a cross-cultural vision of the mother church to begin a second worship site in a rough, inner-city neighborhood in which the population was split fairly equally between Hispanic, White, and Black residents. In the early 2000's, the mother church had a vision of reaching the primarily first-generation Hispanic residents of East Lake, with the goal of gospel-centered racial reconciliation within the city.

New City East Lake (NCEL), Chattanooga, TN
Zip Code: 2.3 square miles of 37407
Population according to 2020 Census: 9,459
Hispanic: 30%
White: 30%
African American: 40%
Ministry Methodology: Incubator

As the mother church itself was cross-cultural, they chose to send out one of their own staff to begin the work in 2008, along with a large group of people and capable leadership. This church planter – a bilingual, bicultural Anglo pastor – had lived in the area for over twenty years prior to his calling, and was thus familiar with the racial tensions and need for reconciliation within his target area.

To reach the new community, the pastor, along with his leadership and core group, immediately began initiating outreach into their new community through ESL, medical clinics, sports ministries, mercy ministries, and art. As their capacity for ministry grew, they also expanded outreach to partner with a local elementary school in order to help with after school care, mercy, and medical needs. Eventually, these outreach areas grew to the specific ministries of East Lake Expression Engine (a music ministry for children), East Lake Montessori School, and Chattanooga Sports Ministries. With expanding outreach especially to the children in this area, summers became the busiest time of year for ministry, with the opportunity to care for and feed children who were not in school.

NCEL also encouraged their core group members to move into the East Lake neighborhood, with the desire to better reach the needs of the community and incarnate the gospel through daily life. One established core value from the beginning was following up with new people in order to share the gospel, and so the site launched a ministry team to intentionally and tirelessly do just that with any who might come to either the outreach ministries or worship services.

In order to serve the diversity of the community in their Sunday worship, NCEL began offering English-dominant bilingual services, with a blend of both traditional and more modern worship, and simultaneous translation for those needing more Spanish. Bilingual staff and members also were able to begin in-home Spanish-language Bible studies, as they worked to bridge the divide between English and Spanish speakers.

Although the mother church shared a budget to cover expenses for the NCEL site initially, the site grew quickly, becoming more financially independent in its growth. Soon the new congregation was even able to purchase an old, rundown church building in the heart of their target neighborhood, which they slowly renovated. Within eight years, the new site had grown to approximately 200 members, and its outreach had also become an indispensable part of the neighborhood. At this point, both the Session of the mother church along with the leadership of NCEL agreed that both membership and finances were healthy enough for NCEL to establish themselves apart from the mother church. Thus, in September of 2016, NCEL became a particular church, fully independent in both finances and leadership.

At the end of 2017, however, the Senior Pastor of the newly-particularized NCEL announced his retirement, and the church began to seek a new pastor who could continue in the mission and vision for cross-cultural ministry and reconciliation. The search proved difficult, and after a year of narrowing down candidates, the one they were anticipating was unable to accept the call. Once again they began the task of searching for a qualified pastor. Understandably, the new church suffered during this lengthy period of transition, struggling to be as involved in the community as previously, and thus experiencing a time of slowed growth. By the Lord's gracious provision, two leaders – an Anglo pastor, along with a trilingual Brazilian leader who was under care in the Presbytery at the time – were instrumental in caring for the church during this period.

Finally, in 2019 after two years of praying and searching, New City East Lake called a gifted, multilingual Kenyan-American, to the role of Senior Pastor. The new pastor, an immigrant himself, could relate on multiple levels with his context, and was desirous to move immediately into the heart of East Lake to better care for the people.

Indeed, the Lord blessed the long, arduous search and patience of the NCEL congregation. In spite of the COVID pandemic, under their new leadership, the church continued to serve their neighborhood with COVID-safe drive-thru clinics; VBS; and sports and mercy ministries. By God's grace, NCEL has even added a large number of new members in the past few years. This includes a large number of students from the adjacent Covenant College campus, many of whom have stayed in the area to become a part of the congregation after graduation.

Although the journey of New City East Lake has not always been easy, it represents an example of the successful use of incubator methodology in cross-cultural church planting. Having a viable timeline for sending out the church plant was instrumental in allowing NCEL to flourish before needing to provide for themselves. Surely if the church had already been struggling financially, they may not have made it through such a difficult period of pastoral transition after particularization. The mother church also exhibited a strong vision (and faithfulness in carrying out that vision) along with a heart to involve and send many of its own members to support the work. Both of these provided great and necessary support in the early years of church planting. Moreover, the church plant and church planting pastor's commitment to becoming truly involved in their new context, has allowed NCEL to reach across many racial and cultural barriers to share the good news of Jesus Christ. In this case, both mother church and church planter worked well through incubator methodology to accomplish God's vision for a new, cross-cultural work in East Lake.

Independent Methodology

Independent methodology (see Figure 4) is the third and final primary category of methodologies for Hispanic church planting. Like integrated and incubator methodologies, it comes with its own positive and negative elements that may make some areas and churches more suited to this strategy than others. Independent methodology refers to the process in which a sending organization (church, Presbytery, or other group) identifies and calls a church planter to start a new work that will eventually become self-governing and self-supporting. This methodology allows a planter to begin his plant with a core group, or to start from scratch, building a launch team* in a virgin territory. Regardless of how he starts, the goal to which both the sending church and church planter is committed is to develop a stand-alone church.

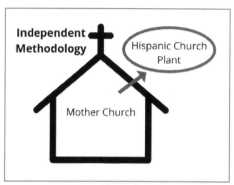

Figure 4

When it comes to independent methodology, there are many positive elements. At the forefront, because the church plant is not tied to a mother church's leadership, location, or congregation, it has more opportunities to develop its own unique flavor from the beginning. It thus has the potential for growing the most culturally inviting

---

Core Group vs. Launch Team?

There is a technical difference between the terms "core group" and "launch team." Most majority-culture churches start with a **core group**: a biblically and theologically trained group of volunteers who are committed to helping the church plant grow and thrive in a particular area. A committed core group is part of what enables majority-culture churches to launch worship quickly and effectively. On the other hand, **launch team** refers to the group of individuals that scratch planters form and train in order to help them be able to reach and disciple individuals prior to public launch. As most Hispanic church planters will, by default, employ a launch team over a core group, this book primarily uses this latter term, although it may also use core group from time to time, recognizing that there may be instances (such as the case of New City East Lake, above) in which such terminology could fit the Hispanic church planting scenario.[3]

church of the three methodologies. It may also be the most evangelistically fruitful since (more so than integrated and incubator methods) it must rely on planting seeds and seeking out new people to eventually join the work. Moreover, as the church planting pastor is working solo, apart from mother church staff, this methodology tends to provide many opportunities for growing and developing leaders, and there is an immediate need for others to come alongside and support the planting pastor. Another great strength of independent methodology is that, since it does not start within a mother church, it allows for church plants to go into areas where majority churches may have a hard time flourishing, thus providing an excellent way for Hispanic church planters to reach a Latino or multicultural context.

At the same time, while the benefits are great, independent methodology comes with the highest risks as well. For the church planter, this methodology may prove quite lonely, particularly if he is working in a virgin territory. He may find himself without the necessary encouragement and accountability that church planters working closely with a mother church leadership might have. Thus, the danger of burnout is considerable.

Financially, independent methodology can also be a risky option. Since there is typically no overlap between a sending church's budget and that of the church plant, it is the most expensive form of church planting. A high budget can prove particularly challenging if the leader does not have the language skills or relational networks to raise sufficient funds. Thus, regardless of his giftedness and qualifications, both he and the church plant may suffer from financial limitations that therefore restrict ministry.

Finally, particularly when starting as a scratch plant, independent methodology tends to take far longer than majority-culture church planting. Without a proper understanding of and commitment to this reality, the mother church (or sending agency) may lose patience and pull support prior to the church plant being capable of standing on its own. Churches and sending agencies must seriously consider whether they are both willing and able to provide support – financially, emotionally, and spiritually – for the long run, when considering independent methodology.

Independent methodology is growing in popularity in the PCA for Hispanic church planting. Christos Community Church represents one example of an independent plant that successfully worked through this methodology to become a particularized church.

Christos Community Church, Norcross, GA Case Study

The seed that eventually grew into **Christos Community Church** of Norcross, GA, was planted in 2006 when a megachurch (over 2000 members) invited an experienced Hispanic pastor to participate in their 2-year Church Planting Residency program. The Residency program itself was not new, but had been originally designed for recent seminary graduates to gain experience, prepare for ordination, and be able to launch a mission church. However, this was the first time the church had invited a pastor who was already ordained to join the program.

> **Christos Community Church, Norcross, GA**
> ***Zip Code:*** 30071
> ***Population according to 2020 Census:*** 17,209
>   Hispanic: 46%
>   White: 19%
>   African American: 25%
> ***Ministry Methodology:*** Independent

The pastor was a bilingual, bicultural, first-generation Mexican immigrant, and was new to Norcross when he accepted the Residency. Over the first six months of the program, besides receiving training for church planting and becoming a part of networks, the pastor invested much time in getting to know the city and determining his target area and context. In his walking the *vecindarios* and spying out the land, he was able to see a great need to target first-generation English-proficient Hispanics. As he came to understand the needs and expectations of this particular target community, the pastor also developed core values of what it might take to reach them.

During the remaining eighteen months of his Residency, the Hispanic pastor continued to identify his target area, while also beginning to serve, raise funds, and develop a core group. In terms of finances, the mother church committed to providing 30% of the needs, while the pastor was able to raise the next 30% from individuals within the mother church, and the remainder of the budget from outside sources, including the local church planting network.

In order to form a core group that might be well-suited to the hard labor of scratch planting in the Latino community, the Hispanic pastor used the core values he had identified to invite individuals to come alongside him. Specifically, he looked for those who displayed at least three of the following five characteristics: 1) Those who were interested in learning from other cultures, and being educated in key values that might be different from their own; 2) those who were appreciative of mental, physical, and spiritual challenges; 3) those who were interested in family life and placed a value on involvement in the community; 4) those who proved to be hard workers and entrepreneurs; 5) those who could see and measure success in more than financial terms.

At the end of his Residency, in 2008, with funding in place and a group of committed core members, the Hispanic pastor was ready to officially launch the work of Christos Community Church. Knowing the work of a solo church planter – and particularly one in a non-majority context – can be lonely and challenging, he also hired a church planting coach for personal support and accountability, and became a part of a vibrant church planting network.

Meanwhile, the pastor also began working with his gifted core group to identify an apartment complex in the area where they could connect with and begin outreach to the residents through education, art, and chess. He also helped the members form ministry teams, and began very intentionally discipling the leaders of those teams to help them be better equipped for leadership and service. In working closely with these individuals, he was able to identify three men with the potential to become Ruling Elders, and thus began to train them as well.

As they continued outreach and leadership development, Christos Community Church launched its first public worship services in a local school. As church membership and participation began to grow, the leaders recognized the need for a more permanent facility that might allow them to minister more effectively. Thus, in 2010, Christos Community Church began renting a warehouse that they were able to use not only for Sunday worship, but also for outreach throughout the week. Continued church growth also necessitated the hiring of additional staff. That same year, they hired a second staff member – an Anglo pastor with a heart for cross-cultural ministry – to join the team and work bi-vocationally, 20 hours per week.

One of the vision points of Christos Community Church was for growth to happen through small groups: places where individuals could study together, serve, evangelize (and also be evangelized). They committed themselves to this type of small-group ministry. Their efforts proved effective, to the degree that in 2011, another local church plant merged with them, growing Christos Community Church to around 100 people, and necessitating the rental of a second space within the warehouse to better accommodate children's and youth ministries.

Although growth had seemed steady, with rising leadership preparing for ordination as elders, the church witnessed a set-back in 2012, with two of the three Ruling Elder candidates suffering tremendous losses that made them unable to continue training. The pastoral staff worked hard and faithfully to come alongside these men and minister to them and their families in calamity, although the losses also meant slowed growth for the church.

After such a difficult period, the pastoral staff found it necessary to recalibrate their focus, and they began to target first-generation, professional, bilingual Hispanics. Though worship services were English-dominant, the Hispanic pastor was also able to organically translate for himself as necessary. As the pastors continued working to form and disciple leaders, they identified new elder candidates in 2014, and began the work of training them for ordination.

In 2017, nine years after its initial public launch, Christos Community Church examined and ordained its first elders, and particularized, even though it was still not fully financially self-sufficient. In 2019, they were able to train and ordain two deacons, and another elder. Unfortunately, however, church finances did not grow at the anticipated rate, and in 2018, the Hispanic pastor also stepped into a bi-vocational role in order to alleviate the financial responsibilities of the church.

In the last years, the COVID pandemic has deeply affected church growth and life, as several core families, including one of the elders, stopped attending. Currently, Christos Community Church has around 60 members, and in spite of the challenges, they are continuing to pursue ministry in their context, and have even recently ordained a new elder.

Though the example of Christos Community Church does indeed demonstrate some of the challenges of independent methodology in Hispanic church planting, such as a lengthened timeline and financial limitations, it also shows success in anticipating some of these challenges, and effectively using this methodology to reach a new community for Christ. It is of note that the Hispanic pastor began his process of church planting by seeking out personal support and encouragement, which is vital to avoid burnout in the long journey of scratch planting. While independent methodology is not a wise or viable option for every Hispanic church plant, with the right context and planter, it can be an encouraging way to reach Latinos with the gospel message.

New Methodologies for Hispanic Church Planting

While integrated, incubator, and independent methodologies comprise the three major categories of Hispanic church planting in the PCA, it is also helpful to examine some newer methods that have not received a lot of attention or use at this point. While each methodology presents with its unique challenges, some of them may also be beneficial to consider for Hispanic church planting, given the right circumstances.

STRATEGY	METHODOLOGY
Partnership	Bi-vocational
	Evangelist for the Presbytery
	Site-Planting
Regional	House Church
	Multi-Church Planting Partnership
	Network Planting

In general, these newer methodologies fall into two larger categories of partnership and regional strategies. In the former, leaders partner together to plant a church with low resources, with each leader donating time to help birth the new work. This would include Bi-vocational, Evangelist for the Presbytery, and Site Planting methodologies. In the latter category, a region with many different pockets of individuals or churches partners with a regional pastor to help start Bible studies and other gatherings in a given context. House Church, Multi-Church Planting Partnership, and Network Planting methodologies would fall into this second category.

Bi-vocational Methodology

Like integrated and incubator methodology, bi-vocational methodology (sometimes also called co-vocational) involves the church planter working under and being paid by an established, local church. Yet different from the integrated or incubator methods, following bi-vocational* methodology (as its name suggests), the church planting pastor actually serves in two separate church vocations: one within the established church, for which he is paid; the second being the work of planting a separate, new work in the Hispanic community. It is also helpful to mention that this methodology is unique from simply being bi-vocational, in which case a pastor might work in a separate space outside of the church to supplement or provide his income.

There are a number of advantages to bi-vocational methodology. Financially speaking, it may be beneficial as having one, steady source of income while planting can allow the pastor to focus on discipleship and relationships rather than funding.

> ***Bi-vocational vs. Co-vocational?***
> While these terms are sometimes used interchangeably, **bi-vocational** pastors typically have the desire to work as a full-time pastor, but are willing to serve bi-vocationally in order to be able to do the work of ministry; **co-vocational** pastors, on the other hand, see their two vocations working together indefinitely as part of the way the Lord has called them to ministry.

While financial necessities can create timelines that may force premature decisions, bi-vocational methodology can help to foster organic growth and spiritual formation, since the pressing goal does not have to be financial autonomy.

Further, bi-vocational methodology can deepen ministry collaboration and cooperation. Since the planter is unable to devote his full attention to the ministry of the church plant, he must move quickly to recruit, train, and deploy helpers. Ideally, this allows the Presbytery to jump in to help in recruiting potential ministry partners and key leaders to help the planter gain quicker traction. A Presbytery might consider bi-vocational church planting to be an "all-hands-on-deck" approach, and use this attitude as the aspirational goal.

Another benefit of bi-vocational methodology can be that it provides good rhythms of life that can help the church planter have patience in the challenging, slow pace of planting a new work in the Hispanic context. Church planting is hard labor, but having the time for organic growth can provide the planter with the needed motivation to engage the community without the demands for seeds to become fruit-bearing trees in impossible timelines. Additionally, in the event that a bi-vocational pastor is working full-time in the community rather than within the mother church, he may be able to leverage his work as an opportunity to develop contacts in his target community.

A church or church planter desirous of using bi-vocational methodology to reach the Latino community should be aware of some of the potential challenges as well. The church planting pastor essentially has two separate pastoral roles. Therefore, if the new work grows quickly, it can lead to overwork, as he must stretch himself to fulfill the responsibilities of ministry in two unique contexts. As he works to balance his attention between both, it may also lead to neither ministry doing well, for the simple reason that there may not be enough time and energy to devote to either one.

For the church planter's family, the increasing demands of the bi-vocational workload may also be difficult. They may suffer if he is stretched thin and therefore has a hard time making time to spend with them, or if he is consistently coming home exhausted and with little to give to his family. Lastly, the church plant itself could possibly struggle to become financially independent, if members are not generous because they perceive that the pastor is already receiving a salary through the mother church.

Considering all the variables, bi-vocational methodology may be effective for reaching Hispanic communities in some circumstances, and offers particularly some financial and relational advantages for the church planter. However, both the mother church and church planter must carefully assess whether the planting pastor will have the ability to step into two unique roles, and whether the mother church will be able to adjust his position within the established church as necessary, so as to not overtax him as the new work grows.

Evangelist for the Presbytery Methodology

Evangelist for the Presbytery methodology involves a church planter receiving a call from a Presbytery to undertake the work of evangelism in a particular area, with the goal of eventually planting a new work. The planter thus begins solo to evangelize his target area progressively under the oversight of the local Presbytery. The prayer is that his efforts in sharing the gospel with an unreached or underreached population would lead to conversions and that, in time, the planter would be able to hand those new believers over to a new pastor within a new church body. This new pastor would then continue to disciple this group, and grow together with them into a particularized church. Meanwhile, the evangelist would begin the work again in a different part of the city or Presbytery to gather a new group.

Owing to the involvement of the entire Presbytery, this methodology offers some unique advantages for planting a Hispanic church. In some ways, it may be likened to independent methodology that takes place in a virgin territory, yet the evangelist has a potential larger advantage of acting himself as a Presbytery (for more details on the role of an Evangelist, see the Presbyterian Church of America's *Book of Church Order* 8-6). Thus, in an area of the community that has few other churches or has not been influenced much by the gospel, as a Presbytery evangelist, he may ordain the necessary Ruling Elders, Deacons, and put together a mission church. Although such work may be quite daunting for a solo pastor, being under the auspices of the Presbytery may offer strong and vibrant connectional support, as the church planter may receive help from not only Presbyters, but their congregations as well.

In this fashion, a Latino church plant happening through evangelist for the Presbytery methodology can become the collective responsibility of the entire region that the Presbytery serves. This can also help establish robust financial support for the work, since multiple churches (and their members) will necessarily be able to contribute more than a single mother church.

Moreover, for the church planter, the benefits of Presbytery oversight yields opportunity for much accountability and support. At the same time, since he is working as an individual evangelist, the planting pastor may also enjoy the autonomy of conducting ministry and evangelism as he feels led, without being overshadowed by being under the care of any one church.

This level of autonomy can, however, also come with negative aspects. Since churches understand this work to be the collective responsibility of a larger group, churches and individuals may feel a lesser responsibility to be involved. Thus the pastor-evangelist runs the risk of actually receiving less ground-level support. Similarly, although he has access to accountability and support from the entire Presbytery, the reality of this methodology is that the planter often is only expected to report to quarterly meetings, with little to no weekly accountability. On the other hand, the planting pastor may find himself navigating tensions within the Presbytery if different churches become competitive in their levels of influence and involvement in the new work.

Evangelist for the Presbytery methodology provides a unique opportunity for reaching a new generation of individuals for Christ, but the realities of navigating such broad oversight may prove difficult for the church planting pastor. The interest in starting such a work also may vary significantly between different Presbyteries. Both a Presbytery and the potential church planting pastor-evangelist must ask themselves whether their own strengths fit this approach in a way that will best serve the Hispanic population they are wishing to target.

Site-Planting Methodology

In site-planting methodology, the church plant becomes an extension of an existing church in a new area of the city. The planting pastor is invited to be a part of a growing Session that is collectively reaching the city as one church (with localized outposts) rather than an entirely distinct Session in a new area. Although this is an older model, it has resurfaced recently in many Presbyteries, and has many strengths that may make it well-suited for church planting in the Latino context.

In the first place, since the mother church and church plant share both a Session and a vision through site-planting methodology, the church planter is able to begin his work with a momentum for ministry, rather than needing to create it. The Session and congregation are already united in their vision to reach multiple areas of the city through different sites, and the plant is an exciting part of this effort. Site-planting methodology can therefore also create a vibrant expression and experience of connectional ministry for the leadership and congregations of both the mother church and the church site.

Moreover, whereas many church planters must spend much time and energy trying to balance ministry with the various logistical demands that come along with starting a new work, sites mean there is leadership and structure already in place. Therefore this system is beneficial in that it allows the planter to focus on reaching his context. While other methods of church planting can also leave the church planter feeling isolated and overwhelmed, the shared Session provides an opportunity for both strong support and accountability.

In terms of financial concerns and timelines that tend to present difficulties for minority-culture church plants, site-planting methodology is particularly useful in such contexts since the shared Session, support, and structure essentially mitigates these challenges. This again frees the church planter to focus on ministry, in a healthy, unhurried fashion. It allows him to spend the needed time planting and watering seeds, without trying to reap a premature harvest, or without the necessary tools.

Like any other church planting strategy, however, site-planting methodology does also come with some potential pitfalls of which churches seeking to use this method should be aware. In particular, there may be unique challenges for using site-planting methodology for planting a Latino site out of a majority-culture church. For example, shared leadership and vision, while useful in many aspects, could also inhibit the localized autonomy and contextualization needed for reaching a minority-culture. If the planting church is unaware of the difference, or cannot understand the need for making changes, it may function more like a mother than a collaborative brother, thus hindering growth in the new context. Similarly, disagreements in leadership regarding what it looks like to reach two different areas may lead to unhealthy splits that leave both congregations and leaders hurt and disillusioned.

Although it does present with some potential problem areas, in general, site-planting methodology has proved quite viable for a church seeking to reproduce in the Hispanic context. The support for the church plant and planter in terms of relationships, finances, and accountability are unique to this methodology, while its lack of need for a particular timeline is also attractive in areas that may take more time than majority-culture church planting. Site-planting methodology goes a long way to address and even mitigate many of the unique challenges of Reformed church planting within the Hispanic context. It can be a good option for churches to consider when looking to reach the Latino populations in their cities.

House Church Methodology

House church methodology usually entails a web of a few or many smaller, interconnected groups that meet in the homes of congregational members. Of all the methodologies, this one is the easiest to reproduce as house churches are small, informal gatherings that simply provide the opportunity to care for and disciple intimate communities. In this methodology, the church planter is responsible for visiting each small congregation to create synergy and connectivity, with the duties of a regional pastor. Once the pastor has found another viable leader and there are enough new families, they can quickly and easily begin a new group, without the need for finding a large space or to establish various ministries to begin worship. Moreover, the small, uncomplicated, and intimate nature of this methodology helps to foster an organic culture that provides opportunities for focusing on gospel relationships, rather than more complex ministry strategies. As church members meet together in their homes, house church methodology also becomes quite locally accessible. Thus it allows for a congregational life that can truly build a sense of neighborly community that larger churches with a commuter population tend to lack. The community aspect, in turn, can foster relational depth and provides excellent opportunity for discipleship and leadership development.

As another positive element, particularly among non-majority cultures that may be under resourced, or have a harder time becoming financially stable, house church methodology proves financially effective. There is no need to rent or purchase large properties, or to spend money on the logistical costs of such properties. The focus on relationship building and discipleship also cuts ministry costs that typically come along with larger church models, such as children's ministry costs, paying additional staffing, or paying a weekly worship leader.

At the same time, house church methodology also presents with some realities that may make it an unviable option for church planting in many scenarios. Planting pastors must consider whether their context will be accepting of a house church, since the religious background of many within the Hispanic community expects a level of visible formality within the church. Thus, the lack of a traditional meeting space or the lack of formal worship can present a barrier to the Hispanic community viewing a house church with legitimacy and credibility.

For the church planter himself, the informality of house plant methodology may make it difficult to set and keep boundaries between ministry and family. Although this can be true in any methodology, the fluidity between daily life and ministry in house church planting may place inordinate stress on the church planting family if they are unable to set aside specific days and times to rest. Additionally, because of the lack of funding and resources, this methodology practically demands that the pastor himself be bi-vocational, thus creating additional responsibilities and potential stressors for him and his family.

While house churches are easy to replicate, house church methodology can also hinder church growth if there is a rapid increase in attendance that leaves inadequate space and insufficient capable leadership for attendees to feel comfortable and cared for. Moreover, the same constraints make certain ministries, such as children's ministry, much more difficult to accommodate. This may be a deterrent for those who want to participate in such opportunities.

A house church planter must also exercise caution that the informality of both space and worship do not foster a church culture that is anti-ecclesiological, or that has a false reverence of simplicity. Furthermore, if the church lacks the proper leadership, or the leadership lacks the proper training, a house church will be unsuited for the proper administration of the sacraments, thus not giving members access to some of the most visible and necessary means of grace. However, the right liturgy, steps, and sufficient leadership may mitigate this problem, allowing the house church to be considered as a proper church service (see the Presbyterian Church of America *Book of Church Order* sections 4 & 5).

Although it does offer some benefits as shown, generally speaking, house church methodology is not viable for the Hispanic context in America. Many Hispanics may struggle to accept this model, particularly if their religious background dictates otherwise. Moreover, if the goal is particularization within the PCA, the methodology will not prove effective, as the church will not have the leadership or financial resources for this process. While it may work in certain target areas or even for a certain time, a pastor looking to plant house churches in the Hispanic context must seriously consider whether he is willing and able to do the work of being bi-vocational, and contend with the challenges that its informality offers, both for his family and for the community.

Multi-Church Planting Partnership Methodology

Another newer approach to planting within the Latino context is multi-church planting partnership methodology. This method involves pastors of various churches coming together to assist a planter in various elements of ministry. For example, they may offer assistance with worship, evangelism, and fellowship. Certainly the structure of involvement offers the potential for significant support for the church planting pastor, as he does not have to do all the work of setting up individual ministries within the church on his own. It can free him to invest in individuals who are coming to the new work, and do outreach to people within his target context.

Another asset to this methodology is that multi-church planting partnership gives the potential for significant support, not simply from the assisting pastors, but from their congregations as well. As pastors of various churches lend time and effort to help the Hispanic plant, they can also help to cast a wide vision for their own church members. These members may decide to help in time, finances, or even by becoming a part of the work. The fact that many are collaborating in one church plant further helps to illustrate the Body of Christ working together as one unit, while simultaneously demonstrating the importance of the church plant and planter. This collaboration may also foster a sense of Presbyterian *connectionalism*, allowing others not simply to see the Hispanic church plant as a missional work, but as an important and mutually beneficial part of the local church.

> ***connectionalism:*** a word used within Evangelical circles to describe the need for pastors and churches to be connected with one another, and seek to make connections with other bodies for the glory of God and building up of the Church.

There are certainly challenges too, however, when it comes to beginning a Hispanic work through multi-church planting partnership methodology. Although many pastors may be involved, difficult situations that inevitably arise from time to time in any church may cause them to need to prioritize their own congregations. Yet this happens at the expense of the needs of the church plant. Moreover, while having an abundance of leadership may be beneficial to some degree, the sheer number of moving pieces may make it challenging to organize efforts, or to organize consistently. Furthermore, this leadership abundance may become unhelpful if the vision or personality of one or more of the assisting pastors begins to overshadow that of the church planter.

Taking all of these factors into consideration, it would be necessary for those considering this methodology first to assess how the multiple willing and available pastors might do working together and under the leadership of the church planting pastor. They also would need to consider whether the supporting churches are stable enough and have sufficient leadership to be able to commit the necessary time to the new work. As with each strategy for Hispanic church planting, multi-church planting partnership methodology requires that the churches and planter considering it both know their context and count the cost before committing to this particular method.

Network Planting Methodology

Network planting methodology involves the establishment of a network of churches that collaborate specifically in planting churches in the Hispanic context. Different from evangelist for the Presbytery methodology, in which a specific Presbytery calls a pastor-evangelist to begin a particular new work within its region, this methodology refers rather to a presbytery-of-sorts, or a network of churches that pool their resources together for a particular endeavor. Thus the network is not necessarily regional, but rather contextual-missional. Such a network can take place within a local Presbytery, or beyond one.

Some of the advantages to network planting methodology include greater support for the church planter and church plant: financially, relationally, directionally, and even organizationally. Since the network of churches has agreed to come together to support the work, it eases the financial burden of raising money on the part of the church planter, as well as lessening the strain on individual sending churches. This coming together of leadership can also give the planter significant personal support to which he may not have access through some of the other church planting methodologies, or that the leadership of a single church may not be able to provide.

Moreover, network planting methodology can help to provide directional wisdom for the new work, as a network that is specifically organizing to reach the new context will have much practical knowledge in knowing how to go about this kind of ministry. They will have other experiences upon which to draw, knowing what has and has not worked in the past, and therefore growing in every new endeavor. On a practical level, the network can also provide a good deal of organization and order that can be difficult to develop, or may even be lacking in many new works, particularly if it is not the strength of the church planter, or if he is already overburdened with responsibilities.

Nevertheless, undertaking network planting methodology within the PCA is highly entrepreneurial; the waters are fairly uncharted, and a planter or church wanting to use this method for Hispanic church planting may have a hard time getting buy-in.

At the same time, if a network for church planting forms either within or outside of the auspices of a local Presbytery, it can run the risk of undermining the local Presbyteries, not taking into consideration the influences as it should. Additionally, as it makes decisions for the church plant and planter, a network could function with a level of ecclesiological autonomy that is misleading and unhealthy. A church planting network must therefore be cautious to act in accordance with the governing standards of the church, while still benefiting from the strengths that its focus provides.

Another challenge for network planting methodology can come if the coalitions are too far apart. In this case, rather than having the benefit of multiple levels of influence caring for the church planter, the participating churches may struggle to provide adequate ground support. Even so, the plausibility of this methodology is very promising, due its unique ability to cooperate cohesively and strategically. While it does have some potential drawbacks, network planting methodology has proven to be effective in other contexts, and could likely offer the same advantages for Hispanic church planting.

Determining the Right Methodology

When it comes to Hispanic church planting, as should be evident given the many examples and approaches, there is no one-size-fits-all methodology. While the three main categories of integrated, incubator, and independent methodologies come with their strengths and weaknesses, and each have stories of successes and struggles within the PCA from which to learn, many of the newer methodologies have their particular attractions as well. Determining the best method for reaching a minority-culture context within the larger structure of a majority-culture church or denomination is complex. And yet, there are many creative and promising methods to think through.

A church planter, church, or group of churches desirous of pursuing ministry within the Latino context must spend time in prayer and seeking wisdom as to which methodology may be best suited for their particular context, and play to their own strengths and weaknesses. It is impossible to determine these factors without first working to count the cost of the different approaches, and without also spending the necessary time to spy out the land and glean valuable insight as to the particular target context. Remember Nehemiah, who made sure to understand the challenges he was up against prior to beginning the work of rebuilding, or determining how the work should take place. The same must happen in choosing a methodology for church planting, as a church and church planter take the next steps for creating a plan for reaching the Latino context. Through much legwork, prayer, and wisdom, they can choose and commit to a methodology that plays to the strengths and needs of a particular area and people, and not simply be tempted to go with whichever method may seem the most glamorous, or even the most familiar.

Determining the *sazón* of the Church Plant

Once the church planter and his sending church have determined the methodology through which they will begin the new work, the next part of creating a plan to reach the Hispanic context is determining what the *sazón* (or heart and core) of the church plant will be. The *sazón* may be determined through asking and answering some fundamental questions that will help to think through and come up with the values, mission, vision, and Strategic Plan for the new work. These four areas not only help the church planter and supporting church(es) understand the task to which God is calling them, but they give a way to begin sharing the vision with others as well.

It is helpful to note that each of these four main steps to determining the *sazón* (values, mission, vision, and strategic plan) build upon one another: that is, each is foundational to the next, and thus should not be skipped or rushed. Furthermore, the first three are foundational for the more detailed work of the fourth and final Strategic Plan. And while answering the questions that go along with each may seem simple, doing it well means truly knowing the context, walking the community, listening, and praying for clarity on what it looks like to reach the target area. Church planters will benefit from taking each step slowly, and in the proper order.

> ***sazón:*** literally "seasoning" or "flavor," but can be used colloquially to speak of something or someone with a full personality or gravitas. Something with *sazón* is filled with just the right flavor and spice, either literally or culturally.

Values Statement

In determining the values statement for a new work, the church planter should strive to answer the question, "Who are we?" While the question is simple, digging deeply and taking the time to word the answer carefully is essential for laying out the core beliefs of the church. These core beliefs dictate how the church should operate, and become foundational to the group's DNA. Sharing a values statement with others also allows potential launch team members to determine if they also share the heart of the church plant. Spending time to determine values is also useful in that, if the church plant has an organizational problem or other disagreement at some point, the leadership will be able to return to their values statement and use it to decide how to proceed.

The following are examples of two church's values statements that help to show how these values may vary in different contexts and churches:

> *"At Christ Central Church we value the Bible and what God says in His word. We value spiritual growth and the discipleship of our people. We value diversity and the picture in Revelation 7 of every tribe, tongue, and nation worshiping together as one. And we value community within the body of Christ as we grow in our relationship with the Lord and with each other."*
>
> (Christ Central Church, Charlotte, NC)

> *"God's grace; Community; Good News; Lordship of Jesus Christ; Spiritual Growth."*
>
> (Christos Community Church, Norcross, GA)

As is evident in the given examples, values statements can be more or less detailed, written as a paragraph, or a simple list; yet their main goal is to give a person a glimpse into what the focus of a church plant will be, and allow the planter to begin to think about how he will focus his work in reaching his context.

Mission Statement

After defining core values, the next step in determining the *sazón* of a church plant is to come up with the Mission Statement. A mission statement should answer the question, "What are we?" or "Why do we exist?" It explains the purpose of the church plant and what it does, and should build off of the given values. Many times, Christian organizations will build their mission statements with the Great Commission (Matthew 28:18-20) in mind, but a church should use their values and context to commit to their particular mission.

A mission statement is particularly important in keeping a church or organization from losing its primary focus. Like the values statement, it provides something to which leadership may return if there is a question or disagreement over a new ministry idea, or focus of a particular ministry. It helps provide the rails to keep the church plant from going off track while pursuing the vision.

Below are examples of the mission statements of three different churches:

> *"Freeing people to enjoy God, hear His truth, grow in diverse community and engage the world with the renewed dignity that comes from Christ."*
>
> (Christ Central Church, Charlotte, NC)

> *"To bear witness to Christ and make disciples of Him from all people with no distinction, to be part of His body. (Acts 15:9)"*
>
> (Emmanuel Presbyterian Church Upstate, Greenville, SC)

> *"Connecting with people and building relationships through community worship, neighborhood-focused ministry, serving local needs, mentoring, and worship."*
>
> (Good News Church, Suwannee, GA)

Like the vision statement, mission statements may be more or less detailed, but provide a general picture of purpose for the church plant. The first of these examples, it bears noting, comes from the same church as the first values statement given above. It is helpful to see how their values then play out and are expanded in the mission statement. The second includes the Scripture passage from which they have chosen their mission, and demonstrates how one might build upon a particular passage to develop a mission.

Vision Statement

Once a church planter can answer who they are (values), and why they exist (mission), the next step is to come up with the vision, by answering the question, "Where are we going?" The vision statement speaks to the church plant's aspirations, and describes where the planter believes the church plant is going, or what he feels God is calling the new work to look like in the future. It may be helpful to think of the vision as what may occur over a 5-year span. Developing a vision statement takes much prayer and discussion. Depending on the method of church planting and context, it may even be helpful for the planter to form some focus groups to help determine the vision.

The following are examples of the vision statements of three different church works:

> *"Emmanuel Upstate will be a covenantal, multi-generational congregation of people from various cultural and ethnic backgrounds, with a common desire to worship the Triune God in the historic, reformed, and confessional manner, who will strive to be an example of the Grace of God by breaking through cultural and ethnic barriers."*
>
> (Emmanuel Presbyterian Church Upstate, Greenville, SC)

> *"Being a community that experiences and expresses LOVE from God to others."*
>
> (Good News Church, Suwannee, GA)

> *"To glorify God by delighting in His grace, and loving the Rio Grande Valley."*
>
> (The Crossing Church, McAllen, TX)

Again, as demonstrated through the examples above, a vision statement may demonstrate more or less simplicity, but it must point to a greater goal and vision for the church. It is worth noting again that the churches listed in the first two examples are the same ones given as two of the examples of mission statements provided earlier. Thus it is helpful to see how a vision grows out of a church's mission, providing direction for the previously determined values and mission. While a mission statement may take much time and prayer to formulate, it will help to keep the church plant headed in the right direction as it takes shape and grows even into a particular church.

The Strategic Plan

A church planter should begin working on his strategic plan only after the other three steps of values, mission, and vision are in place. The temptation for church planters often is to jump ahead into the details of strategic planning before finishing with the other three; yet a strategic plan may be quite detailed and it is easy to get lost in the weeds. So it is essential to be able to fall back on the predetermined values, mission, and vision at this phase.

The Strategic Plan answers the question, "How will we get there?" It therefore becomes less philosophical, and more practical. While it is meant to give a broad overview of how the work of the church plant will play out, it necessarily contains many details. It may be helpful to visualize the Strategic Plan as the route on the roadmap to the destination (vision), that uses the values and mission as signposts to stay en route (see Figure 5). Strategic planning involves coming up with a philosophy of ministry, ministry goals, objectives, and even a financial plan.

Figure 5

Perhaps understandably, the Strategic Plan cannot be encapsulated into a neat sentence or brief paragraph, as it involves many more facets and details than can fit into a small space. While a church may put values, mission, and vision statements on their website or perhaps on a card to give to supporters or potential partners, the Strategic Plan involves more behind-the-scenes planning that will allow the church planter to direct his leadership and members in carrying out the vision. Having such a plan in place will also help the church planter complete the final phase of planning for the new work, which is putting together a church planting proposal.

The following section will help church planters to think through some of the various aspects of the Strategic Plan that they will need to carry out their visions within minority-culture contexts. These include elements of the philosophy of ministry goals and objectives, such as how networking and evangelism should take place, and what discipleship strategies should look like; and also funding strategies for the new work. A church planter should consider each of these elements carefully and with much prayer, keeping his values, mission, vision, and cultural context in mind, as he plans for the new work.

The Strategic Plan: Networking and Evangelism Strategies

An essential part of church planting within the Hispanic context is networking and evangelism. Generally speaking, church planters are self-starters, willing to build something from nothing. Such a personality is particularly helpful within the Hispanic church planting context, as there is an even greater need in these underreached populations for networking within the community and evangelism.

However, a church plant will grow at a slow pace if the church planter is the only person engage in these activities. It will grow at a much faster rate if the church planter engages in personal networking and evangelism, while also training and equipping others on his team to do the same. Coming up with a strategy for networking and evangelism will help a him to be intentional in these critical endeavors; it will also provide him the opportunity and methodology to invite others to collaborate with him in this part of church building.

Admittedly, a reality that Hispanic church planters face in networking and evangelism is that, in most areas, there tend to be few people with the needed cultural and linguistic skills to become part of a core group able to reach the diversity of the community. Ultimately, it is the Lord who opens networks and relationships; it is also the Lord who is able to use and shape willing hearts for the furthering of His Kingdom among the diversity of the peoples and nations He has created. Trusting in this truth, Hispanic church planters should invest significant amounts of time developing a prayer team and communicating with them regularly, as he works with them and others to begin networking and evangelism within the target community.

Although networking and evangelism go hand-in-hand, networking must begin first, as it is the engine which will feed other outreach and evangelism efforts. Networking does not stop when evangelism begins, but it must precede it. Simply defined, networking is meeting new people. The act of creating new contacts may seem simple enough; yet particularly within the Hispanic community, networking must also include the establishment of *confianza*, or trust.

> ***confianza:*** Literally, "confidence" or "trust"; yet in the Hispanic context, this word goes further to speak to a sense of mutual reciprocity in a relationship, in which both parties recognize a sense of deep and abiding trust and commitment to one another through the development of a long-term relationship (aka, *gente de confianza*).

The understanding of the word *confianza* in Spanish, however, goes further than its English definition; ra-ther, *confianza* implies a deep and abiding trust and respect between people. While networking is a necessary start for making new contacts, networking while building *confianza* with individuals and the community is essential for evangelism in the Latino context. The most meaningful evangelistic conversations occur when there is already established *confianza* between the two parties. A person may build *confianza* by showing interest in an individual as a whole; by listening to understand, rather than listening to win an argument; and also though a willingness to be honest and transparent with others. Church planting pastors in the Hispanic context must think through establishing *confianza*, and leading their outreach groups to do the same, as they make contacts in their target areas.

One fundamental opportunity for building relationships and establishing *confianza* is through outreach events. Outreach activities are opportunities for church planters (and their teams, as applicable) to invite those contacts within their circles of influence and in their target communities into their "space," whether that might be a home, or a meeting facility. The goal of these outreach opportunities is to deepen newly-formed relationships, and to establish *confianza* so that the work of evangelism can also take place.

Aside from inviting in, it is also essential that this idea of networking and building *confianza* also incorporates a willingness and readiness to also go out, and be the invitees. While the term "outreach" comes with a connotation of gathering others into the host's space, *confianza* comes not simply through hosting, but through a willingness to "be all things to all people" (cf. I Corinthians 9:19-23) by graciously entering homes, associations, groups, and activities, as there are opportunities and invitations.

As outreach happens within the community, it also gives the church planter and church plant a level of visibility and credibility among the target population. Those who have seen and attended events may begin to invite more friends and neighbors. Thus networks grow, along with the opportunity for strengthening *confianza* in the community and opening new doors for gospel growth (see Figure 6). The work may be slow, but it is critical for becoming a visible, trusted entity within the Hispanic community. The church planter must consider the best ways for networking and

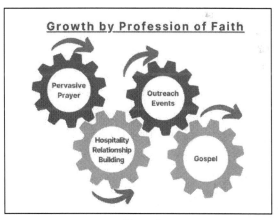

Figure 6

outreach as he builds his strategic plan and seeks evangelistic opportunities. (See Appendix C for more ideas for networking and outreach that may be helpful in strategic planning.)

There are many ways to share the gospel. As the church planter continues thinking through his Strategic Plan, he should come up with some different evangelistic strategies that may work within his context, and that he can share with his launch team. For many people, the work of evangelism often feels uncomfortable, and they may use this feeling as an excuse not to evangelize. Yet the amazing reality is that all believers are called to the incredible task of sharing their faith with others, and a church planter must be willing to lead in this effort of "doing the work of an evangelist" (cf. 2 Timothy 4:5). Still, there are many, starkly different methods of evangelism, and the church planter should come up with evangelistic strategies that fit both his personality along with the needs of his community. As he teaches others to evangelize, he must also examine his own heart and recognize that his efforts will be forced and awkward if they are not an overflow of his own personal relationship with the Lord and desire to see his community transformed for Christ.

The work of evangelism in the Hispanic context takes time and patience. It may be easy for the church planter to grow discouraged if he is not seeing what he deems to be sufficient fruit. Yet the Lord Himself reminds His people through the prophet Isaiah that sharing the Word of God with others is never a lost endeavor; His Word does not return empty, but accomplishes His purposes and succeeds in the Lord's mission (cf. Isaiah 55:10-11). Thus the church planter can trust the work of the Holy Spirit through the Word, even if it does not yield the fruits he was anticipating, or in his expected timeframe. As the church planter himself trusts the work of sowing Gospel seeds to the Lord, he can invite his core team to do the same, encouraging them that it is God who makes things grow (cf. I Corinthians 3:7).

> *"For as the rain and the snow come down from heaven and do not return there but water the earth, making it bring forth and sprout, giving seed to the sower and bread to the eater,* ¹¹ *so shall my word be that goes out from my mouth; it shall not return to me empty, but it shall accomplish that which I purpose, and shall succeed in the thing for which I sent it."*
>
> – Isaiah 55:10-11

Ideas for evangelism within the target population must be a part of the Strategic Plan, but only as the church planter recognizes his responsibility in faithfulness to the call, while it is the Lord who provides the growth. Such a recognition, even given with supporting verses in the Strategic Plan, will help the church planter and church plant remain encouraged when the work of Hispanic church planting seems slow and difficult.

The Strategic Plan: Disciple-Making Strategies

While networking and evangelism strategies are fundamental to a Strategic Plan for reaching the given context, laying out some disciple-making strategies is the next step. Once again, disciple-making does not mean a cessation of networking or evangelism, but rather is a building upon the previous steps, even while the earlier work continues. The Great Commission in Matthew 28 calls on believers to "Go therefore and make disciples of all nations…" (28:19ff), and such a calling is an integral part of the work of a church planter who has the opportunity to reach Latino nations right in his own backyard. In simple terms, discipleship is intentionally investing in people to help them move toward an increasing spiritual maturity. It is a cyclical and ongoing process.

The process of helping Hispanics to grow in spiritual maturity is, like that of everyone else, a lifelong journey. However, there are some potential obstacles particular to the Latino context of which a church planter should be aware and prepared to encounter. First, Hispanic communities that come from a Roman Catholic background will need a reintroduction to the Bible, as many will have little to no biblical knowledge. In many cases, they have been taught to fear the Bible. The church planter should have a clear plan to care for this potential group of individuals, and must be willing to start slowly with the very basics of the Christian faith.

Secondly, there is a segment of the Hispanic population in the USA that is undereducated; in many cases, these individuals may not know how to read and write in Spanish or in English. Consequently, a church planter should think through what it might look like to have a process in place whereby these individuals may learn about the Bible and grow alongside partners who can walk in it with them. Most discipleship materials and processes assume a certain level of education on the part of the disciple. Thus, church planters working in a different context must come up with creative, even oral, ways to disciple people who are in this predicament and help them gain a basic, biblical education.

Finally, those whom a Hispanic church plant may attract who are already professing Christians are most likely coming from a baptistic or Pentecostal background. The challenge here for the church planter will be to not overemphasize Reformed terminology, which they will find unfamiliar and even off-putting, but rather simply to display from Scripture the beautiful, biblical realities that are at the core of confessional Reformed churches.

Thus, in coming up with a strategic plan for disciple-making, a church planter must consider each of these challenges in turn, and design different processes to help those he may encounter within his particular context to grow in spiritual maturity. One key question that may help to guide him in this process is "What kind of disciples does the church plant desire to produce?" As he thinks through an answer, he will be able to determine which discipleship strategies may work best for achieving this end.

While discipleship can look as different as the individuals who participate in it, there are nevertheless four primary ways to invest in the lives of others. These four ways are: one-on-one, small groups, Sunday School, and Bible institutes. These four categories can help a church planter think broadly as he develops a discipleship plan that is tailored to his context. There is a time and place for each of these in disciple-making, and each comes with its own unique benefits:

One-on-one discipleship is particularly suited to smaller groups, allowing the church planter (or other disciple-maker) to truly know and invest in the lives of individuals in a personalized way. As a group grows, it will be difficult for the church planter to maintain one-on-one as the primary means for discipleship, although he may train others to do the same.

Small-group discipleship is an excellent way to blend relationships and learning, to both grow *confianza* within a group, while offering opportunities for deep, gospel growth. If a person came to Christ through an evangelistic Bible study, then inviting them into a discipleship-oriented small group is a logical next step.

> ***escuela dominical:*** While the literal translation is "Sunday school," in the Hispanic community, the idea specifically refers to church instruction for children on Sundays or during the worship service, and does not speak to further adult classes or instruction.

Another opportunity for disciple-making within a church plant is through Sunday schools. However, it is worth noting that, in general, when Hispanics hear Sunday School, they think of *escuela dominical,* or the Sunday teaching offered for children during Sunday worship. Yet being able to invite Hispanic individuals to a Sunday school – even if an explanation is needed – where they can come and learn more about the Bible in a non-threatening environment offers an excellent opportunity for them to know and understand the church's desire for and commitment to their growth.

Bible Institutes are common among many non-PCA churches, and also provide a good method for offering more formal discipleship and training. If his context is suited to it and he has the capacity to do such, a church planting pastor might take advantage of offering formal classes for his community throughout the week to train members for ministry. Bible Institute-type classes offer the chance for students to study, be graded on their endeavors, and receive a certificate of completion at the end of their classes.

As the church planter thinks through his context and the flock that the Lord is drawing to him, he should come up with a prayerful, strategic plan for disciple-making that potentially uses each of these four categories to some degree in a way that creatively caters to his context. In coming up with a strategic plan for discipleship, he should also think through what it looks like not only for adults, but also potential children and youth.

Of course, a single person cannot disciple an entire group, particularly as the church plant grows. It is therefore incumbent on the church planter to invest early on in the lives of others, being prayerful and intentional in the process, so that these disciples will in turn be able to follow the plan for discipleship and invest themselves in the lives of others whom the Lord brings to the church plant.

In thinking through the Strategic Plan for disciple-making, it may be helpful to see an example of how one Hispanic church has thought through helping their flock to grow. The pastor of Christos Community Church describes their discipleship methodology thus: "Our discipleship pathway at Christos Community is not linear but spiral. We do not begin at point A, moving people along a straight line to reach point B and then deploy them as newly minted, mature Christian leaders. Our process acknowledges the reality of the ups and downs of the Christian walk, the challenges of walking in a matter worthy of our Redeemer. Our process has three basic elements, which are visited in each repetition of the spiral, in a much deeper and richer form." The following gives an example of how Christos Community Church has described its discipleship process, and what it hopes to see through discipleship:

Christos Community Church Discipleship Process

We describe our discipleship as follows:

Because of what the Triune God of the Universe has done, and because He is coming back soon, we exist to see, enjoy, and share the Beauty of Jesus Christ in cultural diversity, for the shalom of our communities.

Elements of Discipleship

To See: We strive to know His Person & Work better and better. We desire to know who He is, and what He has done.

To Enjoy: Transformed by a vision of His Beauty, we want to enjoy it by affirming our own hearts with the Gospel. We grow in our desire to give ourselves away through service to others that is humble, compassionate, and generous.

To Share: We long for the opportunity to tell others about His work in us. We want to encourage and support others, to experience the same meaningful spiritual transformation that He is working in us.

Our discipleship process, then, provides the environment where opportunities to experience these three elements take place. Now, since no one can have an encounter with the True Living God and remain the same, there must be evidence of such an encounter. We recognize that the appreciation of this evidence is often affected by our own cultural lenses. With this in mind, we have codified the expected outcomes in terms which are independent of a particular culture.

Expected Outcomes

Humility. This is the ever-increasing ability to set aside our cultural preferences, and sometimes even our rights, for God's glory, our delight, and the blessing of others.

Compassion. As we grow in our understanding of God's mercy and compassion for us, we also grow in the desire and inclination to imitate that compassion so that others may experience it, here and now.

Generosity. God has blessed us immeasurably in Christ Jesus, and because of this, it is our increasing delight to reflect that generosity to others

> so they can see it and enjoy it, particularly in the way we serve others and interact with them.
>
> The fundamental expression of these three expected outcomes is our practice of the spiritual disciplines of fasting and prayer, both personally and as a gathering of His saints.

The discipleship process of Christos Community Church offers one example for how a church intentionally reaches their particular context. While it is a helpful example, church planting pastors must resist the urge to copy and paste someone else's discipleship process. Rather, as with any other part of the Strategic Planning process, they must use their values, mission, and vision as guideposts, also taking into consideration their own personalities, training, and the context of those whom they will train. A strategic plan for discipleship is one that may begin one way, but will need reviewing, and may need adjusting from time-to-time to continue to be the most efficacious in caring for the flock that the Lord brings to the ministry.

The Strategic Plan: Funding Strategies

While every Strategic Plan will be catered to its specific context and the unique vision of the church plant and church planter, the church planter should not neglect to include some fundraising strategies as the final stage of his planning. Most church planters, even if they are receiving significant support from a mother church or sending organization, will still need to raise a portion of the projected funds necessary to begin the work. In the case of Hispanic church planting, this figure tends to be higher than in majority-culture churches, as the timeline is more drawn out. While the task of fundraising can be daunting and does require much time and effort, it will be helpful if the church planter thinks about it as an opportunity to invite others into the Lord's work who may not have a chance to participate in other manners. Incorporating fundraising strategies into the Strategic Plan will help the church planter not only think creatively and envision the time and effort he should set aside for such activities, but also help him think of its integral purpose for sustaining the new work to which he has been called.

Perhaps one of the greatest hindrances to coming up with funding strategies for the Hispanic church planter is understanding the reality of the necessity of money in doing the work of ministry. In the Latino context, there is sometimes an expectation that the work of ministry should just happen, regardless of funding. However, the reality is that someone has to be earning money to support the lives of the planter and his family (and any other ministry workers), not to mention the work of ministry and outreach of the church plant itself. Even (and especially) the months and years prior to an official church launch need funding to allow outreach to occur, and to free the planter to learn his context and invest in the lives of others.

It can be quite surprising to first-time church planters and first-time mother churches that the cost needed to plant and support a church all the way to particularization is so high. For majority-culture church plants, data shows this figure is roughly $100k per year, over the course of three years. But given the realities of the longer timelines required in Hispanic church planting, the overall figure tends to be far larger. Thus, creating a realistic budget for church planting is an essential part of coming up with a strategy for fundraising, as it will be useful both for the church planter, as well as for his potential supporters. (Chapter 16: *Realistic Budgets and additional funding Strategies for Hispanic Church Planting* offers more details regarding practical aspects of creating a budget and raising funds.)

Moreover, church planters and their sending churches may be surprised to find that the responsibility for raising funds belongs both to the planter and the mother church. It requires collaboration, creativity, prayer, and strategy. Support raising is the catalyst that allows the project to move forward. As funds begin to come in, it can also be a very tangible picture of God's provision for the new work, and care for the church planter and the ministry.

In coming up with a strategy for fundraising therefore, the church planter must first confront the reality that the work of raising funds is necessary, and that it requires complete trust in the Lord's provision of such a seemingly daunting figure. It requires a deconstruction of the idea that successful church planting can happen apart from funding, or without adequate resources, along with a firm belief that God is able to provide. It means trusting that "the laborer deserves his wages" (Luke 10:7, and cf. Matthew 10:10, I Timothy 5:18), and it means valuing the calling to reach a certain context to the extent that raising funds to care for them is more than worth it, because it is Kingdom work.

Once the church planter has prayed and is convinced of these things, he will be better equipped to come up with a working strategy for raising the necessary funding. This will look like networking and sharing the vision with any and all who will listen. It looks like making a plan to meet people everywhere to share the vision of what God has called him to do, and then inviting these individuals to be a part of the work through their giving. Knowing clearly the needs of the community, along with the values, mission, vision, and a working budget for accomplishing these things, are essential in seeking financial support. Thus, synthesizing these elements into a compelling church planting proposal or presentation (see below) can be an effective way to invite others into participating financially in the project.

Nevertheless, it deserves reiteration that the most important part of the fundraising strategy is understanding the need, and trusting the Lord's provision. It looks like refocusing the idea not to simply raising money, but raising one's heart to God, and bringing others into the picture of what God is doing and what He can do through the church plant. It looks like bringing churches, organizations, and individuals into the exciting vision of the new work, offering them the privilege of participation, and trusting God to do the rest.

Writing a Compelling Church Planting Proposal

A church planting proposal is where all the hard work of visioning and planning comes together in one, succinct, compelling, and courageous presentation. A good proposal represents the culmination and synthesis of much hard work and research. It can only happen once a mother church (or sending organization) and church planter have committed to the methodology, and the church planter has worked long and hard to establish the *sazón* of his church plant, through coming up with values, mission, vision, and a strategic plan for achieving these goals.

The purpose of a church planting proposal is to be able to share the vision clearly with others, to be able to invite them to participate as prayer warriors, financial supporters, networkers, and even participants in the physical work of church planting. Thus, a good church planting proposal will include more than facts and figures. It should incorporate pictures and stories that engage the listener, along with charts and graphs that help communicate the vision and needs. It should both winsomely and courageously invite others to participate.

The following provides an example of one church planting proposal from Vive Charlotte Church (the story of Vive Charlotte is given as a case study in *Chapter 5: Learning by Example*). While every church plant proposal will necessarily look different to fit the personality and style of the church planter, it is helpful to see how others have synthesized values, vision, mission, and strategic plan into one, succinct presentation to help share the project with potential supporters and participants.

Keep in mind that it may be necessary to update the proposal from time-to-time, as relevant data (like amount of funds raised versus the needs) changes.

VIVE CHARLOTTE
CHURCH

Anna, Benjamin (11/06/19), Daniela (10/10/17) & José Portillo.

I am excited to share with you that we are working in **church planting** in University City, Charlotte, NC with the goal to launch in Fall 2021. We know that only the Gospel of Jesus Christ has the power to transform lives, empowering us and others to be agents of change in our particular circles of influence, while also bringing Gospel life to our community and city.

The word "Vive," is a Spanish word which means "He lives," yet it is also a command for us to live. Thus our church name, "**Vive Charlotte**" becomes the declaration of what we desire to be: those who proclaim His life; those who invite others to be transformed by His life; and those who seek to live and work to bring that message of life to our city.

UNIVERSITY CITY - MINISTRY OPPORTUNITIES:

- 98k people within 10 minutes in a highly diverse community
- 15k people are 2nd and 3rd generation immigrants or new Americans (one of the least churched groups in the US) 16 - 26 years old.
- Over 30 k Spanish-speaking people within 20 minutes.

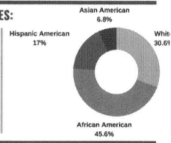

Asian American 6.8%
Hispanic American 17%
White 30.6%
African American 45.6%

We desire to proclaim the Gospel, to walk alongside people in their journey of faith, and to empower them to bring His life into all their circles of influence and beyond.

Please **join us** in entrusting this work to our Lord who has the power to see it through and accomplish what He has purposed through our lives, in this work, in this city, and at this moment in time.

A CHURCH PLANT OF THE PCA TO THE UNIVERSITY CITY AREA OF CHARLOTTE, NC.

UNIVERSITY CITY IN CHARLOTTE, NC

A church for the diversity of the community and for the next generation of leaders.

WE WOULD INVITE YOU, FIRST AND FOREMOST, TO PARTNER WITH US IN PRAYER:

That we would know our deep need for Jesus and that we would live overflowing in grace, mercy, and love from above.

For deep and meaningful relationships that lead people not to ourselves or to an exciting new church, but to the "living hope" (I Peter 1:3)

For us to entrust all of our personal and church planting needs to God:
- Financially
- Relationally
- Missionally

PLEASE ALSO CONSIDER WHETHER YOU MAY BE CALLED TO INVEST AND PARTNER WITH US IN SOME OF THE FOLLOWING WAYS AS WELL:

AN ADVOCATE

Help us connect with others who would:
- pray
- be advocates
- support us, or
- join us "on the ground"

FINANCIAL PARTNER

Would you consider asking God if you should invest in this project?
Our target ministry population is young and (in most cases) in school and unable to work full-time.

JOIN US

We need people who hear and act upon God's invitation to be part of this church planting adventure joining us in ministry with boots on the ground.

"I have found that there are three stages in every great work of God: first, it is impossible, then it is difficult, then it is done."
— Hudson Taylor

FOR WAYS TO GIVE PLEASE REACH OUT AT JOSE@VIVECHARLOTTE.COM

BY MAIL | ONLINE | DONATE STOCK

Not only may the church planter need to update his proposal on occasion, as support progresses, or as new, salient details emerge, but he may also find it helpful to create several versions of the proposal for different types of presentations. For example, in the case of Vive Charlotte, the above reflects a truncated proposal for handing out in conversations; the planter also created a slide-show version for virtual presentations, and also an expanded, four-page proposal with a detailed budget to send to potential supporting churches, networks, and individuals.

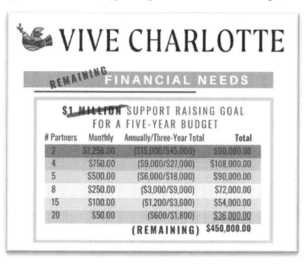

While this example may provide some useful ideas, each church planter should seek to reflect his own personality and that of his target context in his personalized proposal. Some church planters may choose to be more or less detailed, to provide fewer or more pictures and graphics, or to create a proposal following a different layout altogether. (See Appendix D for a suggested outline to help church planters think through the specifics of what to include in a proposal, and how to organize the information.) The most important aspect is that the proposal clearly presents the *sazón* of the project in such a way as to draw others into the project. It should create an exciting picture of gospel ministry that should encourage others to want to be a part, in whichever way the Lord might be drawing them. While not every Christian is called to participate in any one particular work, every work of gospel ministry should be exciting to every Christian, as they see the opportunities for gospel renewal in new areas. The church planting proposal helps to showcase this potential, and allow the viewers to prayerfully consider whether God is calling them to participate in this particular ministry.

Conclusion

Creating a plan for church planting within the Hispanic community (or any other context, for that matter), requires, as this chapter has demonstrated, much prayer, patience, support, and wisdom from the Lord and through the counsel and experience of others. The church planter (along with his supporting church or network, to the degree to which they may be involved) must keep his target demographic at the forefront of his mind, while also considering the type of support he will have from the sending organization and other individuals, as he seeks to plan the ministry. He must keep in mind his own strengths and weaknesses, as well as personality, as he prayerfully plans for the work to which the Lord has called him. Yet overall, throughout the planning process, he must remember that the work is, first and foremost, the Lord's work. Therefore, as the Proverbs say, he must pray and trust that the Lord will direct his path, constantly submitting his plans before the Lord (cf. Proverbs 3:5-6). Ultimately, the plan for a church plant seeking to reach the Hispanic context is to bring glory to God's name!

> *"Trust in the LORD with all your heart and lean not on your own understanding; 6 in all your ways submit to him, and he will make your paths straight."*
>
> – Proverbs 3:5-6

CHAPTER 4:

STEPPING OUT IN FAITH

> *"Then Moses summoned Joshua and said to him in the sight of all Israel, 'Be strong and courageous, for you shall go with this people into the land that the LORD has sworn to their fathers to give them, and you shall put them in possession of it. ⁸ It is the LORD who goes before you. He will be with you; he will not leave you or forsake you. Do not fear or be dismayed.'"* –
> Deuteronomy 31:7-8

Beginning the process of church planting involves much thinking, prayer, and planning, all of which are essential to starting strong. Planning may be daunting in many aspects, but it is also exciting: thinking of all the possibilities, and strategizing how best to reach those whom the Lord is entrusting to the new ministry should make both the church planter and his supporters ready to see what the Lord will do. Yet the end goal of a church planter is not merely to envision the work, but to actually do it, trusting the Lord's guiding hand and leaning into His strength.

Joshua was called to the exciting task of succeeded Moses and leading the Israelites out of the desert where they had been wandering for forty years, and into the promised land of Canaan. Joshua was young, gifted, and a leader chosen by the Lord specifically for this task. Not only Joshua, but also Moses and the people of Israel knew that this was Joshua's role. And yet, as Moses prepared to pass on leadership responsibilities, he recognized that, in spite of the calling, in spite of the knowledge of what was to come and what the Lord would do in and through Joshua, Joshua needed to hear words of encouragement. Joshua needed to be reminded that "It is the LORD who goes before you. He will be with you; he will not leave you or forsake you. Do not fear or be dismayed."

Knowing the task to which the Lord had called Joshua, and in which the Lord would accompany him, Moses charges Joshua to "be strong and courageous." Moses knew by experience that leading God's people, no matter how certain one may be of the calling, requires courage, a stepping out in faith, a trusting that the Lord will not leave you or forsake you; trusting that it is the Lord who goes before you. In fact, this call to be strong and courageous, to trust the Lord's guidance, becomes a theme of the book of Joshua, with the Lord reminding Joshua of this charge three times in the first nine verses of the book! And indeed, Joshua listens and steps out boldly in faith, leading Israel into the Land of Promise, and conquering the Canaanite cities as he trusts the Lord's guidance. It is as if Joshua hears the charge of Moses, and adopts it as his life motto: "It is the LORD who goes before you... Do not fear or be dismayed."

Such must be the motto also of the church planter as he steps out in faith to do the work of reaching the Hispanic community for Christ. While it may feel terrifying to begin putting all the planning into action, if a church planter has indeed been called to the work of ministry in his context, he can move from planning into action, stepping out in faith because it is, in fact, the Lord's work, and the Lord's promise to be at work, in and through him, whatever happens. Recall that Joshua was one of the twelve spies whom the Lord had sent to spy out the land of Canaan earlier; while ten of the spies grew afraid and discouraged, only Joshua and Caleb saw past the fear to the goodness of what God was promising. God allowed the other ten spies to perish in the desert, but He chose Joshua to lead His people into Canaan.

Joshua's work was far from easy, and often it would have been quite simple for him to grow discouraged and even give up. As the Lord God reiterates to Joshua, so must the church planter reiterate to himself, "Have I not commanded you? Be strong and courageous. Do not be frightened, and do not be dismayed, for the LORD your God is with you wherever you go" (Joshua 1:9).

Recruiting ministry partners

After a church planter has spied out the land and created a plan for ministry, it is time for him to step out in faith. One of the first parts of stepping out in faith to do the work of church planting is for the church planter to recruit ministry partners. Ministry partners are individuals who can come alongside the church planter in multiple ways: through prayer, finances, as a personal friend and encourager to the church planter, as a connector to other interested individuals, or even as a member of the church planting project itself. Having ministry partners in each of these categories is a critical part of not doing the work alone.

The church planting proposal created in the Strategic Planning process is the primary tool for the church planter to be able to invite others to be involved in the project. It is the church planter's visual that helps others learn the *sazón* of the project, see the needs in the target context, and ask themselves whether the Lord may be calling them to participate. While telling individuals about the project is far easier than asking them to join, both of these elements are involved in recruiting ministry partners. Even as the church planter himself has seen the fields ripe for harvest and knows the need for laborers and partners, he now has the opportunity to share this vision, and step out in faith by asking boldly for others to join. This invitation does require much prayer, faith, and courage: "Be strong and courageous."

It also may take discernment on the part of the church planter to know how to ask people to participate. Nearly everyone can be a prayer partner; many can contribute financially, but asking someone to join the project as a core member or participant takes more discernment. Can they also see the good fruit of the land? Are their hearts invested in the vision? Asking the right questions and making an invitation takes wisdom and boldness. The church planter must pray, show people how they can be involved, and then trust God to prompt them to invest in the vision.

When it comes to recruiting people to be partners in ministry, it is also helpful to return to the example of Nehemiah, and see his commitment to prayer as he stepped out in faith. Remember that it was the Lord who had put the desire to rebuild the walls of Jerusalem into Nehemiah's heart, the Lord who had given him a heart and vision for the work. Nehemiah knew he would need help, and he was prepared to ask for it; yet prior to going into King Artaxerxes' presence, he fasted and prayed for many days. More than hoping in the help of a powerful king for the task of rebuilding, Nehemiah knew he needed to place his trust in the King of kings, both to provide for the work, and to give him boldness in making the ask.

A church planter must not neglect this crucial step of prayer. A posture of continual prayer becomes a powerful reminder to the church planter that, as daunting as the task may seem, or as unequipped as to ask for support as he may feel, the Lord is in control. Thus, a first step of collecting ministry partners is not only to pray for the process, but even to invite others into this essential task. A church planter might first recruit a prayer team for support, to pray with frequently about and for financial partners and core group or launch team partners. The church planter, and even the group together, could make a list of potential ministry partners in all categories of support, and pray for them together. It may even be that the Lord would move in the hearts of some of these initial prayer supporters to connect others to the work, or to join the work themselves. Regardless, prayer must be foundational as the church planter steps out in faith to recruit others.

Yet Nehemiah's example for stepping out in faith goes further. Even as church planters should start recruiting from within their circles of influence, and looking to those individuals to help broaden their scope, Nehemiah also boldly sought help from his circles of influence – in his case, the powerful King Artaxerxes. Once he received an audience with the king, he wisely waited until the right moment to present his plan. In spite of much preparation in prayer prior to this moment, Nehemiah continued to show his reliance on the Lord in making his request by offering up a brief prayer for help: "Then the king said to me, 'What are you requesting?' So I prayed to the God of heaven. And I said to the king..." (Neh 2:4-5ff). Relying on the Lord's sovereignty, Nehemiah was able to courageously ask for everything he needed to complete the work to which the Lord had called him.

> *"As soon as I heard these words I sat down and wept and mourned for days, and I continued fasting and praying before the God of heaven."*
> – Nehemiah 1:4

While not every potential ministry partner is as powerful or influential as King Artaxerxes, every interaction requires just as much reliance on the Lord's plan. Without this vision, it is easy for a church planter to lack the boldness, or to rely too much on his own eloquence, and to become frustrated and discouraged when those he had deemed the right people are not ready to join forces. Surrounding every potential partner and conversation in prayer allows church planters not only to speak boldly, but also to rest in the knowledge that God is and has been at work, long before the church planter asks anyone to participate physically or financially. While the church planter must be diligent in sharing the vision and asking for help, the Lord knows those whom He will draw as ministry partners for the new work.

Trusting God for the Resources

One final, crucial element of stepping out in faith requires not simply beginning to do the work of recruiting others, but trusting God to provide the resources. This has been the undercurrent already in this chapter on Stepping out in Faith, but it deserves more attention here. Joshua knew the Lord's presence in his task, he knew in general the lay of the land, and he knew where he was going (conquest), but he could not have pictured all that might entail. Nehemiah knew the work of rebuilding to which he had been called; he knew his reliance on the Lord even as he prepared to go, but he could not have envisioned each of the challenges he and those serving under him would face in rebuilding.

Church planting also – in any context, but particularly in the less-charted territories of reaching the Latino community – is a faith-stretching endeavor. Regardless of how meticulous and faithful the church planter is in his planning, fundraising, and recruiting processes, eventually something will come up that he did not consider. A need will arise that he did not plan for, and there will not be resources for the need. Funding promises will fall through; circumstances will change; a key ministry partner will need to step out; a process will take longer than anticipated. These things are not unusual in church planting, yet without the proper support and preparation, they can leave the church planter feeling frustrated or even make him want to give up.

Nevertheless, God's promise is to provide for and care for His people; His promise is to be at work, even when His purposes are hard to see, or the work does not look like what the church planter was anticipating. People may come and go; the church planter may need to readjust strategies; fundraising may have dry periods; "the grass withers, the flower fades, but the word of our God will stand forever" (Isaiah 40:8). Not just at the beginning phases, or during the planning process, but all throughout the hard labor of church planting, a church planter must remember this truth, and remind his ministry partners and supporters to do the same! Remember that God provided manna in the desert each day: exactly enough for the day, never too little, and without excess. He will provide and He will accomplish His purposes. So the church planter can be strong and courageous – not frightened – and unafraid of what may come, "for the LORD your God is with you wherever you go."

> *"The grass withers, the flower fades, but the word of our God will stand forever."*
> – Isaiah 40:8

CHAPTER 5:

LEARNING BY EXAMPLE

"Where there is no guidance, a people falls, but in an abundance of counselors there is safety." –
Proverbs 11:14

"By insolence comes nothing but strife, but with those who take advice is wisdom."
– Proverbs 13:10

"Without counsel plans fail, but with many advisers they succeed."
– Proverbs 15:22

Perhaps one of the best ways of preparing to plant a Hispanic church, either as a church planter or sending church, is to learn through the experiences of those who have already gone through the process, or who are going through it – from the positives as well as the negatives, being encouraged by how the Lord has used it all for His glory. Despite the enormous challenges of planting in the Hispanic context, the PCA has planted Hispanic churches in different regions of the country utilizing a wide variety of methodologies. These include the overarching integrated, incubator, and independent methodologies as discussed in Chapter Two, as well as variants of each. Looking back at these examples, it is encouraging to see what the Lord has allowed this denomination to accomplish already.

Indeed, as the Proverbs say – and as the very recounting of the stories of Scripture demonstrate – it is wisdom to listen to the stories, experiences, and guidance of others. Although nothing takes the place of personal conversations, this chapter seeks to offer a starting point for experiential guidance through multiple examples of various Hispanic church plants within the PCA. These include examples of flourishing, set-backs, and ones that did not survive. Yet even those church plants that might be deemed as failures, humanly speaking, have not happened apart from the Lord's purposes, and also offer an opportunity for learning and growth for new church planters and their mother churches.

Throughout all the efforts of reaching the Latino community, Christ the Lord has been at work. Thus, looking at case studies to see and marvel at the Lord's hand in growing the Hispanic church in the United States throughout past infuses hope for the future, for the Lord's continued faithfulness in building His church.

Church planters and churches desiring to reach the Hispanic context should read these true-life stories carefully, considering the contexts and demographics, methodologies, and strengths and weaknesses of each. It may be helpful to look for patterns that have led to success, as well as identify any potential common denominators that have ended in failure. Reading these case studies should prompt the church planter to specifically consider his own context, using the details of each case provided to think about what may work best (or what may not work) in his own respective community.

Hispanic Church Planting Case Studies

Although there is much to be learned from church plants across denominations, the PCA faces unique challenges with regards to planting Hispanic churches; thus, the examples given below highlight PCA works only, but should prove useful to many outside the denomination as well. Each case study outlines the demographic composition, church planter's profile, target group, model, worship style, finances, and an abbreviated history of the church. The studies also include the rough size of the mother churches, as defined by data from USAchurches.org. The cases selected are also intentionally from various city sizes across different parts of the USA. The charts below are intended as a helpful resource for referencing church and city sizes when considering each example.

Church Sizes*	
Megachurch	2,000 + attendees
Large church	301-1,999 attendees
Medium church	51-300 attendees
Small church	50 or fewer attendees

City Sizes	
Large city	500,000 + residents
Medium city	150,000-499,999 residents
Mid-small city	100,000-149,999 residents
Small city	50,000-99,999 residents

* defined by average weekend attendance

Integrated Methodology Examples

Here are two case studies of Hispanic churches that were planted using integrated methodology (a third appears in Chapter 3 as an illustration of integrated methodology). While both of these church plants have experienced their own difficulties, there have also been benefits for them of using this methodology. Other churches have had less success using integrated methodology, and have actually transitioned to incubator methodology in the planting process, as the subsequent case studies will demonstrate.

Carolina Presbyterian Church, Locust, NC

For many years, **Carolina Presbyterian Church**, a medium-sized congregation in Locust, NC, had been sending individuals on short-term mission trips to Mexico. As they continued these trips and established relationships with the people there, their vision for missions also grew. They began to set aside money in order to be able to support a Mexican pastor to come and train in a local seminary, with the end goal of him being able to return to Mexico better equipped to care for his flock and disciple other leaders.

> Carolina Presbyterian Church, Locust, NC
> *Zip Code:* 28097 & 28163
> *Population according to 2020 Census:* 3,238
>   Hispanic: 1%
>   White: 94%
>   African American: 3%
> *Ministry Methodology:* Integrated

This vision became a reality when a gifted Mexican pastor of a Presbyterian church in Mexico accepted the invitation, moving himself and his family to North Carolina to take the first steps towards his seminary degree by preparing for the Test of English as a Foreign Language (TOEFL). As they settled in Locust, they attended their supporting church, Carolina Presbyterian Church. With a pastoral heart and eyes open to his surroundings, the pastor noticed a small but growing Mexican population within his new community, and began ministering to them while preparing for the TOEFL examination.

Shortly thereafter, as the Mexican pastor passed the TOEFL and began his seminary degrees, Carolina Presbyterian Church experienced a change in leadership, leaving it without a pastor. The Mexican pastor, with another display of pastoral care, began to step in and help to care for the church and its congregation through the transitional period, even at the expense of not being able to dedicate as much time as planned to his own seminary training.

Eventually, Carolina Presbyterian was able to call a new pastor – one who also shared the church's vision for cross-cultural ministry. Meanwhile, as the Mexican pastor continued his studies, his own Presbyterian church in Mexico decided to fill his position, giving him the freedom to find a new calling. Though the situation could have been quite disheartening, Carolina Presbyterian recognized the Mexican pastor's giftedness and faithfulness in his labors; in 2017, they called him to try and establish a local Spanish-speaking congregation under the integrated model. This meant that the pastor would be a part of the Session, and that Carolina Presbyterian, as the mother church, would share their budget to cover most of the expenses of the Hispanic congregation (although the Mexican pastor also took a position teaching Spanish at the church school to complete his salary).

Through the Mexican pastor's efforts in leading Bible studies, and following up with visitors, a Hispanic congregation did indeed begin to grow, reaching primarily first-generation Spanish-speaking Latinos, while the pastor also continued his seminary studies. Upon his graduation, and subsequent ordination by the PCA in 2019, the Hispanic congregation saw growth to the point that the pastor was able to launch Sunday morning worship services.

The pastor, along with Carolina Presbyterian, have worked to establish and maintain their two pillars of ministry as pervasive evangelism, and intentional integration. With regards to the latter pillar, although the church offers two separate worship services by language preference, they also have combined services periodically throughout the year. Moreover, as a part of their core vision, members of the mother church are encouraged to volunteer for outreach events and ministry opportunities.

Once again, as has happened in many churches throughout the United States (and the world), the realities of the COVID pandemic took their toll, and in the fall of 2020, the Senior pastor of the mother church resigned. And once again, the Mexican pastor, while continuing to care for his own Hispanic congregation, was highly instrumental in caring for and helping the mother church congregation through the transition. By the fall of 2021, the mother church was able to call another senior pastor. Meanwhile the Mexican pastor has faithfully continued his work with the Hispanic congregation, which averages around 30 individuals, including children.

Although there have been challenges, and while Carolina Presbyterian's original vision was not for Hispanic church planting, through the vision of the Mexican pastor and the committed support of the mother church, the integrated methodology for Hispanic church planting has proved effective in this example. God has blessed Carolina Presbyterian's commitment to a cross-cultural vision, coupled with the

Hispanic pastor's giftedness, perseverance, heart for service, and heart for both the Hispanic population and the mother church's sheep, to allow Gospel ministry to grow in an area that an immigrant pastor with a vision was able to see was ripe for harvest.

Iglesia La Viña, Orlando, FL

The planting narrative of **Iglesia la Viña** is, like the stories of many Hispanic church plants, long and filled with challenges. Yet commitment to a vision to reach the large Hispanic population in Orlando, Florida, has permitted a new church to grow in the Lord's timing.

For some time, a large, primarily Anglo church in Orlando felt challenged to intentionally reach the Hispanic population in their city, and determined that starting an ESL program might give them some inroads. As the ministry started, second-generation members of the Anglo church stepped in to lead Bible studies for the ESL attendees. Although there was much excitement surrounding the ministry, the students did not attend consistently.

> **Iglesia la Viña, Orlando, FL**
> *Zip Code:* 32817
> *Population according to 2020 Census:* 92,452
> Hispanic: 36%
> White: 43%
> African American: 10%
> *Ministry Methodology:* Integrated

Then, at the end of 2013, a Mexican pastor met with the head of a church planting network, along with the Senior Pastor of the Anglo church, to broach the idea of planting a Hispanic church in Orlando. Encouraged by the pastor's prompting, in 2014, the Anglo church decided to hire a bilingual, bicultural Hispanic seminary student studying at the RTS-Orlando campus, to oversee and invest in the Hispanic group. This he did, faithfully following up with Bible study attendees and ESL students. After a year of service, the student had gathered a consistent group of around 20 individuals, who were meeting regularly for a bilingual life-group. One of these life-group attendees was a Puerto Rican seminary student. Although he was new to the Reformed faith, his participation in the life-group played a key role in his eventual ordination to the PCA. God was indeed blessing the small steps forward in ways perhaps neither the Anglo church nor the RTS student-leader were able to see at the time.

Encouraged by the RTS student's work and the direction of the ministry, the Anglo church commissioned the student to conduct an ethnographic and demographic study of the target context, so that they might be better prepared in taking the next steps of calling a church planter. However, the next steps in planting would take time. Upon graduation from RTS, the student leader accepted a full-time call to ministry in another location. Although it was an appropriate move for the student, without a leader, the growth of the Hispanic group waned.

Meanwhile, the financial situation at the Anglo church was declining, although they continued in their desire to serve the Hispanic population. After a long season of deliberation, in 2016 they issued a call to the Mexican pastor who had communicated with them about the idea of church planting a few years prior. The church would be able to offer him 10% of the budget, with the church planting network providing an additional 15%, leaving the church planter the rather difficult challenge of raising the remaining 75% of necessary support on his own. In spite of the obstacles, the Mexican pastor accepted the call, and began the arduous process obtaining a religious visa.

Continued financial struggles at the Anglo church necessitated their stepping out; yet in God's provision, another church within the local Presbytery agreed to step in as the mother church. Thus, in June of 2017 with his visa finalized, the Mexican pastor and his family prepared to relocate to the United States, while working to raise the remaining portion of the ministry expenses.

Although he had been a pastor in Mexico for many years, the church planter was required to become ordained in the PCA. This presents challenges for many Spanish-dominant candidates (see Chapter 15), yet thankfully, he was able to transfer his ordination and was shortly thereafter commissioned to begin the work officially.

As the church planter and his family adjusted to life in a new country, he also worked to follow up with those who had previously attended the Hispanic outreach Bible studies, ESL classes, and the bilingual life group. His faithful investment paid off, and by April of 2018, the group had grown into two life groups, and they were ready to launch public worship as Iglesia la Viña. Services were held in one of the mother church's classrooms, and took place on Sunday mornings in Spanish, with around 30 launch team members in attendance.

The launch of Sunday worship was only part of how Iglesia la Viña was serving the community, however. The members of the new church, under their pastor's leadership, became quite active in proclaiming the gospel and ministering to the needs of the surrounding first-generation Latino immigrants. As a result, they had the opportunity of witnessing many coming to Christ. Though their labor and reach were quite fruitful, as is often the struggle within transient immigrant communities, Iglesia la Viña did not experience numerical growth within their own body.

By the end of 2019, church attendance remained consistent at around 35 individuals, although outreach and ministry efforts included another 40 or more people. The church planter and his congregation rallied together in a vision to maximize outreach efforts in 2020, but the realities of COVID soon made them have to refocus ministry efforts. Moreover, as COVID continued to surge, the Senior Pastor of the mother church took another call, and was replaced by an interim pastor. Nevertheless, the Mexican church planter continued faithfully proclaiming the Word of God, and serving his community. By God's grace, in spite of the challenges, the congregation's numbers did not dwindle, but remained consistent throughout the pandemic.

In recent months, Iglesia la Viña has witnessed exciting growth. Not only has church attendance remained consistent, but there have been visitors every week, and they have received an average of one new member each month, such that some Sunday services have seen more than 40 people filling the meeting room to capacity. Not only that, but in 2021, after much effort and prayer, Iglesia la Viña was able to come to a place of financial stability, even to the point of being able to hire a part-time lay-worker to assist with youth and Sunday school.

Certainly the journey to growth and stability for Iglesia la Viña has been long and difficult, with many transitions and many potentials for questioning the Lord's plans. Yet it is encouraging to see how the Lord has delighted to provide for and maintain this vision, allowing faithful members of a small church to do much with little. The story of Iglesia la Viña should offer hope to church planters to see that the Lord can use what may look like small efforts to accomplish great work for His Kingdom.

Integrated-to-Incubator Methodology examples

While typically it is most effective when churches commit to one methodology for church planting, sometimes there are situations that necessitate reassessment and flexibility in methodology for the health and growth of the church plant. The following two case studies provide examples in which the mother churches felt that such a change would benefit the church plant. It will be helpful to read the case studies and ponder what made these changes necessary, whether such transitions could have been avoided, or where being able to reevaluate and recalibrate proved helpful for these churches.

Rey de Gloria, Miami, FL

The story of **Rey de Gloria** is unique among the case studies in that it not only demonstrates a change from integrated to incubator methodology during the church planting process, as well as a transition from mother church to Presbytery oversight, but also provides an example of pulling a second methodology (in this case, bi-vocational) under the umbrella of one of the three main categories.

Rey de Gloria, Miami, FL
Zip Code: 33127
Population according to 2020 Census: 442,241
Hispanic: 72%
White: 11%
African American: 15%
Ministry Methodology: Integrated to Incubator

The vision for Rey de Gloria began when a large church in Miami, Florida, feeling the need to reach the majority-minority Hispanic population of their city, decided to search for a Spanish-speaking pastor to help them reach cross-culturally. With the desire to operate via integrated methodology in a way that would work financially for the church, the mother church thus issued a bi-vocational call for a pastor willing to work as a security guard at the mother church during the day, while seeking to gather a second group for an evening service. In 2012, they hired a first-generation Spanish-dominant pastor to fill the call.

Although originally from Argentina, the new Hispanic pastor had lived in the area for ten years prior to accepting the call, and therefore already had much familiarity with his target demographic. As he began his roll, he felt convinced that the primary need of the Hispanic community in the area was theological training, and so he began teaching seminary classes at Miami International Seminary in the evenings to be able to open doors for ministry. The Lord blessed his observation and work, opening many relational networks through the students who were attending his classes. By 2014, he was able to launch a public, Spanish-speaking worship service in the evening at the mother church with a group of around 40 individuals.

Throughout these first years of building relationships and gathering a group, the church planter was working in and paid by the mother church, although the mother church members were uninvolved in his outreach events and ministries. While he attended Session meetings on occasion and had the opportunity to meet with the Senior Pastor as needed, he was not a part of the Session. Moreover, just as the church planter was launching his Spanish services in 2014, the Senior Pastor retired, and the mother church called a new pastor to replace him the following year. The new Senior Pastor started a process of assessing all the church ministries. Along with his Session, he determined that the Hispanic pastor needed to be able to dedicate all of his energy to growing the Hispanic congregation. Thus, in 2016, the Hispanic pastor was able to stop working as a security guard, and focus his efforts on his flock.

This change from bi-vocational work proved highly beneficial for the Latino congregation, which began to grow rapidly both in number, and in their spiritual depth. By the end of 2018, the Hispanic congregation numbered around 75 members, and were able to ordain two qualified candidates to the office of Ruling Elder. Moreover, the demands of shepherding this growing group well led the church planter to leave his role of teaching at the seminary to be able to devote more time to his sheep.

As the Hispanic congregation grew, the mother church continued to assess the work, and began to feel that perhaps the integrated methodology they had been following was actually restricting the potential for further growth in the Hispanic community. They therefore encouraged the church planter to begin to prayerfully search for a new location for worship services in an area of the city with more first-generation Hispanics.

By 2019, the Hispanic pastor had found an ideal location for his congregation, which now, as a new church plant, he had named Rey de Gloria. He and the mother church set plans in motion for the Hispanic congregation to leave the mother church and transition fully to incubator methodology. As a part of this process, the mother church pledged to support Rey de Gloria for three more years, using a declining scale, while also transferring oversight to the local Presbytery. At the end of 2019, Rey de Gloria thus became a church plant of the Presbytery, being sent out by the mother church.

Although the church planter felt confident that Rey de Gloria would be able to be financially self-sufficient, self-governing, and ready for particularization in under two years, he (like any other church planter) could not have anticipated the realities of the COVID pandemic. Unfortunately, the pandemic significantly affected the church plant. By the end of 2021, Rey de Gloria's congregation had shrunk to 45 members. While the pastor attempted to raise support during this time, the realities of trying to do so as a monolingual, minority pastor in a majority-culture, English-speaking denomination proved insurmountable. Understandably discouraged, he turned from support-raising to looking for a job in the community to be able to serve his congregation again as a bi-vocational pastor.

The example of Rey de Gloria demonstrates many of the challenges and opportunities that are realities of church planting in the Hispanic community. Indeed, there is much to glean from this example, both positively and negatively. The transition between methodologies, and even transition of oversight from mother church to Presbytery show the need to be flexible even after a church planter and mother church have established a vision. The move from bi-vocational work within the mother church, to full-time ministry, and the need to return to seek bi-vocational ministry demonstrate the challenges Hispanic church planters (and especially monolingual pastors) may face as they seek to serve their flocks. At the same time, the flourishing and growth of the Spanish-speaking congregation starting from the very beginning speak to the need for church plants among the Latino community. Indeed, the fields are ripe for harvest, and church planters and sending churches alike must work to ensure they understand well the needs and challenges of their particular Hispanic demographics.

Emmanuel Presbyterian Church Upstate, Greenville, SC

The groundwork for **Emmanuel Presbyterian Church Upstate** began in 2007, when a large church in Greenville, South Carolina, noticed a promising pastor from Peru, who was also a seminary student, and asked him to develop a Hispanic congregation within their church using the integrated model. As the student himself was first-generation and Spanish-dominant, the group would target the needs of first-generation Spanish-speakers in the area. The mother church committed to supporting the pastor with a space to use within

Emmanuel Presbyterian Church Upstate, Greenville, SC

Zip Code: 29687
Population according to 2020 Census: 23,222
　　Hispanic: 9%
　　White: 70%
　　African American: 15%
Ministry Methodology: Integrated to Incubator

the church. In turn, the seminary student worked with members of the mother church congregation to make contact with Greenville's Hispanic population.

Through this networking, the student was able to begin some home Bible studies, although he found his time limited by his studies and progress was slow. Even so, the group began to grow. By 2010, as the student finished his degree and was ordained, there were around 45 individuals involved in the ministry, and they enthusiastically agreed it was time to launch public worship, which took place in one of the classrooms at the mother church.

Meanwhile, the mother church was growing exponentially, to the point where they found it necessary to build a much larger sanctuary in order for their congregation to worship together. This transition on the part of the mother church gave the Hispanic congregation the opportunity to move services into the old sanctuary, which had a seating capacity of 500. While they had started as a small group gathered in a small space, they now had much room in which to grow. Nevertheless, the transient nature of the immigrants who were the primary target of the church plant made it difficult to see numerical growth.

In 2015, the Senior Pastor of the mother church accepted a new call, and the mother church went through a period of realignment as they searched for and called a new pastor to fill the role. The following year, under new leadership and assessing the situation of the Hispanic congregation, the mother church felt that their Hispanic congregation might flourish more through incubator church planting methodology. To make this happen, they pledged a significant amount of seed money spread over the first three years, requesting that the church planter raise the remainder of the budget. They also allowed the Hispanic congregation to continue meeting in the old sanctuary for as long as necessary, while transferring oversight of the church plant from the mother church to the Presbytery, as a mission church.

Working within the new methodology and surveying his greater context, in 2017, the church planter decided that a bilingual church would best serve his demographic, and named the church plant Emmanuel Upstate. As he worked diligently to both raise support and expand outreach efforts, the Lord blessed the transition, and by the end of 2019, the group had grown to around 80 individuals. After much prayer and surveying of the land, Emmanuel Upstate was ready to leave the mother church, and they settled in Taylors, South Carolina, approximately 15 minutes north of the mother church. In Taylors, they found an old church building for sale. With the financial support of the

Presbytery, they were able to purchase it, trusting that a permanent facility and presence in the area would help them grow further.

Unfortunately, the COVID pandemic soon put limits on the use of the new space, and the church plant witnessed a significant drop in membership. However, they remained committed to working hard within the community. Continued financial support from the church planter's fundraising efforts allowed Emmanuel Upstate to remain financially afloat, even during the challenges of pandemic ministry. Though the church plant was already bilingual, with translation of services from Spanish to English (and vice versa, as necessary), the transition to Taylors, along with the realities of COVID, helped direct Emmanuel Upstate to desire to better reach also the English speakers of the community. Thus they began searching for a bilingual, English-dominant pastor (or seminary student) to help fulfill this mission.

Like Rey de Gloria, the story of Emmanuel Upstate also reflects a shift in church planting methodology as leadership watched growth and reassessed what might best serve the Hispanic congregation. For Emmanuel Upstate, this transition to more autonomy proved successful, as they were able to move to a more strategic area for reaching the Hispanic community. By God's grace, the church planter has been able to raise sufficient funding to continue serving the church full-time, and even consider hiring a second pastor to help in ministry. While the timeline of planting and growth for Emmanuel Upstate has been long, it is encouraging to see the Lord's blessing of the mother church and church planter's faithful commitment to serving the context to which they have been called, even as they remain flexible in their strategies.

Incubator Methodology Examples

While the previous two case studies transitioned to incubator methodology over the course of time, the following case study provides an example of a church plant that has successfully used this methodology from the beginning (see Chapter 3 under the incubator methodology description for another example as well).

El Buen Pastor, Dallas, TX

The vision for ***El Buen Pastor*** church began when a large mother church in Dallas, Texas, saw a need to reach the sizeable Hispanic population and decided to search for a Hispanic pastor who would be able to reach the many first-generation Spanish speakers within this context. So in 2017, they hired a first-generation Mexican pastor who was both bilingual and bicultural, and who had been living in the area for ten years prior to being called.

Using incubator methodology, the plan was for the pastor to worship for a year within the mother church, while networking in the community and raising funds, and then eventually launch a second, Spanish-speaking worship service. The mother church agreed to provide 40% of the budget, while the church planter would be responsible for raising the remaining 60%. As he began worshiping at the mother church and learning his context, he also had the opportunity to regularly cast the vision of the new work for the mother church congregation, encouraging and intentionally teaching them to give.

El Buen Pastor, Dallas, TX
Zip Code: 75227
Population according to 2020 Census: 1,304,379
Hispanic: 41%
White: 29%
African American: 25%
Ministry Methodology: Incubator

As the church planter came to understand his demographic better, his strategies for reaching the community included English as a Second Language classes (ESL), kids' ministries, and guitar classes, all of which he was able to launch from a local recreation center in the summer of 2018. As ministry participation grew, he also launched Financial Peace University classes that began to take place in homes. Besides being encouraged to give to the project, members of the mother church were also encouraged to volunteer for these ministries and other outreach events. Outside of the mother church, volunteers came from other local PCA churches as well to help, seeing themselves as missionaries within their own city.

The church planter strategically chose to hold ESL classes on Sunday afternoons, and made sure to include a devotional and gospel presentation during each class. He also was tireless in following up with the ESL students, and eventually was able to invite many of them to participate in home Bible studies. God used the efforts of this church planter and many volunteers mightily and quickly; by December of 2018, just six months after beginning outreach ministries, El Buen Pastor launched worship services, which took place on Sunday afternoons at the recreation center following the ESL classes.

For the next year, the church plant continued worshiping and outreach. In 2020, the reality of the COVID pandemic forced them to move their worship services from the recreation center to a local park. While the pandemic has been a period for many of disconnection and falling away from the church, the church planting pastor demonstrated his concern and care for his new community well by systematically calling or visiting everyone involved both in the church and outreach ministries on a weekly basis. Again, the Lord used his faithfulness, and in a period of great uncertainty, he had the great privilege to see and be a part of many making professions of faith.

While the loss of the recreation center for worship at first seemed temporary, the realities of COVID made it a permanent reality, and El Buen Pastor had to move their worship services into the mother church. By the end of 2021, the Hispanic congregation was averaging around 80 weekly attendees. Although the volunteer pool has shrunk after three and a half years of ministry, the church planter continues to recruit more missionary-minded volunteers.

In spite of being birthed shortly before the COVID pandemic, El Buen Pastor is an encouraging example of incubator methodology working well, as the planting pastor navigated and cared for his context, with the support of both his mother church and other local congregations. Indeed, the Lord has used both the heart of this pastor, along with His foreknowledge of the needs that would arise through COVID, to grow a new work in the heart of a Spanish-speaking community ripe for gospel ministry.

Independent Methodology Examples

The independent model has been growing in popularity in recent years; as such, there are multiple examples from which to learn. The first two given below were scratch-plants that made it all the way to become particular churches; the third example has faced innumerable challenges, but continues to await the Lord's guidance; while the final two cases have the unique and challenging experience of launching during the pandemic.

La Travesia, San Juan, PR

The story of **La Travesia** differs from the other Hispanic church plant case studies here in that, firstly, the intent for this church plant was not to start a single work, but an entire new Presbytery; and secondly, that the plant was to take place outside of the contiguous United States in the majority-Hispanic territory of Puerto Rico.

The vision began with a megachurch in Birmingham, Alabama, when the

La Travesia, San Juan, PR
Zip Code: 00920
Population according to 2020 Census: 322,854
Hispanic: 98%
White: 2%
Ministry Methodology: Independent

missions committee saw the need for churches in Puerto Rico, and identified the island as a strategic place to begin a Presbytery. They began to search for a church planter who might fit the position, and in 2010, they called a second-generation Mexican pastor, who was also both bilingual and bicultural, to lead the work.

Fully funded by his mother church, the church planting pastor moved to San Juan to spend his first year spying out the land and creating a plan for ministry to suit his new context. Without a Presbytery on the island or other PCA churches in the area, the planter and the mother church were using independent, scratch-plant methodology. Although the mother church was committed to supporting the planter, it still would necessarily mean much hard, creative sowing of seeds on the part of the church planter. His first year therefore involved much networking; studying Puerto Rican culture, as well as learning and understanding their unique religious history; casting a vision for the new ministry; and pouring into the lives of gifted men and women as he formed relationships with them.

As the pastor began discipling individuals, they were able to open deep, rich connections with others, such that a strong core group was born out of this work. The majority of this core group had not been attending other churches. Therefore, they launched public worship quickly (a Spanish-speaking service), with about 30 individuals in the group. Moreover, with the desire to multiply church planting in a new Presbytery throughout the island, the church planter recognized the need for deep discipleship, and a focus on teaching the doctrines of grace to be core values for the church plant.

Incredibly (or perhaps, not surprisingly, as the Lord works), God honored this vision by providing a brilliant, charismatic seminary professor to join the launch team. Shortly after becoming involved in La Travesia, he was ordained to ministry within the PCA, and able to come alongside the church plant in hosting theological conferences to teach winsomely the doctrines of grace. These conferences were well attended, and those who were interested in learning more were then offered the opportunity to study further in small groups. By the Lord's grace and blessing of faithful labor, La Travesia began growing rapidly.

Although the planter did not need to raise money for the church plant itself, as a Presbytery planter, he had a vision to be able to identify and train new leaders, and provide funding for them to attend seminary. Thus, he did spend time and efforts fundraising for this endeavor. In this way, he was able to create an internship program for potential Puerto Rican ministry candidates, to identify competence, calling, and character. Once again, the Lord blessed this vision, and the first two interns in the program (who were also members of La Travesia) sensed a call to ministry, and were able to attend Covenant Seminary through the funding the pastor had raised. They were followed a few years later by a third student.

In 2016, La Travesia had grown to 150 individuals, and the original two seminary students graduated from Covenant and returned to San Juan and the church. When Hurricane Maria devastated the island a year later in 2017, La Travesia was able to galvanize the efforts of the entire Christian community within Puerto Rico to provide relief work and mercy ministry. Just as God so often uses catastrophe for His glory, indeed He used these turbulent times to deepen the faith and commitment of the members of La Travesia to serve the community both in word and in deed. With the growth and support, the leadership sensed the call to begin a second church plant.

The second church would serve a different demographic, focusing on the expat community living in Dorado, just west of San Juan. It was named Trinity Church, with services taking place in English rather than Spanish. The original church planter made the move to begin preaching at Trinity Church, while one of the Covenant Seminary graduates took over leadership at La Travesia. The work of the ministry and new Presbytery continued to expand, and in 2020, La Travesia launched their third worship site, Igelsia Comunión, another Spanish-speaking congregation located in the city of Caguas, to the south of San Juan.

After eleven years of faithful service in Puerto Rico, and overseeing the establishment of three churches, a Presbytery, and the growth of many new leaders, in 2021, the original church planting pastor accepted a new call. At this point, his Presbytery transferred oversight of the work to the South Florida Presbytery, who oversaw the ordination of two Puerto Rican Teaching Elders. The process of leadership transfer went smoothly, and the South Florida Presbytery continues working with these Puerto Rican leaders with the goal of eventually forming their own Presbytery. Meanwhile, the churches have continued to serve the island for the glory of God.

Although the story of La Travesia differs from many of the case studies presented here, both in its overwhelmingly Hispanic context, as well as in its mission as an entire new Presbytery plant, it represents an encouraging example of how the Lord is working to grow new churches and raise up new leaders in virgin territories. It further speaks to the Lord's blessing of a vision and faithfulness in pursuing that vision on the part of both the mother church and church planter. It is certainly a picture of hope where a small seedling has sprung up to multiply across an island.

Las Tierras Community Church, El Paso, TX

The seeds for **Las Tierras Community Church** were planted with a Mission to the World missionary, who had been serving for the past 22 years in Spain. After so many years of service abroad, the missionary – originally from Puerto Rico, and both bilingual and bicultural – sensed a call to return to the United States to plant a church for the Hispanic community. In 2006, the Lord answered this vision when the Southwest Church Planting Network called the pastor to begin a work in the majority-Hispanic border city of El Paso, Texas.

Fully funded by the church planting network, the pastor was able to devote his first year in El Paso to spying out the land and creating a plan: he learned his demographic and began networking, recognizing that his target should be primarily second-generation English-speaking Latinos. Thus he also began casting a vision for the church plant, and doing the work of evangelism and service within his target community. Through this initial year of groundwork, the church planter was able to form a strong launch team, who in turn was able to come alongside him to serve their community and share the gospel.

Las Tierras Community Church, El Paso, TX
Zip Code: 79925
Population according to 2020 Census: 678,815
Hispanic: 81%
White: 12%
African American: 4%
Ministry Methodology: Independent

By 2008, the group was ready to launch the public worship of Las Tierras Community Church at a local school. Given their demographic, services were English-dominant, with translation to Spanish offered as needed, and with some songs in the Spanish language as well. As he assessed the needs of the community, the church planter set the core values of the Las Tierras Community Church to be intentional and deep discipleship focused on learning and practicing the doctrines of grace. The launch team carried out this vision particularly through sharing the gospel regularly and intentionally in small groups. As they did so, the Lord blessed the work and encouraged the hearts of the church members, as they saw new people coming to faith, and their group growing as a result.

Internal growth also meant a need for new leadership, so the church planter began identifying and training potential new leaders. Moreover, growth necessitated a more stable place for worship and ministry. Financial stability allowed Las Tierras to be able to purchase five acres of land on the east side of the city, to begin casting a vision for a future in that location.

By 2013, there was sufficient internal support and leadership that Las Tierras Community Church was able to particularize, as one of the few multi-cultural, bilingual, self-governing and financially self-sufficient churches within the denomination. As a particular church, they continued focusing on developing servant leaders, and in 2016, they ordained two qualified candidates to the office of Ruling Elder, and two to diaconal ministry.

For the next several years, Las Tierras continued to serve the community. In 2021, after fifteen years of faithful service in El Paso, the original church planter accepted a new position with a missions agency. Yet the transition was smooth, as Las Tierras, already well-established, called a bilingual, bicultural Anglo pastor to take over leadership. The ministry of this church has continued to flourish as Las Tierras continues to carry out the original vision of seeing their community transformed and renewed by the gospel.

Las Tierras Community Church represents an encouraging example of how the Lord united the vision of a missionary and a church planting network to reach the diversity of an unreached area in El Paso. In this case, independent methodology worked well with the personality and gifting of the church planter, and with funding from the church planting network, as a way to reach a new area for Christ.

Misión Vida Nueva, Escondido, CA

The idea for **Misión Vida Nueva** was birthed when the South Coast Presbytery recognized a need for a church to reach the large population of first-generation Spanish-speaking Latinos in Escondido, California. In 2002, they located a potential church planter – a Mexican pastor who was also first-generation and Spanish-dominant – and issued a call for him to begin the work. A mother church in the Presbytery had agreed to support the

Misión Vida Nueva, Escondida, CA
Zip Code: 92025
Population according to 2020 Census: 151,038
Hispanic: 52%
White: 31%
African American: 2%
Ministry Methodology: Independent

planter financially, and he also would receive a large amount of funding from the Presbytery itself; still, the pastor would be responsible for engaging in significant fundraising efforts yearly, in order to adequately meet the financial needs of the church plant. Undaunted by these requirements, the Mexican pastor accepted the call and moved to Escondido to begin the work.

During the first year, he devoted time to getting to know his community, learning cultural differences, casting a vision, and raising the necessary funds. While he worked hard making connections, the church planter found it difficult to gather believers to join forces with him in reaching his target population. Undaunted, he and his family worked tirelessly to minister to the large and needy immigrant community of Escondido. As dictated by the context, a large part of this ministry was mercy-based. One outlet became a regular food bank that would distribute over 10,000lbs of food each Saturday in the Grove Park neighborhood. Each distribution included gospel presentations, and follow-up with those who received the food.

Though the labor was hard, the church planter was able to launch public worship in Spanish with a very small group of people, using the facilities of a nearby PCA church on Sunday afternoons. Through mercy ministries, individual conversations, and worship services, Misión Vida Nueva had the privilege of witnessing conversions year after year. Yet growth of the church community itself proved difficult, hindered especially by the reluctance of the immigrant community to travel to the more affluent part of Escondido where the host church was located.

Thus, in 2008, Misión Vida Nueva decided to take steps to rent their own space in Escondido. This act of faith became a new beginning for the church plant, which began to grow as it had not previously. Excited by the growth, the church planter was able to identify potential leaders, and eagerly began to train them to assist with the work of outreach and discipleship. However, even before the completion of their training, the realities of immigrant life forced each of these potential leaders to relocate in turn, leaving the church planter and his family once again to do the bulk of the work of outreach and ministry.

As new individuals continued to replace those who had moved on at Misión Vida Nueva, the church planter was encouraged to identify a new group of promising leaders, and to pursue their training for ministry. Yet in a transient context, the story inevitably repeated itself, and the church planter was once again alone.

Meanwhile, although Misión Vida Nueva had become an integral part of the life of the community, through outreach and evangelism, the lack of a stable body also meant a lack of steady income, and the church plant had to rely on outside financial support for survival. After a decade in the rented facility, these financial challenges necessitated the church to not renew their lease, returning instead to worship at the former host church. Ten years later, however, after the opportunity to gather more committed members in a more accessible area of the city, the transition back to the PCA church proved more effective. There, Misión Vida Nueva was able to maintain a steady group of around 60 each Sunday.

From this group of sixty, unshaken by previous loss, the church planter again identified potential leaders for training. This time, the leaders were able to complete their training. With both stable leadership and stable income without the added burden of paying rent, Misión Vida Nueva was ready to particularize. Nearly twenty years after its inception, they set their date for particularization for December of 2021.

As the Lord would have it, two weeks before the particularization service, the church planter pastor was faced with the unforeseeable, and underwent open heart surgery. Necessarily, the service was postponed until further notice. Though this was certainly a set-back, the Lord in His impeccable timing allowed the pastor's health to take him out of ministry only after a caring leadership team was already in place. Where it might once have meant the end of Misión Vida Nueva, the church is currently continuing to serve its members and community through these faithful leaders, as they wait for the Lord's continued guidance and provision.

Certainly, the journey of the **Misión Vida Nueva** church plant has not been simple, yet there is little doubt that the Lord has used this mission to serve the Hispanic community of Escondido, California. God has provided continually through the unrelenting efforts of a faithful church planter. Though the road has been long and hard, He has allowed a group to emerge that is caring for the community even outside of the ability of their pastor to care for them during his illness. While some could see the twenty years of ministry in Escondido without particularization as a failure, the reality is that the Lord has mightily used Misión Vida Nueva and its members to show Christ to the surrounding community.

Vive Charlotte Church, Charlotte, NC

The seeds for **Vive Charlotte Church** were planted in 2018, when a gifted, second-generation Salvadorian pastor shared a vision for reaching the rapidly-growing Hispanic community in Charlotte, North Carolina, with several of the PCA churches in the city. In 2019, two churches from the Presbytery came together to sponsor the pastor for a church planting residency, during which time, he would have the opportunity to move to the city, learn the community, and choose a target area. Though the mother churches would provide significant support, the church planter would be responsible for raising the greater part of the financial needs.

Vive Charlotte Church, Charlotte, NC
Zip Code: 28212
Population according to 2020 Census: 874,579
Hispanic: 14%
White: 41%
African American: 35%
Ministry Methodology: Independent

In the summer of that year, the new pastor and his family relocated so that he could begin his residency. Aside from fundraising, he spent the first several months networking in earnest with any and all who would meet with him, and got to know the layout of the city. After much groundwork, it became apparent that the Lord was calling him to target second- and third-generation Hispanic-Americans, particularly focusing on the influx of Latino university students attending the city's large community college and local university. As a second-generation bicultural and bilingual Hispanic himself, he had a natural affinity for this group, understanding many of their unique struggles as the children of immigrants.

At the end of 2019, however, the planter's vision was threatened when a transition in leadership at one of the sponsoring churches had the unintended consequence of needing to close the church planter residency program. In spite of the set-back, the church planter was convinced of his calling to plant in the city, even if it meant working bi-vocationally. However, the Lord affirmed the call when the second sponsoring church affirmed the church planter's giftedness, and agreed to launch him as the official mother church.

As the church planter continued raising funds, networking, and gathering a core group, the COVID pandemic hit, and once again, it would have been easy to question how church planting could continue. Yet the planter and his launch team used COVID as an opportunity to immediately implement a strategy of fervent, intentional, weekly prayer held outdoors on the campus of the local university where they hoped to eventually launch. Moreover, the Lord allowed the planter to serve the local community in unique ways during this period. The pandemic had hit the Latino community particularly hard in this city, forcing eight local Hispanic churches to close their doors. Looking for opportunities to serve, the pastor and his parents (first-generation Salvadorians, who had spent most of their lives church-planting throughout Central America) were able to minister to many who were without a church. God further blessed the planter with additional funding such that the small group was able to be actively involved in mercy ministry for members of the Hispanic community who had experienced significant loss through COVID.

As the core group continued meeting, praying, growing, and serving, the planter continued finding other avenues for ministry within the city and its surroundings. In 2021, he, with the help of two other Hispanic Teaching Elders in the area, started a discipleship ministry, *Multiplicadores*, to disciple Spanish-speaking lay-leaders, particularly from the churches who had closed but were hoping to re-open. Through this ministry, the church planter's father – a member of the launch team and ordained PCA minister – was recruited to begin helping with preaching, teaching Bible, recasting the vision, and assisting with the search for a new pastoral candidate at one of the Hispanic churches who had lost their pastor.

In the summer of 2021, the core group began worshiping together on a monthly basis at a non-denominational church next door to the university that opened its doors to the group free of charge. Although they were growing and excitedly hoping to launch public worship from this facility, a new wave of COVID caused the host church to pull their offer. Public launch was delayed as they searched for a new facility, but dealing with a small budget and sky-rocketing rental prices proved fierce. For several months, they were hosted by another, non-denominational church fifteen minutes southeast of the University, in another area of the city with a large immigrant population.

The hope was again to launch from the new facility in the spring of 2022, but once again, plans changed when the second host church was unable to provide the flexibility for services that the church plant needed. As they searched between the University and the eastern part of the city, the Lord gave the church planter eyes for a dirty, large old house located in the heart of the immigrant community and along the main road. Investors had recently purchased the house along with its two acres of land as an investment property, planning to sit on it for a few years before rezoning and rebuilding. The church planter approached the owners in faith, and offered to rent the property in the interim, and fix it up. By the Lord's grace, Vive Charlotte Church found favor in the eyes of the non-Christian owners, and the planter and launch team worked diligently to fix the house into a place of worship and house of peace for the community. They launched public worship from the house in May of 2022, with a team of around 20 individuals. Although worship is primarily in English, many of the songs are in both Spanish and English, to speak to the hearts of native Spanish-speakers.

While the original vision was to reach second- and third-generation Hispanic immigrants, the Lord has drawn a diverse group of individuals to Vive Charlotte Church, ethnically, culturally, socioeconomically, and even in age and stage of life. While the movement from one area of the city to another had its challenges, it has also opened the opportunity and vision for reaching also the needs of the large Spanish-speaking population in the area. The church planter is working with his father to establish a second, Spanish-speaking worship service during the week to serve this population. Meanwhile, they are also working to start mentoring cohorts that will better equip Hispanic pastors within the community.

The road to planting Vive Charlotte Church has come with many unexpected turns and detours; there have been many chances to experience frustration or to give up; and yet God has used each of these as further opportunities to open eyes to the needs of the community, and allow a small church plant to serve in large ways. It is encouraging to see how God has already used the vision and work of this faithful church planter, his father, and small launch team, to make a difference in a hurting Latino community.

The Crossing Church, McAllen, TX

The story of **The Crossing Church** is unique in that, though it started with the intention of using integrated methodology, this approach quickly led to a dead-end, and church-plant efforts later re-launched using independent methodology. So the case study belongs here among the independent

The Crossing Church, McAllen, TX
Zip Code: 78539
Population according to 2020 Census: 142,210
Hispanic: 90%
White: 7%
Asian: 1%
Other: 2%
Ministry Methodology: Independent

methodology examples, although the initial phases looked different. These initial conversations regarding The Crossing Church started in 2014 when a mother church in the heavily Hispanic border town of McAllen, Texas, issued a call to a Mexican pastor to become an Associate Pastor and help reach the Hispanic community.

The new pastor was a bilingual, bicultural first-generation Mexican man. After serving as Associate Pastor for two years, the Session of his church felt a need to take further steps at reaching the Latino community, and began encouraging the Hispanic pastor to consider planting a new work using integrated methodology. He agreed, and enthusiastically step-ped into the role of church planter in 2017. Yet it quickly became apparent that the target community was not responding well to the work, as it was playing out within its methodology. Thus, a year later, in 2018, the church leadership decided to stop the initiative, and the Hispanic pastor continued to serve the Hispanic context as an Associate Pastor.

At the end of 2019, the church went through a period of transition as the Senior Pastor accepted a call elsewhere. During this time, the Associate Pastor was quite instrumental in helping the church navigate the change. After a new Senior Pastor had been installed, the Associate Pastor sensed it would be an appropriate time to try the church plant again, but using an alternate methodology. In preparation, he attended the MNA Church Planter's Assessment, and was approved for church planting in the summer of 2019. That same year, the Reach South Texas Church Planting Network further affirmed his desire by calling him to plant The Crossing Church in McAllen, following independent methodology.

As a church planter, the Mexican pastor would receive support both from the mother church as well as the church planting network, but he would be responsible for raising the church budget. Having spent at this point six years in McAllen serving the Hispanic community, the church planter felt compelled to target especially second- and third-generation English-speaking Hispanics.

Just as the church planter was in the early stages of core group formation and networking at the beginning of 2020, the pandemic hit. While such an event surely could have been a reason for the pastor to abandon plans of church planting, he remained convinced that the Lord had called him to plant, and he continued with plans in spite of and through the additional challenges. He and his core met regularly, as they could, throughout 2020 for fellowship, Bible studies, and prayer. Although COVID restrictions hampered the ability to network or practice hospitality on a large scale, the group devoted themselves to prayer and mercy ministry. In 2021, they were able to begin offering hospitality and meeting new people. These efforts eventually led to hosting weekly Bible studies in the pastor's home.

By October of that same year, the group had grown to such an extent that they could no longer meet comfortably at the church planter's home, thus necessitating a search for a larger space. They were able to find a facility to rent for Sunday evenings, in order to continue meeting and growing there. The Crossing Church's vision within this facility and for the future is to create a deeper community with those who are committed to the work, to offer hospitality, and to evangelize. The prayer is to launch public worship, potentially at some point in 2022, when the group has reached 25 regular adults.

A "false" start followed by a start during COVID might be enough for many to feel discouraged from the call to church planting, particularly in the Hispanic context that comes with its own challenges. Yet even the beginning of the story of The Crossing Church demonstrates that God is at work, in His timing, and through His means, directing the paths of His people to serve this population. Certainly, the Lord has blessed the persistence and vision of this church planter, and this open-ended story can only leave one wondering how the Lord will continue to use this pastor, launch team, and fledgling church plant to reach the diversity of McAllen and beyond for His glory.

Learning from "Cold Cases"

Even as it is helpful and encouraging to learn from cases in which churches and planters have witnessed success, it is also useful to examine some of those stories that have come to their end. Thus the following three examples are case studies of mission churches that were shut down, referred to in this book as "cold cases," each from a different size city. (A fourth cold case example appeared earlier in the book as an illustration in Chapter 1: *Counting the Cost*.) While including as many helpful details as possible, the identities of the churches and individuals involved in these painful and sad cases have been carefully protected.

Often, the failure of a minority church plant is seen as proof that the denomination should simply stop trying because this type of work is so much more difficult than majority-culture church planting. Yet the truth is that majority church plants also tend to fail, and the reaction from the mother church to those failures is far from a call to give up on church planting in the area. The aim in discussing "cold cases" is to avoid the mistakes that cause pain and suffering to all who were once part of the dream of planting a church. Even as the Proverbs say, "By insolence comes nothing but strife, but with those who take advice is wisdom" (Proverbs 13:10). May these difficult examples provide a chance for reflection, advice, and gleaning wisdom for moving forward in Hispanic church planting.

Cold Case: Mid-Small City Church Plant

The narrative of this cold case began when an established church in a mid-small city had a cross-cultural vision to reach the Hispanic population of their city. They began searching for a Hispanic pastor to lead a Spanish-speaking congregation. Following integrated methodology, the mother church would cover the entire budget, and bring the Hispanic pastor to be a part of the Session. The man they called was a first-generation, Spanish-dominant Hispanic pastor who moved to the area to accept the role.

Cold Case: Mid-Small City Church Plant
Population between: 100,000-149,999
Population Breakdown:
    Hispanic: 15%
    White: 44%
    African American: 31%
Ministry Methodology: Integrated

As a way of reaching the Hispanic community, the mother church and Hispanic pastor began an ESL ministry, although it never experienced much traction. Moreover, the church planter worked hard to evangelize and start Bible studies within the target population. Soon he was able to launch a Spanish-speaking worship service that came alongside the English-speaking service on Sunday mornings, with a joint-congregation Sunday school in between the two services.

The first threat to the new congregation happened, however, when the landlord of the mother church's meeting space increased the rent, and the mother church experienced financial strain as a result. In order to make ends meet, the Session made the decision to move to a new location; moreover, to further cut costs, they made a switch from Sunday morning worship, to service on Sunday evenings, and combined the Spanish and English services into one worship service that would be bilingual. As one might expect, such drastic changes proved difficult, and as a result, over half of the English-speaking congregation did not make the transition to the new facility.

With the loss of so many members, the church began to spiral into greater financial trouble as well. The English-speaking pastor accepted a new call, and the Hispanic (and Spanish-speaking) pastor was left to care for the congregation on his own. Naturally, the congregation eventually became majority Hispanic, but was unable to support their pastor financially. Determined to continue serving, the pastor sought to lead the church while working bi-vocationally; however, the work eventually proved too demanding. Under-supported and burnt out, the Hispanic pastor resigned, and those members who had remained throughout the transitions found and joined other church bodies.

Certainly this story represents the sad case of a Hispanic work that was unable to thrive, yet knowing its details yields some valuable insights. In the first place, it is incredibly important to take adequate time to count the cost: while a church may genuinely buy into the vision of cross-cultural ministry, the reality is that the work requires readjusting of majority-culture mindsets and expectations, and for the mother church members to learn to feel uncomfortable before they feel at home. Although there may be much up-front enthusiasm, moving too quickly may dampen this excitement, and prompt the majority-culture church members to consider moving to a body where they will again feel more comfortable. In the context of Hispanic church planting, slow is typically better.

Secondly, the sad reality is that it is often quite difficult for a minority leader to lead a majority-culture body, as became the case in this study when the English-speaking pastor vacated his position. Majority-culture church members may struggle to follow a minority leader, particularly if his cultural ministry style butts up against that to which they may be accustomed. Naturally, the addition of language barriers can make it nearly impossible. While minority leaders certainly can lead majority-culture members effectively, it requires the church planter to embody the cultural aspirations of his target. A church in any context must seek a pastor who can winsomely engage the culture of the target, regardless of who represents a minority or majority culture. To assume that a Hispanic pastor will be able to draw together two different groups by nature of his country or language of origin does a disservice both to the pastor, and the target population.

Finally, this example highlights the need for having clear-cut values, mission, vision, and strategic plan. While certainly a church planter must always be reassessing and leaving room for flexibility as needed, radically modifying a vision – such as suddenly moving from two separate language services to a single, bilingual service – is typically quite problematic, and even disastrous. Unfortunately, but not without the Lord's providential control, the vision for church planting among the Latino population in this mid-small city did not materialize as hoped; nevertheless, the lessons learned are valuable in providing insight and wisdom for future works.

Cold Case: Medium City Church Plant

In a medium-sized city in the United States, an established majority-culture church had the cross-cultural vision to reach the relatively large Hispanic population in their city. Thus they began the search for a Hispanic pastor who would be able to incubate a Hispanic congregation, with the expectation that this new work would launch itself out within 5-7 years. The church planter they called was a bilingual, bicultural pastor who was new to the area when called, and his target demographic were specifically first-generation Spanish-speaking Hispanics. While he was not a part of the Session, he did attend the Session meetings on occasion, and had the opportunity to meet with the Senior Pastor as needed to discuss the work and ministry.

> **Cold Case: Medium-size City Church Plant**
>
> **Population between:** 150,000-499,999
> **Population Breakdown:**
>   Hispanic: 15%
>   White: 41%
>   African American: 35%
> **Ministry Methodology:** Incubator

As the mother church was covering the entire budget, the church planter was able to devote himself to the work of ministry itself. With eagerness, he began evangelizing and starting Bible studies among the Spanish-speaking community. In time, these efforts allowed him to begin a second worship service at the mother church for these individuals, that took place in Spanish. Services continued, but as is so common particularly among first-generation immigrant communities, there was constant turnover as attendees came through the city and moved to the next place. The transient nature of the context made it difficult for the Hispanic congregation to grow, and also meant that giving was minimal. Furthermore, although lay-leaders emerged from time-to-time, they all eventually moved away, and the Hispanic pastor was left to do all the work of ministry unsupported.

Meanwhile, as the Hispanic congregation remained small and struggled financially, the English language congregation of the mother church was growing rapidly, and outgrowing their space. To accommodate their growing population more comfortably, they began a building campaign, while simultaneously reappropriating the budget for this new direction by cutting the

Hispanic pastor's salary. While they continued to offer the Hispanic congregation a free space for meeting, the church planter was now responsible for the difficult task of raising the budget for the work. Perhaps unsurprisingly, his fundraising efforts fell flat, as seemingly the project was not as attractive to potential supporters as other new church plants in the area.

As the mother church completed the new building, it necessitated a change of locations. And while the location served the majority-culture congregation, the new facility proved too far away for Hispanic members to attend. Financially struggling and with a rapidly dwindling congregation and no optimal meeting space, the Hispanic pastor resigned.

The lessons from this sad example point back to some of the key steps in preparation for launching a Hispanic church plant. Namely, it is indeed necessary to count the cost and to create a plan. In this case, while the mother church had committed to a certain time-frame for support, and while it may have felt the initial excitement of cross-cultural ministry, numerical and financial success within its majority-culture congregation led them to abandon the critical support needed for the Hispanic plant. Indeed, for the mother church it was too costly (not simply financially, but in terms of vision as well) to focus on a second ministry at the expense of not growing its own congregation.

This example also demonstrates how creating a plan and having predetermined values, mission, and vision can help mother church, church plant, and church members to stay on target when faced with options and obstacles. In this case, since the church planter was not a member of the Session, he did not have much weight in the mother church's decision to devote their resources to the new building campaign. On the other hand, it seems that the mother church and mother church members were also not committed to the values and vision of the church plant, allowing the church planter to wade through the obstacles on his own. Having a pool of volunteers from the mother church aligned with the values, mission, and vision of the church plant may have helped to keep the church planter from burning out when first-generation immigrants were unable to maintain stability.

Of course, it is impossible to say what might have been, and it is helpful to rest in the assurance that the Lord's plans were greater. Yet it is certainly helpful to look at this example, assess the challenges, and seek the Lord's wisdom in growing and avoiding some of the same mistakes in undertaking new Hispanic church plants under similar circumstances.

Cold Case: Large City Church Plant

In a large American city with a sizable Latino population, a majority-culture church saw the need for reaching the first-generation Spanish-speaking immigrants. They desired to launch a Spanish-speaking church plant using independent methodology. Thus they called a Spanish-dominant first-generation Hispanic pastor to move to the city and begin the work. Although it would be a scratch-plant, the church committed itself to full financial support for the project, and also offered their facilities as a meeting space for the new congregation. The Hispanic pastor would not be a part of the Session as a scratch planter; however, he would be permitted to attend as desired, and was encouraged to meet with the Senior Pastor as they determined necessary.

> **Cold Case: Large City Church Plant**
> ***Population between:*** 500,000+
> ***Population Breakdown:***
>   Hispanic: 29%
>   White: 32%
>   African American: 24%
> ***Ministry Methodology:*** Independent

The move to a new city and new culture proved difficult for the church planter, and he struggled to adjust to his new settings. Nevertheless, he set to work attempting to start some outlets for networking and evangelism. Yet it became evident that the Spanish-speaking community that he had been commissioned to reach were actually more acculturated than the new pastor, and thus many of them struggled to follow his lead. While he was eventually able to start a small Bible study, later efforts to launch worship services did not gain any traction.

After three years of hard labor with little visible fruit or encouragement, both the mother church and church planter agreed that it was time to end the project. Tired and discouraged, the Hispanic pastor moved from the city, and decided to leave ministerial life.

The story of this attempted church plant and the burnout of the Hispanic church planter demonstrates a sad, harsh reality in Hispanic church planting. Like pastors in any context, it bears remembering that not all Hispanic pastors are the same. A pastor may have great success within his own context, but it may not necessarily mean that he is suited to a particular work of church planting. It is critical that both church planter and mother church compare the church planter's nationality, level of acculturation, and previous ministry context to that of the target demographic, and assess whether or not the pastor may be able to thrive in the new environment. To simply plant a pastor in an area because he may speak Spanish, without regards to his connection to the community, does a disservice to the pastor, the church plant, and mother church alike.

Moreover, this story helps to draw out a subtler piece of wisdom that may prove helpful when calling any pastor to do the often-lonely work of church planting, and that is: invite to the table. Alone and unsupported, a church planter can burn out easily, but fed with food – along with fellowship, encouragement, and prayer – he may have strength to do what would otherwise be impossible. Particularly in the Hispanic context, this idea of inviting to the table is important in the literal sense, as the dinner table is a place of intimate conversation and connection. Being invited to the table fosters a unique sense of connection to one another, and can help provide the needed *confianza* and even help with learning a new context that a Hispanic church planter may crave when moving to start a new work. Inviting to the table could be a strategic part of mother churches and supporters caring for the church planter and his family not just financially, but mentally, emotionally, and spiritually as well. Sadly, in this cold case, the lack of connectionalism sped the process of burnout for a lonely pastor struggling to adapt to a new setting and new challenges.

Conclusion

Reading through these case studies and listening to the experiences of church planters who have come before should give a new church planter or mother church desirous of reaching the Hispanic community pause for thought and reflection. There is much to glean both from positive and negative experiences, and from the long, arduous journeys that most of these church plants have gone through. They help to illustrate some of the unique challenges of planting Hispanic works in a majority-culture denomination, yet also how the Lord is using faithful workers to accomplish His mission of reaching all the nations. The next section of this book will look more in depth at some of the challenges of Hispanic church planting represented in these stories, and discuss ways of preparing for and facing them in the process of planting, growth, and maintenance.

At this point of reflection, however, it is helpful to remember Paul's words to the Corinthian church, regarding the roles of different individuals and growth. While one could be tempted to read through some of these case studies and judge different settings or individuals and praise others, it bears remembering that reaching the Latino context is (like any other gospel mission), first and foremost, the Lord's work, conducted by God's grace through individuals who are "God's fellow workers" (I Corinthians 3:9). As one author puts it, "Our mission is not fulfilled because of the adequacy of our financial and intellectual resources, but our mission is guaranteed by the supernatural resources of a God who promises his presence to fulfill that mission." 4

Through different cities, unique scenarios, and different methodologies, each of these laborers have been faithful servants whom the Lord has used to bring others to faith. Aside from visible church growth, this incredible reality is filling the Church triumphant with new believers from every people, tribe, nation, and language (cf. Revelation 7:9)! Moreover, for each of these servants, the Lord has indeed "assigned to each his task" (I Corinthians 3:5, NIV). While some may plant, some may water (and some may approach the task of planting and watering from different directions), it is "only God who gives the growth" (3:7, ESV).

> *"What then is Apollos? What is Paul? Servants through whom you believed, as the Lord assigned to each. I planted, Apollos watered, but God gave the growth. So neither he who plants nor he who waters is anything, but only God who gives the growth. ... For we are God's fellow workers. You are God's field, God's building."*
>
> – I Corinthians 3:5-7, 9 (ESV)

Therefore, while helping current and future planters observe themes and think through approaches, these stories should above all point to the marvelous, persistent work of the Lord Jesus Christ in growing His church through His people to all nations – through financial struggle, through lack of resources and lengthy timelines, through COVID, through language barriers – for indeed nothing is impossible for God. Reflect on these stories that they may offer encouragement to continue the work of reaching the Hispanic community for the glory of God!

PART 2:

PLANTING THE CHURCH

"I am the LORD; I have called you in righteousness; I will take you by the hand and keep you; I will give you as a covenant for the people, a light for the nations, [7] to open the eyes that are blind, to bring out the prisoners from the dungeon, from the prison those who sit in darkness." – Isaiah 42:6-7

"Go therefore and make disciples of all nations, baptizing them in the name of the Father and of the Son and of the Holy Spirit, [20] teaching them to observe all that I have commanded you. And behold, I am with you always, to the end of the age." – Matthew 28:19-20

"As for you, always be sober-minded, endure suffering, do the work of an evangelist, fulfill your ministry." – II Timothy 4:5

CHAPTER 6:

THE EVANGELISM STAGE

"How then will they call on him in whom they have not believed? And how are they to believe in him of whom they have never heard? And how are they to hear without someone preaching? ¹⁵ And how are they to preach unless they are sent? As it is written, 'How beautiful are the feet of those who preach the good news!' ¹⁶ But they have not all obeyed the gospel. For Isaiah says, 'Lord, who has believed what he has heard from us?' ¹⁷ So faith comes from hearing, and hearing through the word of Christ." – Romans 10:14-17

Following the Preparation Stage come the next several stages of church planting that involve putting all the visioning and strategizing into practice. It may be helpful at this point to refer back to the Church Planting Timeline given at the beginning of this book to visualize how each stage of the work of church planting builds upon the former. It may also be helpful to note the anticipated timeframe for each of these stages, that offers a realistic glimpse into how the length of these phases may stretch out longer within the Hispanic, non-majority church plant context.

The first of these stages involve networking and evangelism. These are the primary work of the church planter for the first year or so of church planting. As discussed in the section on developing a Strategic Plan, they are a crucial, fundamental element of the work of church planting – in any context, but particularly when reaching the Latino community. This is true because, while many majority-culture church plants serve populations with a somewhat churched background, the immigrant experience often comes along with a disillusionment of who God is. That is, even if individuals had a church background in their country of origin, oftentimes, the circumstances surrounding their decision to leave, coupled with the difficulties of adapting to life in a foreign country (not to mention a lack of easily-accessible churches willing to serve them) may cause them to abandon the church as disconnected from the reality of their experience. For second- and third-generation Hispanics who have seen their parents struggling, the experience of God and church in their lives becomes even further removed. The need for hearing the Good News in new ways, or even for the first time, is great.

The Priority of Evangelism in Hispanic Church Planting

A church planter desiring to reach the Hispanic context must prioritize evangelism, not simply at the beginning of the church plant, but as an ongoing part of ministry that becomes a part of the church's DNA. Yet the starting place for evangelism cannot simply be a necessary stage in church planting; it must go much further, as a deep, heart-calling and privilege. While the word "evangelism" may sound terrifying to some, the work of evangelism is actually one of the greatest privileges of gospel ministry, as it reflects the Lord's heart for the world.

Paul makes a compelling exhortation for evangelism in his epistle to the Romans. A church planter cannot simply plan for ministry among a hurting people group, and expect people to show up. As Paul asks rhetorically, "How then will they call on him in whom they have not believed?" (Romans 10:14). If the trials of the immigrant experience have led them to believe that their God has failed them, they will not call on His name unless someone will show them a bigger, grander, more loving picture of the Lord. "And how are they to believe in him of whom they have never heard?" (10:14). How easy it is for second- and third-generation Hispanics busily working in a post-Christian society to create a life and experience distinct from that of their parents to not hear the word of hope that God's Word offers! "And how are they to hear without someone preaching?" (10:14). It is this preaching, this reaching people with this breath of life of the Gospel message that is not only the responsibility, but the great privilege of the church planter.

Indeed, Paul echoes the words of the prophet Isaiah when he speaks to the beauty of the work of the evangelist: "How beautiful are the feet of those who preach the good news!" (Romans 10:15). This has been the Lord's incredible plan even from the Old Testament: to allow sinners redeemed by His grace to play a part in bringing other sinners into His work of redemption, as He draws all nations to Himself. The work of evangelism, as Isaiah describes it, is the incredible work of publishing peace, of bringing good news of happiness, of showing forth the Lord's salvation, of pointing to the God who reigns over and above all the hurt, disappointment, and bitterness of the immigrant—or human—experience (cf. Isaiah 52:7ff). It is a chief priority and calling, yes, but also a beautiful, transformational

> *"How beautiful upon the mountains are the feet of him who brings good news, who publishes peace, who brings good news of happiness, who publishes salvation, who says to Zion, 'Your God reigns.'"*
>
> – Isaiah 52:7

privilege for the church planter to commit to the work of evangelism within his target context.

Thus, regardless of church planting methodology, nothing else in the church planter's schedule should come close to the priority of evangelism. To neglect evangelism both at the outset of church planting, but also as an established, ongoing focus of the church plant, not only robs the church and church planter of an incredible experience of participating in the beauty and grace of gospel witness, but will eventually lead the church plant in an unhealthy path of intense, inward focus. As a leader, the church planter must continually model the priority of evangelism, and intentionally train others in it. Seeing the privilege and beauty of playing a part of publishing the good news of salvation will help evangelism move from being a necessary action that takes place on occasion, to something written into the very DNA of life as a church planter and Christian in an unchurched context.

> *"Oh, taste and see that the LORD is good! Blessed is the man who takes refuge in him!"*
>
> – Psalm 34:8

Possible Hindrances to Evangelism in the Hispanic Context

When seeking to evangelize within the Hispanic community, the church planter must (as in any other aspect of church planting) consider the culture of his context. While the majority culture in the USA is heavily individualistic, Hispanic culture tends to be far more collectivist, and this has implications for the work of evangelism. In majority-culture churches, the American, individualistic attitude tends to seep slowly into the church planting world, with the result that many view evangelism as a solo sport. That is, perhaps a gifted evangelist has particular strategies and tools that prove effective for him, and he then teaches them to others and sends them out alone to "save" people. Yet what works in one context may not be accepted in another. While some may respond well to to-the-point gospel presentations, for others, the message of the gospel will not be compelling without being able to tangibly taste it first through meaningful relationships and experience in gospel-centered community.

Within a family-oriented, community-based context like the Latino population, this is especially true, and it hearkens back to the discussion of *confianza* from Chapter 3. In general, Hispanics need to be invited into fellowship first, to experience belonging as part of a group, to have the opportunity to build and grow *confianza* within that group, before they may be ready to hear the gospel message. As one author writes, "When it comes to hospitality, the church exists to display the goodness and peace of God in Jesus by making family out of strangers, friends out of enemies, and homes out of brokenness."[5] Being invited into Christian community allows the non-believer to "taste and see that the Lord is good," as they experience the fellowship, care, and grace expressed to them through the working and active Body of Christ (cf. Psalm 34:8). Developing relationships not just in individual, one-on-one settings, but within a group comprised of a variety of individuals with unique stories builds *confianza* with the church, and reinforces the message of the gospel.

Evangelism within the Hispanic context, therefore, cannot be rushed; it cannot be seen as one-size-fits-all, or take an individualistic approach. Doing so ignores the reality of the immigrant experience and the Hispanic culture, thus offering a message that feels too far removed or unapproachable. Rather, reaching the Latino context for the gospel must involve the slow, meaningful work of inviting people in to the point where they feel comfortable sharing their heart struggles, and seeing how Jesus enters into those places to bring redemption.

Assessing Evangelism in the Hispanic Context

Part of the groundwork of creating a strategic plan during the Preparation Stage of church planting allows the church planter to think through strategies for evangelism within his context ahead of time, so that, when it is time for the work to commence, he will already have ideas in place upon which to act. Preparation is good and critical, but the actual work of evangelism will require constant assessment and strategizing, as the church planter sees what is working, and what needs improvement.

At this stage of church planting then, the church planter should have already selected his prayer, networking, outreach, and evangelism strategies. Chapter 3 has already discussed some ways to plan for networking and evangelism, while Appendix C gives more practical ideas. The remainder of this chapter provides ways of assessing the functionality of evangelism strategies for both himself and his launch team, as the church planter does this essential work to which he has been called. While engaging in this exciting but challenging task, it is important that the pastor continue encouraging the work by preaching the gospel of grace to himself and to his team. Constant reminders of the Lord's grace will encourage pastors and core members to put evangelism strategies into action, while also enabling them to measure the results through the lens of grace.

Prayer Support in Evangelism

In the first place, it is crucial that the pastor implement prayer support for both himself and his team of fellow evangelists. Without prayer, it is easy to become sidetracked with measuring human results; prayer helps to maintain a Kingdom focus, shifting the work of transforming hearts from a human effort, to the Lord's work that He chooses to accomplish through jars of clay. Moreover, maintaining a focus of prayer is a good way to bring others into the work of evangelism. The church planter may want to grow a prayer team to pray for transformation in his target context. As a group begins to meet together regularly in prayer, perhaps even in the center of the target community, it becomes a powerful way of relying on the Lord's strength, desires, and timing for building His Kingdom. Regular, organized prayer for the community among a body of believers not only serves the community, but molds the hearts of those meeting in prayer to care in new ways for those for whom they are praying, as the Lord meets them in their prayers.

As the church planter and his team begin building relationships, growing in outreach, and having gospel-conversations with unbelievers, a prayer team provides an excellent place to unload the excitement, the concerns, and the desires before others and ultimately before the Lord. Maintaining regular contact with this prayer team will give them the privilege of being involved in the work of evangelism behind-the-scenes. Moreover, the work of evangelism, though exciting, will certainly prove difficult at times. Like Aaron and Hur holding up Moses' arms in the battle as he grew tired, a prayer team will provide encouragement for the church planter, as he and his fellow evangelists experience these prayer warriors supporting them and bearing them along through their prayers.

> *"But Moses' hands grew weary, so they took a stone and put it under him, and he sat on it, while Aaron and Hur held up his hands, one on one side, and the other on the other side. So his hands were steady until the going down of the sun."*
>
> Exodus 17:12

Prayer support could look a number of different ways; the planter might plan days of prayer and fasting throughout the first year of evangelism. He might choose different strategies for training and growing his group. He may choose to recruit only individuals already involved in the core group for prayer, or invite a broader group of individuals to meet and pray regularly. He may choose to organize prayer walks through the target demographic, helping both he and the prayer team lift up the needs of the community as they physically witness them, while becoming witnesses in the community as they pray. Regardless of how prayer support works, it is an essential part of evangelism, and an essential way of being able to accurately assess and measure the work. Apart from prayer, the work of evangelism becomes little more than a reliance upon human efforts, yet only the Lord accomplishes the work of salvation!

Assessing Networking and Evangelism

As the church planter (and his team, as applicable) walks the community, as he begins building relationships, conducting outreach events, establishing *confianza* in his context, he will need to engage in the work of assessing the reach and effectiveness of his efforts. Some pastors will have a tendency to be too lenient in self-assessment, while others may be too critical; hence, such assessment should take place again only under the auspices of established prayer support, to both hold him up before the Lord, and keep him accountable.

Some helpful ways for assessing efficaciousness of strategies would be for the planter to set realistic goals regarding the number of contacts he anticipates through community engagement at the end of his first year. Working backward from that number, he might set goals for a reasonable number of monthly, weekly, and even daily contacts needed to reach the year-end goal, keeping in mind that the day-to-day meetings must necessarily involve much follow-up with new contacts, along with further networking. Of course, constant assessment of goals will prove unhelpful and most likely stressful. Some days will be full of encouraging meetings, and an assessment would look quite promising. On the other hand, other days will look quite unfruitful, in terms of numbers or depth of conversation, and constant assessment at the end of the day could cause a planter to lose sight of the big picture and despair. Rather, stopping and reflecting at consistent intervals will allow the planter to ask: how is God at work? Is the Lord opening doors through these efforts and in these spaces?

Earnestly asking such questions and measuring them against expected goals before the Lord will allow the church planter to humbly and honestly measure the fruitfulness of his labors. As he prays through them and brings them before the Lord, time and time again, it will allow God to shape and reshape the work into the work that He has envisioned for those whom He will bring. At the end of the day, honest assessment asks the question, "is the Lord at work?" It invites His presence to guide and constantly reform goals and strategies as He directs the path to church planting. Through assessing the efficacy of networking and evangelism, the church planter may find that the Lord is opening the doors he had anticipated, as well as or perhaps those he least expected, as He builds His church.

Conclusion

While doing the work of evangelism – not only in the first year, but throughout an entire life of ministry – it is necessary to bear in mind the balance between human responsibility and the work of the Holy Spirit. "And how are they to hear without someone preaching?" (Romans 10:14). God sends out workers into the harvest fields, but it is the Lord who opens the eyes of the blind and unstops deaf ears. Tim Keller compares the work of evangelism to Elijah's work of building the altar at Mount Carmel in 1 Kings 18. Elijah built the altar before Ahab and the 400 prophets of Baal, but it was God who sent the consuming fire from heaven.[6]

> "...Elijah the prophet came near and said, 'O LORD, God of Abraham, Isaac, and Israel, let it be known this day that you are God in Israel, and that I am your servant, and that I have done all these things at your word...' Then the fire of the LORD fell and consumed the burnt offering and the wood and the stones and the dust, and licked up the water that was in the trench. And when all the people saw it, they fell on their faces and said, 'The LORD, he is God; the LORD, he is God.'"
>
> - I Kings 18:36-39

So it is when it comes to evangelism: while church planters and believers have the responsibility (and glorious calling) to share the good news with others, it is God who pours out His Spirit. He delights to use everyday, common people to spread the glorious message of the gospel. The church planter is not able to control who is born again through evangelism efforts any better than anyone else. Rather, it is God who removes the blinders from the minds of the unbelievers, so they can see the light of the gospel of the glory of Christ. It is God who sovereignly and supernaturally rebirths individuals, moving them from darkness to light, and from death to life.

What this means for the church planter, as he engages in the work of reaching the Hispanic community with the gospel message, is that certainly, he must evaluate and measure how he is doing in building his "altar." According to an old business axiom, anything that is measured and watched is improved, and this is true in evangelism as well. The church planter can look and see where the Lord is giving fruit and opening doors, and where doors are closing, adjusting his strategies to fit this work. He must continually pray for the Lord to work through his efforts and provide results. And then, he can rest assured as he works that the work of church planting, the work of evangelism, is first and foremost the Lord's work. He can trust that the Lord has delighted to use His servant to accomplish this task within a particular community, all for His glory.

CHAPTER 7:

THE DISCIPLESHIP STAGE

> *"Now an angel of the Lord said to Philip, 'Rise and go toward the south to the road that goes down from Jerusalem to Gaza.' This is a desert place. ^{27} And he rose and went. And there was an Ethiopian, a eunuch, a court official of Candace, queen of the Ethiopians, who was in charge of all her treasure. He had come to Jerusalem to worship ^{28} and was returning, seated in his chariot, and he was reading the prophet Isaiah. ^{29} And the Spirit said to Philip, 'Go over and join this chariot.' ^{30} So Philip ran to him and heard him reading Isaiah the prophet and asked, 'Do you understand what you are reading?' ^{31} And he said, 'How can I, unless someone guides me?' ... ^{35} Then Philip opened his mouth, and beginning with this Scripture he told him the good news about Jesus." – Acts 8:26-35ff*

In the book of Acts, Philip, following the prompting of the Holy Spirit, encountered a man in need of guidance in understanding the Scriptures. Upon engaging in conversation, Philip discovered that this man was reading the Old Testament prophet Isaiah. While the words of Isaiah might have been quite familiar to any literate Jew in that period, this man's background and cultural context was quite different than that of a Jew. He carried the high position of a royal official in the court of the Ethiopian queen. Acts 8, without offering explanation as to why, finds him far from home, traveling through Jewish land as a foreigner. As a eunuch, he would have been unwelcome in the inner courts of the temple; yet here was a God-fearing gentile, engrossed in Scripture, but without the knowledge to make sense of all that he was reading.

Thus, as Philip joined the eunuch's company, he had the incredible opportunity of discipleship. The Lord allowed Philip to quite literally enter into this man's space (his chariot), to sit alongside him as he journeyed, and to help him grow in his faith as he helped the eunuch understand the meaning of Scripture. Notably, the eunuch was reading from a passage in Isaiah, and his initial question to Philip dealt specifically with what he was reading: "About whom, I ask you, does the prophet say this, about himself or about someone else?" (Acts 8:34). Perhaps Philip knew some of his own discipleship methods with which he felt comfortable; perhaps he may have had strategies of how to start a course of discipleship; but here, it is fascinating to note that Philip met the eunuch exactly where he was in his knowledge and questions. He did not redirect the question, or ask to start elsewhere, but "beginning with *this Scripture* he told him the good news about Jesus" (8:35, emphasis added). In short, Philip followed the Spirit's prompting and open doors to disciple this gentile eunuch into a deeper understanding of Jesus.

And Philip's obedience in discipleship bore fruit! Coming to a deeper understanding of the work of Jesus in his life (or perhaps, as a seeker, understanding the work of Jesus in his life for the first time), the eunuch expressed his desire to be baptized (Acts 8:36). Philip therefore had the joy of performing this outward, visible sign and seal of the covenant for the eunuch (8:37), witnessing the transforming work of the Word of God in the life of this man, as He reveals it through Scripture and discipleship. Moreover, while eventually it was time for Philip to depart, the eunuch continued on his journey "rejoicing," changed by a greater understanding of the work of Christ on his behalf (8:39). Although there is no further mention of this man in the Bible, one can only imagine the influence that his transformed life may have had, as he returned to his work and his context, able to bear witness to Christ in a way he could not have without the Lord's placing Philip in his path.

Truly this story illustrates well the picture of the work of discipleship to which church planters – and all believers – are called. The Discipleship Stage of church planting follows on the heels of the Evangelism Stage, but even as the story of the Ethiopian eunuch demonstrates, moving into this second stage does not mean abandoning the work of outreach and evangelism, but rather building upon it. Ultimately, discipleship looks like coming alongside others in their journey of life, and helping make sense of their questions through the lens of Scripture, such that they are transformed in increasing measure into the image of Christ, whether they are just beginning to learn about Jesus (like the eunuch), or whether they have been a Christian for some time.

Complexities of Discipleship within the Hispanic Context

When it comes to discipleship in the Hispanic church context, the story of Philip and the eunuch provides additional helpful insights. Firstly, it is helpful to see Philip's willingness and ability to meet the eunuch exactly where he was. The eunuch was not majority-culture, and did not have the knowledge or background of many of the Jews Philip frequently encountered. In the Hispanic context, as noted at multiple points already in this book, individuals are coming from many different backgrounds with respect to gospel knowledge, from unchurched, to disillusioned, to loosely Roman Catholic. The church planter therefore must be prepared to hear the heart and stories of his disciples, and adjust his strategies and teaching to meet their unique backgrounds. As with evangelism, a one-size-fits-all approach will not prove effective.

Secondly, it is an encouragement to pay attention to the end of the story: the Lord permitted Philip and the eunuch to each go their separate ways. However, as noted earlier, the eunuch had been transformed by the grace of God in his life through Philip. Particularly in first-generation communities, the transient nature of immigrant life can prove quite frustrating for the church planter, as demonstrated by the constant ebb-and-flow of leaders in some of the Hispanic church planting case studies in Chapter 5. Yet the reality is, more than the work of building a particular church plant, the work of discipleship is to build up the Church as a whole. That is, even when the church planter necessarily witnesses some of his disciples moving on, he can be encouraged in trusting that the Lord has allowed his investment of time and ministry into these people as a way of reaching the Hispanic community. While disciples may need to leave the church plant for various reasons, as they go out, they will be better equipped to bring the message of Christ into their new communities.

The Church Planting Timeline for Hispanic church planting dedicates approximately two years to the Discipleship Stage of ministry. While this may seem like a lengthy period to some, it is appropriate for the context. Like in other aspects of church planting, discipleship within the Latino context is often a lengthier process than in majority-culture church planting. Many majority-culture churches gather group members who come from churched backgrounds, ready to learn and become involved in ministry of the new plant. But the common life experiences of the Hispanic community may mean that there is a need to drink long and deeply first from the well of life, before being ready to share a drink with others. Circumstances that may have hardened first-generation immigrants to the gospel message also mean that the work of discipleship may involve the process of uncovering trauma and applying the balm of the gospel to these wounds. For second- and third-generation Latinos who feel neither a part of their mother culture, nor fully accepted by their fellow Americans, discipleship may look like working through questions of race and identity, and how the gospel transforms the understanding of these categories.

Whatever the backgrounds, church planters in the Hispanic context will have both the difficult and rewarding work of bringing the gospel to bear in individual experiences and unique stories, as they help to mold these church plant members further into the image of Christ. Regardless of how long the Lord allows the church planter to walk alongside these individuals in their journeys towards maturity in Christ, he can trust that the Lord has determined and used their interactions to grow the gospel in places and ways he may never see.

Engaging in the Work of the Discipleship Stage

The work of discipleship in the Hispanic community does come with unique challenges, but also with many rewards, and is a necessary process in Hispanic church planting. While evangelism (and along with it, networking and outreach) is the focus of the first year or so of Hispanic church planting, the transition into the discipleship focus of the next two years requires a critical shift for the church planter. Certainly the work of outreach and evangelism continues, but as new members and believers join the work, they need the opportunity to grow up into spiritual maturity, both for their own health, but also the health of the church plant (cf. Ephesians 4:15-16). Indeed, God calls the church to present every person complete in Christ (Colossians 1:28), meaning that making mature and equipped disciples is

> *"Rather, speaking the truth in love, we are to grow up in every way into him who is the head, into Christ, ^{16} from whom the whole body, joined and held together by every joint with which it is equipped, when each part is working properly, makes the body grow so that it builds itself up in love."*
>
> - Ephesians 4:15-16

the primary work of the church. The church planter must never lose sight that the goal is the transformation of individual lives so that they become engages in God's story – the larger story – for the rest of their lives.

The key in the Discipleship Stage is for the church planter to help his people move towards spiritual maturity as he intentionally trains other disciple makers. These disciples will in turn be able to teach others, allowing the reach of the church plant to grow and multiply. Without training disciples, the church plant will be unable to grow in depth and will simply stagnate; without training other disciple makers, the church planter will eventually burn out. Thus, intentionally investing in a lengthy period discipleship will allow the church planter to invite others to come alongside of him in the ministry of the church, as they share the burden of reaching the community for Christ. Moreover, as he and other believers disciple these individuals, the church planter may begin to prayerfully identify those in whom he may see a potential for leadership, thus readying them and the church plant to move into the next stages of church planting and growth.

Even in discipling new Christians, or those who are immature in their faith, it will be helpful for the church planter to recruit others to assist in the work of discipleship. If there are members of his core team who already exude spiritual maturity, he may help and encourage them to come alongside these new believers to invest in their lives. This may be especially helpful in the case of discipling women. In Hispanic culture, the reality of church planting is that (typically) more women will attend church than men; yet they will respond best to discipling from other, more mature women in the faith. Thus the church planter must pray for and help equip women in the church to disciple other women who are in need of spiritual mothers who can relate with their unique struggles and encourage them and help them grow in their faith (cf. Titus 2:3-5).

As the Discipleship Stage begins, the church planter may be excited and tempted to start big. Yet the work of discipleship, particularly in this context, must be slow and measured, working at a pace that hears the unique stories of the disciples, and that will not lead to burnout for those who are doing the discipling. For this reason, the timeline suggests two years over which the church planter may slowly implement his discipleship strategy, rather than trying to start everything at the same time.

Firstly, it is essential that the church planter invest in his launch team, caring for them and equipping them to have the capacity and vision for coming alongside him in the work of ministry. As he spends time with these individuals, intentionally investing in their lives, he will begin to see their strengths (as well as encourage them in their weaknesses) and thus be able to play to these in empowering them in the appropriate places of leadership. The church planter should furthermore ensure that he is communicating clearly with these individuals, creating a relationship in which they are able to express their needs, and that he is able to give clearcut, loving, expectations. It will be helpful for him to remember that the manner in which he cares for and disciples these individuals will necessarily model how they will care for and disciple others. At the same time, as relationships grow, he must be willing to relinquish some control and allow these individuals to mature through experience, as he begins to delegate leadership functions to them in the specific areas where they may be gifted.

As with any stage of ministry, the Discipleship Stage requires constant assessment and readjustment of strategies as necessary. The Strategic Plan for discipleship provides a helpful starting point, but the church planter must be ready to adjust as he learns more specifically the hearts of his core group members, and listens to the stories and needs of his demographic. As he leads others in discipleship, he will need to ensure that his discipleship plan is clear, yet he must also allow room for questions and flexibility as they arise. Different gifts and ideas among emerging leaders, or unique stories within the community, may necessitate starting, stopping, reworking, or consolidating different discipleship programs to better fit the context. This work of intentionally helping others live in a more Christlike manner requires much patience, prayer, and possible revision of plans as the Spirit gives guidance.

Conclusion

Without purposeful, dedicated investment in the lives of launch team members and new believers, the church plant will be unprepared to move into the next stages of church planting. Over the course of two years, the church planter will see some disciples come and go, but with the Lord's guidance, he will be helping to mature and equip believers to serve in the church and community, and further the witness of the gospel. Like Philip with the Ethiopian eunuch, even the discipleship of those whom God allows to leave and go their separate ways will not be in vain. While the church planter will not see the end to every story and interaction, as he faithfully disciples others, he will have the joy and privilege of seeing the Lord redeeming hard stories for the glory of His Kingdom, even as God begins to raise up individuals to love and serve the church plant community. May he not grow weary in this ministry, knowing that, as he seeks the guidance of the Holy Spirit, the Lord will accomplish His purposes in bringing the harvest He has determined (cf. Galatians 6:8-10).

> *"...the one who sows to the Spirit will from the Spirit reap eternal life. 9 And let us not grow weary of doing good, for in due season we will reap, if we do not give up."*
>
> - Galatians 6:8b-9

CHAPTER 8:

THE WORSHIP STAGE

"After this I looked, and behold, a great multitude that no one could number, from every nation, from all tribes and peoples and languages, standing before the throne and before the Lamb, clothed in white robes, with palm branches in their hands, [10] and crying out with a loud voice, 'Salvation belongs to our God who sits on the throne, and to the Lamb!' [11] And all the angels were standing around the throne and around the elders and the four living creatures, and they fell on their faces before the throne and worshiped God, [12] saying, 'Amen! Blessing and glory and wisdom and thanksgiving and honor and power and might be to our God forever and ever! Amen.'" –
Revelation 7:9-12

John Piper has famously written that "missions exist because worship doesn't," that worship is ultimate over missions "because God is ultimate, not man." Therefore, "worship is the fuel and goal of missions."[7] Church planting is indeed a mission work, and Hispanic church planting is an opportunity to reach the nations right in the community. Church planting involves much outreach, evangelism, and discipleship; yet the objective of this work, as Piper rightly points out, is the glory of God in worship of Him.

In the book of Revelation, John is given a glimpse into what consummated worship of God will look like, and the depiction is glorious. This worship involves "a great multitude that no one could number, from every nation, from all tribes and peoples and languages" together with angels and heavenly beings coming together in eternal worship before the throne of the Lord God Almighty (Revelation 7:9ff). While nothing can compare to consummated worship, the act of worship within the church invites people in to experience the presence of God and fall before His throne of grace as a quite literally heavenly taste of what is to come. A diverse body of believers worshiping together provides a place where unbelievers and believers alike can get a glimpse of what it means for people of distinct backgrounds to be united under the headship of Christ.

Indeed, as a church planter witnesses God's hand at work in his target context, in spite of and through the challenges, it should be a cause for celebration in worship, as he and his launch team can see and confess that "Salvation belongs to our God who sits on the throne, and to the Lamb!" Worship is the celebration of who God is, what He has done, and what He promises He will do. It is an invitation to fall on one's face before the throne in recognition that all blessing, glory, wisdom, thanksgiving, honor, power, and might belong to the Lord, and to Him alone. Who else but God can plant a seed in the heart of a pastor to work through the difficulties of reaching a Hispanic community in a majority-culture setting? Who else but God alone is able not only to plant that seed, but to cause it to spring up and bear fruit, in spite of the rocks and thorns that might threaten its growth? As the church planter and his group witness this mighty work, it will cause them to break forth in worship of the Creator.

Timing for Launching Public Worship

Even as Revelation depicts, worship is the highest, most sacred, and most joyful experience of a believer's existence. While worship can and should happen individually and in fellowship organically and informally throughout the week, organized, Sunday worship is the culmination of Christian worship. Thus, a church plant group that has experienced the hand of God in their midst will push to launch public worship early on. But launching public worship in a healthy way requires patience and wisdom. Although it is a good and healthy desire, there are many factors to take into consideration first. Church plants that launch public worship prematurely often find that their works struggle and remain small, as they have not taken the time to lay the appropriate foundations. Of course, it is necessary to mention here that the metrics of "small" used by majority-culture churches are not the appropriate measuring rod here. Realistic Hispanic church sizes are small by comparison, as the case studies in this book demonstrate. Rather, the goal is to have a consistent group of committed launch team members prior to launching.

Another risk of launching public worship too soon is that of exhausting the church planter, if he has not garnered adequate support, or of burning out his launch team, if they are not yet large enough or sufficiently prepared to do the work that comes along with public worship. Starting Sunday worship too early runs the risk of taking time away from the essential groundwork of networking, evangelism, and discipleship, as the church planter will need to focus sufficient time to Sunday preparation. It may also run the risk of not actually inviting in the target community, if the church planter has not invested adequate time to both understand their context, and develop the *confianza* needed to be able to invite them to a worship service.

Thus, investing the first three years of the church plant's existence in evangelism and discipleship before launching public worship will pay off in the long term. While this timeframe may seem lengthy in comparison to majority-culture church plants who typically launch public worship in under a year, it bears remembering that the Hispanic demographic dictates a more drawn-out approach in order to be fully ready. As seen in the discussions regarding the evangelism and discipleship stages of church planting, it is during these pre-worship service phases that the church planter is able to devote most of his time to the critical work of reaching new people. The Hispanic church planter must push back against majority-culture pressure to launch worship before his community is ready, recognizing instead that the soil needs greater preparation before fruit is ready for harvest.

Aside from external pressure to launch prematurely, the church planter may also experience pressure from within the community itself. For many Hispanics, and particularly those from a Roman Catholic background, the belief is that the work of the church equates to worship services. They may struggle, therefore, to understand the role of the pastor and church plant without being able to participate in Sunday worship. Yet in this aspect, the church planter has the unique opportunity to be able to draw his community into a greater understanding of the church not just as a weekly event, but as the Body of Christ being built up together. Lending enough time to the evangelism and discipleship process will help to demonstrate to the community what active church life looks like on a daily basis. Only after investing significant time in growing and building up a core group will the church plant be ready to enter the Worship Stage of church planting.

Planning for Public Worship

Of course, preparing to launch public worship does not mean an abandonment of the work of evangelism and discipleship, but once again, it does necessitate a shift in focus and reappropriation of the church planter's weekly schedule. The suggested timeframe, then, for launching public worship in a Hispanic church plant (following the Church Planting Timeline), is during years four and five of the church plant. As the church plant moves into this stage, the first steps look like preparation for worship itself. While the first three years of experience in the community will work to inform the process of how formal worship should look, the leadership team should begin the actual work of planning for the first public worship service approximately six to nine months prior the expected date of the first worship service.

Finding a Worship Location

There are several aspects involved in planning for the launch of public worship. One of the first objectives involves finding a space for worship itself to take place. Of course, if the church plant is following integrated methodology, the church plant will already have a confirmed space within the mother church; similarly, church plants using incubator methodology may be able to push the process further down the road, if the plan is to initially launch from the mother church site. For all other church plants, however, the search for an appropriate space can be a difficult and lengthy process. Seeking a viable location within the target area that will both fit within a budget, and be easily accessible to the Hispanic community requires much wisdom, prayer, and potentially creativity.

Indeed, the needs of each church plant will differ given their demographics, and it need not always look like a traditional worship setting. While some contexts may be open to using a space only available for afternoon worship, this may provide a hindrance to other church plant demographics. While some church plants may have the financial ability – and need – to acquire a facility for use throughout the week, it may be preferable for others to rent a space only during the time of worship itself. Once again, the time that a church planter has invested in his community, establishing *confianza* and getting to know his demographic may prove quite helpful here. Knowing where neighbors spend time, the local bus routes, and areas they avoid will be helpful in determining which pockets of the community provide the most strategic spots to look for real estate. At the same time, connections within the community may be helpful in providing ideas, identifying a trusted local realtor, or even offering some of their own space.

As the church planter visits and visualizes a potential worship space, he and his team must also think through the logistics of Sunday set-up, potential space for children's ministries, Sunday schools, or even meals. As he considers the needs of his group and weighs what options may be available, he must pray for eyes to possibly see beyond what he had envisioned as ideal. Various Hispanic church plants, as seen through the case studies in Chapter 5, have found a home within other churches, schools, recreation centers, converted warehouses, or even repurposed houses! Ultimately, the Lord can use any space as a place for people to join in worshiping Him, as they follow His guiding and direction.

Selecting a Worship Model

While finding a space to hold public worship is an important step in preparing for public launch, another critical element is determining a worship model to meet the needs of the target community. In the Hispanic context, this looks like assessing the level of assimilation and English language proficiency of the church plant's context, in order to determine the church may best communicate with members and visitors.

Thus it is helpful first to understand the diversity of language skills and preferences in order to think through which model (or model variant) may work best. Thinking through a group's language proficiency in terms of a **_Language Continuum_** (see Figure 7) may prove quite useful here. As seen through the diagram, there are several stages of language proficiency and comfortability that factor into choosing how a church plant should pursue worship. Some target contexts (i.e., first-generation immigrant communities) may lean towards the righthand side of the continuum, with primarily Spanish-only speakers, and perhaps a few individuals who can communicate in English, but feel more comfortable in their mother tongue (Prefers Spanish). On the other hand, if a church planter is working within a demographic

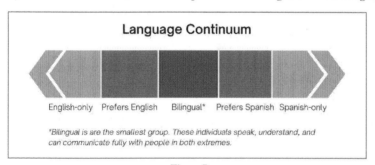

Figure 7

that has more second- and third-generation Hispanics, they may lean more towards the middle or left-hand side of the continuum, necessitating the incorporation of more English into worship. Other contexts may have a good mix of individuals from all stages of the continuum. A further consideration is that, while a church plant may serve a community of first-generation Spanish-only adults, the reality is that many of their children (who are attending English-speaking schools and spending time with English-speaking friends) may actually fall into the "Prefers English" category. Reaching both the parents and their children requires creativity in thinking through worship models, especially as parents may have prejudices or insecurities regarding their children learning in English. All of these factors must come into consideration when thinking through worship models.

While there are a variety of effective ways to do this, three primary methods of balancing English and Spanish in worship are the Distinct Model, the Joint Model, and the Connected Model, each discussed in turn below. Each model has its unique advantages and disadvantages. The church planter and his launch team must prayerfully consider these before selecting which model (or model variant) may be best suited to their target demographic. It is also helpful to note that there is some fluidity between models. Even as some of the case studies given in this book illustrate, it may be necessary for a church plant to start with one, with a willingness to move into another later, as necessity dictates and resources permit.

The **Distinct Model** for worship refers to two separate (or distinct) congregations meeting in their respective languages (in this case, either English or Spanish), with no interaction between the two groups (see Figure 8). The two worship services could start at the same time, meeting in different locations of the same facility, or perhaps meet in the same location, but at different times. Often, church plants using integrated methodology will follow the distinct model, with members of the mother church meeting for one, English-speaking service, and the Spanish-speaking congregation meeting at the same facility as a separate service. Incubator methodology also lends to a version of the Distinct Model for worship as well, at least in so long as the church plant is meeting ("incubating") within the mother church. Notably, in these cases, the Distinct Model for worship does not refer to two services within the church plant itself, but for the mother church and the integrated or incubating Hispanic church plant. However, a church planter could also choose to incorporate distinct worship into the church plant itself.

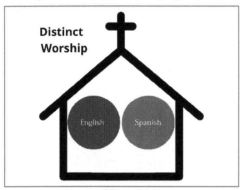
Figure 8

Some of the benefits of the Distinct Model for worship are that individuals are able to worship and hear the preaching of the Word in their heart language. Without language barriers getting in the way of understanding, there is a low level of discomfort for the participants of either service. Thus, Spanish-speakers will find it easy to invite their Spanish-speaking friends, while English-speaking individuals will feel comfortable inviting other English speakers (Hispanic or otherwise).

At the same time, the church plant must exercise caution when using the Distinct Model that they do not end up with not simply two worship services, but two churches. In fact, it can be difficult to avoid this trap as each language-group feels content within their particular settings, and may be reluctant to interact with one another, or may simply find it too uncomfortable. A church planter with a mixed-language launch team must weigh these potential positives and negatives, to determine whether having two distinct language-specific services will best serve his church plant.

In a near-opposite method as the Distinct Model, the **Joint Model** for worship means that a group is always together, regardless of language preference (see Figure 9). While there are a number of ways in which this can play out, it typically looks like an English-dominant service with translation provided for those who are not fluent in English. In some majority-Hispanic contexts (like Hialeah, Florida, in Miami-Dade county), the language structure might be reversed, with the greater part of the service taking place in Spanish, and translation to English as needed. Understandably, this model tends to work best in church plants where one language-group is dominant over the other (i.e., a Spanish-dominant service if first-generation Spanish-speakers are the main group, or on the other hand, English-dominant services, if second- and third-generation English proficient Hispanics are the target demographic).

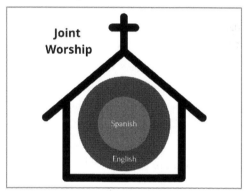

Figure 9

Positively, the Joint Model for worship means that the church body is always together, thereby avoiding the tendency of the Distinct Model for members of two different services to view one another as two separate churches. Moreover, Spanish-speakers and English-speakers alike in congregations following the Joint Model for worship have the benefit of experiencing a little discomfort, as they both learn to worship in new ways, and have the opportunity to interact with those of different backgrounds. Particularly when the church plant represents a diversity of cultures, Joint Model worship provides a good opportunity for members to learn about different backgrounds and cultures, to see how different cultures worship, and to grow through the experience.

On the other hand, one of the challenges to Joint Model worship is that translation of services is difficult: even a good translator will not be able to fully translate all of the nuances of a sermon and worship. Thus the minority culture hearing the translation may not reap the full benefits of worship. Moreover, in this model, it is the minority culture that is always having to make sacrifices. Not only may it be difficult to glean everything from a translated service, but even sermon applications and illustrations may not be relevant to the minority group, if the pastor is not diligent in actively engaging those of the minority language. Additionally, there may be some disconnect for worship participants, as they will find it challenging to sing in a language in which they are not proficient, or to fully engage in what they are singing.

Some of these challenges may be lessened if there is a fluidity of language skills within the congregation – that is, if many of the Spanish-speakers also are at least comfortable understanding some English, and vice-versa. Again, it will take discretion on the part of the church planter to know if his congregation might benefit from some version of the Joint Model for worship.

The **Connected Model** for worship describes a setting in which the group meets together for a portion of the worship service, and then separates during the preaching in order to hear the sermon in the language of their choosing (see Figure 10). How the remainder of the service is split between languages will vary from church to church and depending on the context, but the idea is for members of the same church body to be able to hear the critical preaching of the Word of God for their unique context and in their mother tongue.

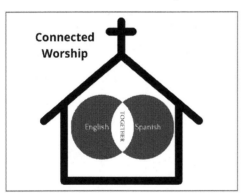

Figure 10

One of the greatest benefits of the Connected Model for worship is that, like the Joint Model, it promotes intentional interaction between members of different backgrounds and languages, in a way that the Distinct Model struggles to do. At the same time, like the Distinct Model (and different from the Joint Model), there is no translation barrier to prevent Spanish-speakers or English-speakers from understanding the preached Word. Rather, the Connected Model focuses on the priority of hearing the sermon without hindrance of language or translation. Thus in both interactions and hearing the preaching, the group experiences most of the benefits of the Always-Together model (i.e., the majority-context model, where there is no need to differentiate between languages because practically all members are English-speakers).

Nevertheless, like the other worship models, the Connected Model also presents with some potential negative aspects. In the first place, it may prove difficult for the majority culture of the church (whether that be Spanish-speakers or English-speakers in a Latino church plant context) to accept the inconveniences of a split worship service. Moreover, there will still be a level of discomfort for at least one group within the congregation during the joint section of the worship that is not in their language of preference. When it comes to the preaching of the Word, the Connected Model for worship may prove difficult in that it demands multiple staff and adequate space to accommodate two sermons happening at one time. Both of these requirements may be particularly challenging for a young, Hispanic church plant to provide. On a very practical level, having two simultaneous sermons makes it difficult to time the end of worship services, and that challenge can trickle down into timing for nursery and children's classes. Thus, in considering the Connected Model for worship, the church planter must consider whether his church plant has the bandwidth and capacity to carry out its complexities, if he thinks the model may prove beneficial to his demographic.

Selecting the best model for worship takes time, wisdom regarding the needs of the church plant's demographic, and much prayer. As seen above, any model will come with its own challenges and advantages; the church planter must know his people to such a degree that he can determine which model may stretch them in the appropriate ways to help and not hinder their growth. While these are the three primary models for worship in the Hispanic context, both the church planter and his launch team will need to prayerfully nuance how the model should play out specifically within their context, and then trust the Lord to be at work.

Developing Church Ministries

As the church plant finds a facility, chooses a worship method, and moves closer to launching publicly, the church planter must also help his core group to develop the ministries that will be necessary to facilitate Sunday worship. These ministries might include hospitality, children's ministry, a music or worship team, set-up/tear-down crews, even potentially a team trained in leading liturgy. Necessarily, a church planter must determine which teams are essential (and which are either non-essential, or could potentially wait) through assessing both his resources as well as the needs of his demographic. For example, if the community is abounding with young children, it may be difficult to launch a welcoming worship space without a plan for caring for children, but in other communities with older populations, children's ministry may not be an immediate consideration.

Part of the process of developing these ministries will include identifying and training launch team members to lead and participate in areas where they may have gifting – or at least willingness. A church plant will only be able to develop the ministries for which there are adequate, dedicated volunteers to staff them, so the church planter must also take into consideration where each team member is serving, such that no one individual overcommits themselves either through enthusiasm or through feeling compelled to volunteer.

Regardless of what ministry teams the church plant determines are essential for public worship, there must be a plan for welcoming and following up with visitors. This may include having materials and resources to hand out (which, in turn, involves finding or creating, and providing these resources), but also should include a robust team of members who are willing and ready to engage new faces. Reaching new people for Christ, after all, is one of the primary goals of church planting!

Another essential part of preparing for Sunday worship includes music ministry. When it comes to music ministry, there are nearly as many methodologies (and opinions) as there are churches; yet the church planter and his launch team must determine how they will use the resources God has provided (individuals, finances, etc.) to help lead people in the praise and worship of the Lord. If the worship model will be any other than the Distinct Model, this will include a discussion of what worship will look like in a bilingual, multicultural context. For some church plants, simply using digital worship soundtracks may be appropriate, while others may develop a group of trained musicians, or even decide to pay a worship leader or staff. Insofar as the Lord provides the resources, it will be helpful for the worship team to reflect the makeup of the congregation. Also importantly, as the pastor (and potential worship leaders) learn their context, they must consider what sort of musical style and "songs, hymns, and spiritual songs" will best direct the hearts of the congregation in worshiping and making melody before the Lord (cf. Ephesians 5:19).

> *"[address] one another in psalms and hymns and spiritual songs, singing and making melody to the Lord with your heart..."*
>
> - Ephesians 5:19

It is helpful to bear in mind that no one style or leader will satisfy everyone all of the time; yet one of the goals of a worship leader or team is to help transcend those preferences by pointing everything to the incredible act of being able to fall before the throne of the living God together in praise, adoration, confession, and thanksgiving. In visioning worship and training a team, or even preparing the resources, the church planter and his team must again bring everything before the Lord, praying for His wisdom, and trusting Him to use the talents He has provided to lead people in the worship of Him.

A final, but also necessary, step to preparation for public launch requires having a team of individuals ensuring that the space is ready and welcoming for public worship. Depending on the facility, this could require quite a lot, or very little, from the church plant launch team. If the church plant is not using a mother church facility, they will need to ensure that they have all the necessary equipment (for sacraments, sound, hospitality, nursery, etc.,) and furniture to host Sunday worship. Potentially this could involve many launch team members coming together to prepare the space, whether that means cleaning and setting up a semi-permanent rented facility, or working together to vision and prepare a weekly set-up and tear-down. It need not be elaborate, but certain team members may prove quite gifted in making a space hospitable and ready to welcome the community.

Launching Public Worship

There is certainly much planning involved in the preparation for the launch of public worship, and this planning takes time, wisdom, knowledge of the demographic, training of team members, and prayer. Yet the end goal is the powerful opportunity to publicly proclaim the Word of God, and invite the community into the worship of the Lord. As the church plant readies for this day, the church planter will have the exciting task of preparing his first sermons, and determining how the Lord is leading him to address the church plant in the first months and year of worship. Once again, knowing the stories and heart of his demographic will help him in choosing what biblical book or theme may best benefit his hearers from the outset of public preaching. Determining these initial sermon series' must also be a process bathed in prayer!

As the core group gears up for public launch, it may be helpful to hold a number of "preview" services, in which the team together in the acquired space for series of trial-runs of Sunday worship and its respective ministries. Such a period of practice will help both the church planter and his team feel more prepared for welcoming the community on the day of public launch. They will have the opportunity to work through some of the unanticipated hiccups prior to inviting the community to participate. It may also be a good time for allowing individuals to share their testimonies as an encouragement to everyone regarding how the Lord has been at work in preparing for this phase of church planting.

Indeed, the launch of public worship is an incredible time for celebrating the work that the Lord has done and will do through the church plant in the target community. It is a time for the church planter, launch team members, and community to come together and give all "blessing and glory and wisdom and thanksgiving and honor and power and might" to the Lord God for His care and plans for the church plant's community.

Conclusion

This public launch of worship will usher the church plant into a new stage of ministry, as the church not only continues to reach out to the community, but now has the opportunity to invite them into the glorious, formal worship of the Lord. It changes the focus of the church planter from primarily evangelist and disciple-maker, to a pastor who is evangelizing and discipling not just through conversations and outreach during the week, but through the preached Word. It gives him the opportunity of opening his community to a contextualized exposition of "the implanted Word" which has the power to save souls (cf. James 1:21). While the process of launching may be lengthy and involved, the work is exciting, and it is the work to which the church planter has been called. As the Worship Stage takes off, the church planter can trust that he has been sent by God to be the prophetic voice to the community in which the Lord has placed him, so he may boldly proclaim the message the Lord has given to him. The words that the Lord spoke to Moses at the burning bush are appropriate for the church planter here: "Now go; I will help you speak and will teach you what to say" (Exodus 4:12). Entrust the work of worship to the Lord; He already knows what He will say to the communities He has chosen for the work!

> "Then the LORD said to him, 'Who has made man's mouth? Who makes him mute, or deaf, or seeing, or blind? Is it not I, the LORD? Now therefore go, and I will be with your mouth and teach you what you shall speak.'"
>
> - Exodus 4:11-12

CHAPTER 9:

THE LEADERSHIP STAGE

*"Moses' father-in-law said to him, 'What you are doing is not good. *[18]*You and the people with you will certainly wear yourselves out, for the thing is too heavy for you. You are not able to do it alone. *[19]*Now obey my voice; I will give you advice, and God be with you! You shall represent the people before God and bring their cases to God, *[20]*and you shall warn them about the statutes and the laws, and make them know the way in which they must walk and what they must do. *[21]*Moreover, look for able men from all the people, men who fear God, who are trustworthy and hate a bribe, and place such men over the people as chiefs of thousands, of hundreds, of fifties, and of tens. *[22]*And let them judge the people at all times. Every great matter they shall bring to you, but any small matter they shall decide themselves. So it will be easier for you, and they will bear the burden with you. *[23]*If you do this, God will direct you, you will be able to endure, and all this people also will go to their place in peace.'"* – Exodus 18:17-23

Moses, as God's chosen servant for bringing the Israelites out of Egypt and leading them through their wilderness wanderings, had a great responsibility. The Lord entrusted him with a vast group of men, women, and children who had experienced much trauma in Egypt, and were now living a nomadic life in the desert. Although the Lord was at work rescuing and leading them, as their repeated grumbling demonstrated, they were not particularly good at seeing and remembering His guidance or provision. The need for wise, God-fearing leadership was great.

As Moses settled into the task of caring for the wandering nation – hearing their complaints and helping to decide their daily disputes – he was at risk of burning out. The responsibility was too great for him alone, and would also not be beneficial to the people he was leading. His father-in-law, Jethro, wisely noted the problem: "What you are doing is not good. You and the people with you will certainly wear yourselves out, for the thing is too heavy for you. You are not able to do it alone" (Exodus 18:17b-18). Thus, as Exodus 18 relates, Jethro helped Moses to oversee and divide the responsibility of caring for the people between a number of able-bodied leaders, who could help bear the responsibility in hearing and judging the people, and defer to Moses' wisdom in larger matters.

Moreover, Jethro helped Moses see the qualifications for these leaders. Notably, they were not the men who perhaps had been the most successful in their work in Egypt, or from any one particular tribe. Rather, they were to come from "all the people," to be "men who fear God, who are trustworthy and hate a bribe" (Exodus 18:21). By establishing such qualified, upright men to assist in leadership, Moses was able to share the burden of responsibility in caring for God's people, increasing his own ability to "endure," and in turn, also allowing the people to better flourish and live "in peace" (18:22-23).

Jethro's advice to Moses provides wisdom also for the church planter – in any context, but perhaps particularly within the Hispanic context in which the needs for training, discipleship, outreach, and mercy ministry are especially high. At this stage in the work of church planting, as the work of outreach, evangelism, and discipleship continue, and as the pastor prepares weekly for Sunday worship, there are simply not enough hours in the day for the church planter to accomplish everything that needs to happen. And like the Israelites, God's people need much wise counsel and reminding of God's provision, protection, and plan. The risk of burnout for the church planter at this stage – of losing his sanity, or not caring adequately for his family – is high, if he is not developing leadership to come alongside him in the work of ministry. Thus, the next stage of church planting is the Leadership Stage (years 5-8 of ministry, following the Church Planting Timeline), which involves identifying and training both lay-leaders and ordainable leaders (Ruling Elders/Deacons) to assist in reaching out to the community, and caring for those whom the Lord is bringing.

Well-trained leaders who embrace the church's values, mission, and vision, take time to identify and develop. Like the other stages of church planting, the church planter must not rush this stage or be too quick to appoint leaders. The risks in moving too quickly are in appointing leaders who are not ready, thus necessitating the church planter to spend more time in conflict resolution than in the work of growing the church. This chapter, then, will look at some strategies for both identifying and training potential lay-leaders and leaders who might be ordained to the offices of Ruling Elder and Deacon.

Identifying and Training Lay-Leaders

While there is certainly overlap in the process of identifying and training both lay-leaders and potential Ruling Elders and Deacons, the criteria for ordainable leadership is more specific, so it is helpful to look at these overarching categories in turn.

In the first place, a church planter must find those lay-people who are willing to lead in lay-ministries (i.e., visitor follow-up, hospitality, children's ministry, etc.,) as the church plant has need. The right kinds of people are those who are already serving the church in diverse ways, without being asked. They are those who have not only a heart for service, but a humble spirit, ready and willing to learn more about the interaction of faith and work, and ready to be taught. In short, they are those who are growing in the grace and knowledge of the Lord, and serving with willing hearts as they grow (cf. 2 Peter 3:18, 2 Corinthians 9:7).

> *"But grow in the grace and knowledge of our Lord and Savior Jesus Christ. To him be the glory both now and to the day of eternity. Amen."*
>
> *- II Peter 3:18*

It is critical to remember in Hispanic church planting that the best leaders are not necessarily those whom a majority-culture church might recognize as such. There are many people who are ready to be greeters at the door, or to work on the setup of coffee and snack ministries. When such individuals approach the church planter to ask to serve in such ministries, it is a noble request. The church planter should be excited to place them into the respective ministries, and allow them to flourish, potentially shifting them through different ministries as the needs arise, or as their giftings and interests develop and mature.

In a church plant, there is always a need for volunteers. Some potential leaders may desire to serve, but feel unsure as to where they are called. A church planter and other mature leaders can help by listening to these individuals and helping them test different ministries to see where they can flourish. As they rotate through ministries, they may grow in their capacity to identify needs and fill those roles, emerging as new leadership. Spending time with both new families and individuals, as well as those who have been in the church for longer, will help the church planter to be able to encourage these people to use their gifts to serve the church in the manner best suited for them. Although not all will become leaders of any particular ministry, helping to identify gifts and encouraging them in these areas as they grow in the Lord will help to shape individuals for lifelong service in the church and within their spheres of influence.

One particularly important demographic to look for and encourage rising leadership within is the younger generations and children of the church. In Hispanic church plants, these are often second- or third-generation Hispanic-Americans, who have the potential to become the future leaders of the church. Without investment in their lives early on, these children may be tempted to leave the church feeling that they do not fit. On the other hand,

> "The wolf shall dwell with the lamb, and the leopard shall lie down with the young goat, and the calf and the lion and the fattened calf together; and a little child shall lead them."
>
> - Isaiah 11:6

drawing them in and showing them their importance and ability even as children to serve within the greater church body will encourage and embolden them for future life and ministry as Christians. Seeing young people in ministry and leadership also serves as an encouragement to older members and the community, as they see all of the Body of Christ growing and serving together. Moreover, it serves as a witness to the families of these young men and women regarding the importance of being intentional with their children, and remaining connected to the church. Involvement of young people in service and leadership may encourage the involvement of others as well, as they see that the Lord uses even little children to lead (cf. Isaiah 11:6).

It is also essential not to overlook the identifying and training up of women for leadership roles within the church plant. This is important in any context, but particularly within the Hispanic community, where, statistically and sociologically speaking, women will lead the family in spiritual life and coming to church. According to one study, in many cases, "the women in the family are the ones who inculcate values and keep religious rituals alive. While the structures of Latino families may have a patriarchal exterior, the foundational base is often formed by the influence of the mother, grandmother, or other female figures."[8] This, coupled with the tendency for the Hispanic community to be full of broken families, often creates a complex dynamic in a society that is both *machista* and matriarchal. Thus, the need to invest in women who may be treated pejoratively by their spouses, and/or who have uninvolved

> **machista:** literally, a "male chauvinist," or within the Hispanic community, typically referring to men who have the need to prove themselves as the *jefe* (boss) within a relationship and show excessive dominance (potentially with aggression), resulting in damage both to the relationship of the couple, but also to any children who may be involved.

husbands and are attempting to lead (and potentially provide for) their households is high. Church planters need to be especially sensitive, therefore, to the needs and giftings of these women. The church should provide maximum opportunities to shepherd them in ways that they are encouraged to use their giftings to find joy in service and leadership both at church and at home. As women are likely to comprise the majority of a Hispanic church plant, it is especially important that they are considered, included, and encouraged in the service and leadership of the church as appropriate. Such investment can prove redemptive for these women and their families, even as they help the women grow in their faith and flourish in their giftings.

Identifying and training lay-leaders in the church will not only serve the church plant itself, but will help these individuals to grow in grace as they are encouraged in a life of service to the Lord. While lay-leaders will come and go, the work of identifying their gifts and helping them flourish in these areas will continue to bear fruit throughout their lives. It may even help to raise new leaders for future church plants within the Latino context and beyond, as even children discover a heart for and joy of service to the Lord.

Identifying and Training Ordainable Hispanic Church Leaders: Qualifications

The identification and training of lay-leadership may provide the first steps in finding candidates for the offices of Ruling Elder and Deacon. When it comes to identifying and training these candidates, the PCA provides abundant resources, building on the qualifications given in 1 Timothy 3, and Titus 1. The *Resources* page at the end of this book provides a list of several of these widely-available resources that will prove useful for a church planter in practically any given context. Thus, the goal of this section is not to summarize any of these materials, but to speak to some of the considerations and challenges surrounding ordination to these positions that may be specific to the Latino context.

In the first place, the church planter must keep in mind that potential ordainable leaders need not look like those found within the majority-culture church. What is meant by this statement is that, without any built-in stipulations as such, the overwhelming majority of men who become ordained to the office of Ruling Elder in particular, but also Deacon within the PCA, are fairly affluent, successful, upper-class, white, older men. While the goal is not to cast aspersions upon these God-given leaders, the fact is that position in society can direct a congregation to see a potential candidate. Yet leadership within a Hispanic church plant must reflect the culture of the church members, and these qualified candidates will reflect a number of diverse backgrounds.

Recall the specifications for leadership that Jethro gave to Moses: he was to "look for able men from *all the people*, men who *fear God*, who are *trustworthy* and *hate a bribe*..." (Exodus 18:21, emphasis added). Qualified men for leadership in Israel were not chosen based on any social status (all Israel had been serving in slavery immediately prior to this time!) or even tribal affiliations. Rather, Moses was to consider *all* the people, and look specifically for those who were of outstanding moral and spiritual character, who would thus have the humility and wisdom to help lead and shepherd the people well. Although the pastoral epistles speak to more of the specifics of qualifications, these overarching qualities should guide the church planter as he seeks to find leaders to train for ordination.

Identifying and Training Ordainable Hispanic Church Leaders: Challenges

One of the challenges to training and ordaining men to the offices of Ruling Elder and Deacon in Hispanic churches is the transitional nature of most immigrant communities. Many of the church plant case studies given in Chapter 5 speak to this reality, as church planters trained groups of potential leaders, only for those individuals to move on before even reaching ordination. This reality may feel frustrating to the church planter, especially if he is unprepared to see people come and go, but this is one of the reasons that training leaders in the Hispanic context can take more time than it might in a majority-culture church plant. Moreover, as discussed in other contexts, the church planter can rest assured that, in the Lord's guidance, his labor is not in vain (cf. I Corinthians 15:58). Whether these men serve in his church plant, or elsewhere, he has had the opportunity to help them move towards a deeper understanding of what it means to live as God's servants. Moreover, if God has truly called a church planter to the work within his given context, then God will indeed provide the right leaders, in His timing and according to His plan. Thus, fear of them leaving should not be a reason to pass over a potential candidate.

> *"Therefore, my beloved brothers, be steadfast, immovable, always abounding in the work of the Lord, knowing that in the Lord your labor is not in vain."*
> - I Corinthians 15:58

Another potential difficulty when it comes to training potential candidates involves levels of education and the materials available for training. Again, most majority-culture ordained leaders are coming from middle- to upper-America backgrounds, which typically indicates high levels of continuing education, and ability to read at a level commensurate with that education. Thus, many of the books and resources available for their instruction target these levels of training and understanding. Yet in the Hispanic community, life demands and backgrounds may mean that some men who are qualified as potential ordained leaders may not have the educational foundation to be able to work through the available materials on their own. Many have not had the opportunity to attend college, while some have not finished high school. In fact, according to the 2003 US Census Bureau, Hispanics are among the least educated group in the United States, with only 11 percent over the age of 25 with a bachelor's degree or higher (cf. 17% of Blacks, 30% of Whites, and 49% of Asian-Americans within the same age bracket), and more than 25% of Hispanic adults have less than a ninth-grade education.[9] Reading and studying materials that a church would typically provide for Elder/Deacon candidates thus becomes burdensome if the reading is too heady, or if extracurricular reading has not been a normative part of life for these individuals. For the church planter, this reality will mean approaching officer training with flexibility. Most likely, it will include more classroom-type and one-on-one instruction, to help cover the necessary material in a clearer fashion. The church planter may also consider incorporating video instruction, using videos (either as an at-home assignment or within a classroom) as a starting point for discussion and growth.

Similarly, language barriers can also be a challenge in training potential Hispanic ordainable leaders. Even if candidates come with a high level of education, if their primary language is Spanish, the resources available will not be accessible. The *Resources* page again lists some materials that have either been translated, or written specifically with the Hispanic community in mind, which may prove helpful in overcoming this obstacle. Still, the church planter may find himself needing to create some of his own resources, or adapting some materials to better fit the language needs and context of his candidates. Additionally, the church planter may again need to spend more time in verbal instruction (through classes or individual meetings) to help train these candidates.

One helpful manner of training that can help to overcome both language and educational barriers comes through experiences and observation, rather than simply learned knowledge. That is, Elder and Deacon candidates can learn much through accompanying (and eventually assisting) the church planter in different aspects of ministry. This might look like participation in visitations, Bible studies, prayer meetings, and so forth. As the candidates accompany the pastor, he will have the opportunity to invest further in their lives, and encourage them to take leadership in these areas as well. Participation in Bible studies, and seeing the pastor's methodology in action, will give the candidates the opportunity to then begin to replicate that under the pastor's leadership, and then on their own. Training in this manner takes time and dedication on the part of the church planter, but it is fruitful. Interestingly, Jesus did not train His disciples through simply giving them reading materials, but by bringing them with Him in ministry, helping them understand what He was doing, and then giving them the opportunities to go out and do the same!

Another consideration in identifying and training ordainable leaders within the Hispanic context is the religious backgrounds from which they are coming. Oftentimes, within majority-culture churches, Elder and Deacon candidates are transplants from another Reformed church, or have spent many years in the Presbyterian or Reformed church prior to nomination. Yet in a Latino context, this may look quite different, thereby necessitating a different foundation of instruction. Many will come from non-Reformed backgrounds – whether Pentecostal, Roman Catholic, or other – and others will have non-Christian backgrounds. In any of these cases, the candidates may need more basic instruction in biblical knowledge and Reformed doctrines than the average PCA Elder/Deacon training materials offer. Again, this will simply take more time and creativity on the part of the church planter (see again the *Resources* page).

One final challenge in training potential leaders is that many qualified Latino candidates are working long hours, leaving them exhausted and with little time to commit to outside work or a formal training process. Moreover, these jobs may be through odd hours of the day and week, thus making it hard to come consistently to a training. The church planter will need to be creative and flexible in thinking through times and layout for leadership training. Again, he may need a longer timeline, and more one-on-one meetings, to help these individuals prepare for ordination. Rushing the process will prove frustrating to the candidates and the church planter alike, and may result in burnout from both ends.

Conclusion

Identifying and training lay-leaders and ordainable leaders is an exciting next step in the phases of church planting, and it is necessary both for the growth of the church plant, and the sanity of the church planter. However, in the Hispanic context, it does require patience and creativity. Yet recognizing the leadership abilities of individuals within the target demographic and helping train them to use these gifts for the Lord will have great payoff. The church planter himself may not get to see all the fruits of this training, as some of these rising leaders will need to move early in the process, while younger leaders may build on this initial investment of a caring pastor for decades to come. Nevertheless, although the process takes time, the church planter and church plant can pray and trust for God to provide the right leaders, and for the investment of time and energy into leaders to bear fruit for God's Kingdom, within the Hispanic context, and beyond.

CHAPTER 10:

THE CHURCH FORMATION STAGE

> "Now in these days when the disciples were increasing in number, a complaint by the Hellenists arose against the Hebrews because their widows were being neglected in the daily distribution. ²And the twelve summoned the full number of the disciples and said, 'It is not right that we should give up preaching the word of God to serve tables. ³Therefore, brothers, pick out from among you seven men of good repute, full of the Spirit and of wisdom, whom we will appoint to this duty. ⁴But we will devote ourselves to prayer and to the ministry of the word.' ⁵And what they said pleased the whole gathering, and they chose Stephen, a man full of faith and of the Holy Spirit, and Philip, and Prochorus, and Nicanor, and Timon, and Parmenas, and Nicolaus, a proselyte of Antioch. ⁶These they set before the apostles, and they prayed and laid their hands on them. ⁷And the word of God continued to increase, and the number of the disciples multiplied greatly in Jerusalem, and a great many of the priests became obedient to the faith." – Acts 6:1-7

The apostles in the book of Acts were very much learning what it looked like to church plant, in different demographics, to different people groups, and all from scratch and without any handbooks for guidance. As the church grew, and as "the Lord added to their number day by day those who were being saved" (Acts 2:47b), the need for organizing the church became clear. In Acts 6, there was discord between Greek and Hebrew Christians, as the Hellenist widows were being overlooked in mercy ministry. In short, a lack of sufficient organization and oversight in the face of rapid growth was playing out in this case as a preference for the needs of one ethnic group over another.

Hearing the complaints, the apostles determined that they must set structures in place to ensure sufficient resources for all people and aspects of mercy ministry, without coming at the expense of the ministries of prayer and preaching. Thus, they set apart and commissioned men for diaconal ministry, while being able to continue the essential preaching and teaching to which they had been called. Indeed, the Lord blessed the apostles' wisdom and organization of the church! As the deacons cared for physical needs, the apostles were free to focus on the spiritual needs of the people, and the result was further multiplication of disciples and new believers (cf. Acts 6:7).

The organization of a church plant into a particular church is much like this organization of the early church in Acts. After a period of growth and development, there comes a point when the church can best care for a growing congregation and continue to reach the community through the ordaining of Ruling Elders and Deacons to assist in the work of ministry, and through becoming a church no longer dependent on a mother church to accomplish the work. In Hispanic church plants, as the previous chapters and case studies in this book have shown, reaching this Church Formation Stage is a long process. Hispanic church plants typically can expect to be ready for particularization somewhere between years 7 and 10 of planting (refer again to the Church Planting Timeline here).

After the years of planning, learning the context, networking and evangelizing, gathering and discipling a core group, and raising up leaders, the time for official church formation should be exciting. Although the actual process of becoming a particular church within the PCA is complex and can feel burdensome, it is also a joyous time of celebrating what God has done in bringing the church plant to this point. Prayerfully, and by God's grace, it will be a new stage of ministry that will allow the church to further expand the reach of God's Word, such that believers within the church plant's specific Hispanic community and beyond "multiply greatly" and become "obedient to the faith" (cf. Acts 6:7).

Hispanic church planters who are within the PCA should consult with their temporary government body, the *Book of Church Order*, and their Presbytery in navigating the unique process to church particularization. Non-PCA planters will have other guidelines for organizing the church. However, regardless of denominational structures or affiliations, the two key indicators that a church plant is ready to organize as a particular church (or no longer under the auspices of a mother church or sending agency) are the church plant's ability to be self-sufficient in both finances and government. The remainder of this chapter will speak to what is involved in both of these aspects of readiness particularly as it relates to Hispanic church planting, as well as the challenges to self-sufficiency that are peculiar to the Latino context.

Financial Self-Sufficiency: Preparation and Obstacles

After years of fundraising and receiving outside support from a mother church, Presbytery, individuals, and other sources, the ideal is for a Hispanic church plant to get to the point of being financially self-sustaining through internal giving. As a church planter works towards this goal, he must be aware of the church budget and needs, while also considering how he may best prepare his congregation for self-sufficiency.

While most majority-culture church plants are able to be financially self-sufficient within three years, here again the timeframe within Hispanic church plants tends to be significantly longer. The budgeting for this expected timeframe was a part of building a Strategic Plan and raising funds, but as the time for Church Formation nears, the church plant will need to reassess the initial expectations versus actual financial state. As the church planter examines the budget, measuring the church plant's dependency on outside giving versus internal giving, and taking into account current and projected ministry expenditures, he will be able to build a more accurate picture of what goals the church plant might realistically accomplish in a given timeframe.

While economic self-sufficiency of churches and church plants in the Hispanic community is thought to be critical for the growth, formation and multiplication of mature and prepared leaders to reach this highly diverse community, data shows that it is not actually a determining factor.[10] Being able to rely on their own sources of income rather than remaining dependent on outside giving is thought to free churches to focus on the work in their demographic, rather than taking time for fundraising, while also permitting them to become grounded within the community as a self-sustaining entity. Nonetheless, a church planter can work early to build self-sufficiency by training members in the biblical doctrine of giving to the church. In fact, such training is necessary throughout the church as a whole, as fewer than 25% of American Evangelicals are in the practice of tithing to their churches – and evangelicals tithe more than any other group in the United States![11] Yet whereas most majority-culture PCA churches tend to attract middle- to upper-class Americans, and a reliance on 25% giving proves fairly stable, it goes without saying that even the same giving statistics reflected in the Hispanic community would not be sufficient for supporting a church.

While challenging, it is possible for a Hispanic church plant to achieve financial stability, but there are other obstacles that are helpful to understand and be able to treat. A study among refugee communities in the United States named the two greatest reasons for financial insufficiency in Hispanic communities to be a lack of financial literacy, and language barriers (which, in turn, exclude Spanish-speakers from high-paying jobs for which they would otherwise be qualified).[12] According to this research, and the experiences of many Hispanic pastors, addressing these two issues provides the best results in generating a community that enters the path of generosity.

Benefits of Teaching Faith and Finances

With respect to financial literacy, a new church plant (as well as an established church) can serve its members by helping them to become financially literate, helping them to understand how the gospel affects finances, and how managing finances well (regardless of how great or small one's income) are a part of the Christian life.[13] One of the top reasons the immigrant community does not have money to give to the church is that they are working hard to send money back to support friends and family in their countries of origin.[14] Offering biblical, financial training can help the community to rightly manage their finances, and appropriately budget the money that they will be sending home.

Moreover, as a church plant teaches financial literacy to the community, it will help to demystify conversations about money, by showing how God's generosity towards people transforms them into a new creation with generous hearts. This is particularly helpful for the immigrant community with respect to their background. Socioeconomically speaking, individuals who have emigrated have often done so because of a lack of access to money. Therefore, not only were they not financially literate in their home countries, but the problem is compounded when they arrive in a new country with a different financial system, operating in a new language. The idea of financial stability is therefore far from their understanding, and they will seek to make the most, spend the most, and use it quickly, in case it is gone. The church plant has the opportunity to ground people in understanding the basics of financial systems and giving.

As the Hispanic community becomes more financially literate, there will be many positive repercussions, for themselves in daily as well as spiritual life, but also for the church. In the first place, it will help to prepare these individuals for any financial crises that may arise, and that typically can devastate a family. Moreover, it will help individuals to be set free from the guilt, shame, and legalism that often surrounds giving, and rather be motivated to give by grace. Finally, having a foundation of financial literacy can help immigrants overcome an antiestablishment and anti-commitment culture, as they come to understand that they are responsible before God to give cheerfully as members of the local church.

Benefits of Teaching English as a Second Language (ESL)

Teaching faith and finance can help to grow a church's financial self-sufficiency, while also providing powerful witness and impact to the community. Offering ESL classes provides another means to also work towards these goals. In fact, they may go hand-in-hand, as ESL classes can also be a way to teach financial literacy while participants learn related English. There are many written materials in English that may serve as simple yet powerful resources for teaching about finances and the gospel. Such materials allow individuals to become aware of the market conditions of local and national municipalities, even as they are learning English, thus preparing them better for the workforce and personal life in the United States.

As immigrants learn English, ESL classes have the opportunity to demonstrate how generosity drives many of the social benefits, such as parks, public museums, mercy ministries, even ESL classes, and so forth. From a church perspective, ESL classes can also provide a way to give participants a better panoramic view of the history of the church, reasons for membership, denominations, and why it is important to become a member of and support the ministry of the local church.

> *"And he said, 'Truly, I tell you, this poor widow has put in more than all of them. ⁴ For they all contributed out of their abundance, but she out of her poverty put in all she had to live on.'"*
>
> *- Luke 21:3-4*

Even as they prepare for financial self-sufficiency, church planters within the Latino context have the great opportunity and privilege of continuing to reach their community with practical teaching that will greatly benefit the lives of these individuals, while also inviting them into a way of living by the gospel. This will, in turn, help those who are coming to the church plant consider what it means to live in a way that glorifies God through their finances, regardless of how large or small their income, and serve the church in that way. Indeed, Jesus recognized the heart of the widow's mite, and God will indeed provide for His church through what He has given to His people.

Self-Governance: Preparation and Obstacles

The work of Hispanic church planting, while wrought with challenges, is a great blessing, and preparation for self-governance is a celebration of the Lord working through difficult circumstances to reach a new community for Himself. As the church planter approaches this stage, he will look back and see people who had never attended church before coming regularly, and getting involved. He may see those who had nominal Roman-Catholic backgrounds now accepting Jesus as their personal Lord and Savior, and becoming church members. Though the work has been long, looking back, the church planter will be able to look at those who have become active in the church plant, and recognize that the grace of God has been at work, week after week, year after year.

Preparation for self-governance starts the first day of church planting, as it builds upon the previous stages of evangelism, discipleship, and leadership stage. In the case of the former two stages, the church must have enough committed members, as determined by the overseeing Presbytery. In the case of leadership, there must be sufficient qualified candidates for the office of Ruling Elder to adequately care for the body without the support of the temporary church government. When the church plant oversight (Presbytery) has determined that adequate persons and financial support exist, the church plant can move forward in this phase. (Refer to the PCA *Book of Church Order* Chapter 5 here for more specifics as it relates to the particularization of a Presbyterian church). Arriving at this stage is indeed a cause for celebration.

At the same time, as the church planter readies his Hispanic congregation for self-governance, he will face challenges that would not come into play in majority-culture church plants. As the previous chapters have addressed, there are a number of obstacles for Hispanic church plants that lengthen the earlier stages of church planting, and the same is true in the preparation for self-governance. Many of these challenges have already presented themselves in previous chapters, again because the work of preparation for self-governance is ongoing. Yet it may be helpful, specifically when it comes to thinking of the Church Formation stage, to view some of these factors as opportunities, rather than obstacles.

The Question of Transience

While many may come through the doors of a Hispanic church plant over the years, once again, the transient nature of Hispanic immigrant communities may make it challenging to achieve self-governance for some time. The process of continually discipling new individuals and families as they come and others leave means that, while overall church attendance numbers may remain stable, it may take some time to establish a core-base of trained, serving members ready for particularization. Although the lengthy process can feel disheartening, the beauty is in the opportunity to reach so many, even if for a short time. The church plant may also grow in its ability to find a way to lovingly send people out as they move on, while thinking through strategies for quick assimilation for new faces. There will be a constant need for drawing new people in, and both a challenge and encouragement to the church to develop simple methods for training them in the basics of the faith. With creativity and the Lord's guidance, a transient community does not necessitate an inability to grow individuals into flourishing members of the church.

The Question of Immigration

A potential pitfall for church planters when considering self-governance in a Hispanic church plant is to get stuck in the immigration question trap. That is, there can be a tendency to see a whole community through the lens of an issue that the church plant is not responsible for solving. Out of 60 million Latinos in the United States, 49 million are American citizens, and the rest are somewhere in the immigration process. The trap is that focusing on the question of legal status puts this entire people group under a description that belongs to the minority, while also allowing the church to miss out on the opportunity to shepherd, disciple, train, and deploy new leaders to serve the Kingdom of God. Hispanic church planters must recognize their calling as members of the body of Christ to start, plant, and revitalize churches within the Hispanic community. They must not allow smaller issues to cloud Jesus' calling to develop qualified men, women, elders and deacons for the service of God's bride.

Necessarily, there are many positions on what it looks like to ordain undocumented leaders to church positions. Yet to lead with the question of immigration status in the Hispanic community is out of accord with the mission of the church. If a church plant does find itself in a situation of needing to make a decision, they will not only need to use discretion and wisdom in caring for those involved, but perhaps more so, they will need to protect their own hearts from assuming that an experience with one person will necessarily be the case with those who may look or sound similar. Regardless of what the decision regarding ordination might be, the church must continue to equip and encourage these newly trained leaders to hold positions in the church, and to continue serving in key roles and positions for which God has equipped them. (The *Resources* page provides a list of further reading to help church planters and their governing bodies think through this topic.)

Another temptation regarding the question of immigration – particularly when it comes to preparation for self-governance – is to simply give up and look for non-native leadership. While involving missional-minded elders or deacons from around the local Presbytery to serve on the Session or temporary Session might serve as a temporary fix, it will not serve the Hispanic church in the long run, and can actually become quite detrimental. It communicates to the community that Hispanics cannot offer the same sort of qualified leadership as majority-culture individuals. Rather, church planters in the Latino context must operate in faith and prayer, training those whom God puts in their path, and knowing the grace of God in using all their own weaknesses and struggles, as well as those of their church members, to accomplish His great purposes in putting to shame what the world deems strong (cf. I Corinthians 1:18-31).

> *"For consider your calling, brothers: not many of you were wise according to worldly standards, not many were powerful, not many were of noble birth. But God chose what is foolish in the world to shame the wise; God chose what is weak in the world to shame the strong; God chose what is low and despised in the world, even things that are not, to bring to nothing things that are, so that no human being might boast in the presence of God."*
>
> - I Corinthians 1:26-29

The Question of Knowledge of Reformed Christianity

Something else that can appear as an obstacle when seeking to become a self-governing church is the fear that church participants have not heard of "Presbyterian" or "Reformed." In fact, while many majority-culture church plants may have transplants from other Reformed churches thus making the statistics appear different, the reality is that most people are unfamiliar with these words. Rather than being an obstacle, however, this provides a great opportunity to demonstrate true Christianity within the community, becoming true salt and light. It gives the chance for the church plant to teach the doctrines of God's grace and kindness not only through teaching terminology, but through becoming the hands and feet of Jesus within the community. Indeed, it gives the church plant the privilege of seeing lives transformed through understanding the grace of the Covenantal God, as He speaks of Himself throughout the Bible.

Conclusion

Becoming a particularized Hispanic church does require much time; it involves many years of loving and caring for the community to which God has called the church planter. Over and above all, it must involve prayer. Latinos make up the fastest growing group of American evangelicals,[15] and are thus a perfect victim for Satan's attack. It is therefore crucial to spend time in prayer with the leaders of the church, trusting that God will bring the right people, the right finances, the right leaders, all within His perfect timing: that He will establish His church. And when the church plant does indeed particularize, it is a time for the church planter, his congregation, and supporters to fall to their knees in adoration of the God who has brought about such a wondrous work!

CHAPTER 11:

THE REPRODUCTION STAGE

> *"But you will receive power when the Holy Spirit has come upon you, and you will be my witnesses in Jerusalem and in all Judea and Samaria, and to the end of the earth."* – Acts 1:8

> *"When they had preached the gospel to that city and had made many disciples, they returned to Lystra and to Iconium and to Antioch, ²² strengthening the souls of the disciples, encouraging them to continue in the faith, and saying that through many tribulations we must enter the kingdom of God. ²³ And when they had appointed elders for them in every church, with prayer and fasting they committed them to the Lord in whom they had believed."* – Acts 14:21-23

Jesus' final words to the apostles prior to His ascension come at the beginning of the book of Acts, and are, to some degree, a reiteration of the Great Commission given at the end of Matthew's gospel narrative (Matthew 28:18-20). As Jesus prepares to ascend, He promises the presence of His Holy Spirit, even as He sends the apostles to bear witness to His name not simply "to all nations," as recorded in Matthew, but "in Jerusalem and in all Judea and Samaria, and to the end of the earth." This naming of places and the order in which Jesus names them is highly significant. Whereas in the Old Testament, the nations were to be drawn to Jerusalem to see the glory of the Lord in His temple (cf. Isaiah 60:1-3), now Jesus is showing a reversal of events. The gospel message is to go forth from its epicenter in Jerusalem, creating a ripple effect into the surrounding Judea, and then the neighboring Samaria, until it reaches the end of the earth.

Indeed, the goal of gospel ministry – and what begins happening through the witness of the apostles in the book of Acts – is the planting and then reproduction of churches, as the church expands its reach increasingly further into the ends of the earth. One small snapshot of this reproduction is found in Acts 14, as Paul and Barnabas travel through the Roman province of Galatia. While Paul certainly had many opportunities to stay with one church, he was continually strengthening and encouraging the believers of the churches (Acts 14:22), and then appointing appropriate leaders and elders (14:23), in order that he might continue to go out and bring the gospel to the ends of the earth.

Moreover, Paul was continually sending others out, even from his own ministry, to grow, strengthen, and multiply the church. While Timothy was a disciple and companion of Paul (cf. Acts 16:1-3), rather than keeping him always at his side, Paul sends Timothy out to strengthen many other churches (e.g., Philippians 2:19-25ff), and eventually to care for the church at Ephesus. Certainly, Timothy is only one example among the myriads of others whom Paul sent out to encourage, care for, and grow new churches. Clearly the goal was not to build up Paul's ministry in any one particular area, but to see the reproduction of the gospel via church growth throughout the world.

When it comes to church planting in the Hispanic context (or any other context for that matter), the end goal is not simply to create one successful church plant. Rather, the goal is to seek to develop leaders whom the church can then send out, not simply to reproduce another church in the Latino context, but to multiply the church, even to the ends of the earth!

Once a church plant has made it all the way through the exciting stage of Church Formation, the church can look towards the ripple effect it may have through reproduction and multiplication.*

Most church plants begin with the goal of becoming a reproducing church, but the reality is that very few achieve that goal. Recent church planting research showed only 7% of the churches as reproducing, with less than 1% going further to the stage of multiplying (this data refers to Protestant churches in the United States, but does not give the data specifically for Protestant Latino churches).[16] Although there are many factors that make reproducing (much less multiplying) within the Latino context particularly hard, Hispanic church planters cannot afford to lose the chance to multiply leaders, churches, and continue impacting this rapidly-growing segment

> **Reproduction vs. Multiplication?*
>
> A **reproducing** church is defined as one that has been directly involved in supporting, providing for, and opening a new, autonomous church work within the past year. a **multiplying** church takes this definition a step further by being involved in a greater number of church plants per year, while also being significantly active in raising up new church planters: preparing them, sending them, and financially supporting them.

of the American population for Christ! The Reproduction Stage is essential for the future growth of the Latino church and beyond. Thus it is helpful to look at some of the factors that inhibit reproduction in order to be able to prepare for them, combat them, and not be content for the work of church planting in the Hispanic context to stop with one church.

Tensions for Reproducing Hispanic Churches

Perhaps one of the first of many factors contributing to the lack of reproduction within Hispanic churches is that, after the long journey to Church Formation, many leaders find themselves tired. It may be easy to feel that the church has arrived, and rather than continuing to think missionally and pursue reproducing, the temptation may be to enjoy growing in and loving on the new church itself. And certainly, there is no lack of work within the church simply because it has become a particular church! There is still constant need for outreach, evangelism, discipleship, and leadership development. Yet one of the beauties of reaching a stable point in the life of a church, is that it now has the capacity to reach its own community, but also to reach beyond this community by equipping and sending others out to replicate and multiply the work.

Nevertheless, sending out qualified members and leaders requires sacrifice on the part of the church planter as well as the church body. The tension in a newly formed church body is for the church planter to want to focus his time and energy into growing this new body. He may fear that releasing some of the leaders in whom he has invested so much to "go and do likewise" (cf. Luke 10:37), and letting go of some of his most gifted members will be costly. And in reality, it does require sacrifice and an act of faith! Yet just as Paul trained Timothy (and so many others) not simply to keep him by his side, but to send him out to multiply the work of the church, so must church planters see their call in training qualified members and leaders.

The example of Hannah in the Old Testament provides a powerful illustration and encouragement here. For years, Hannah was barren and yearning for children; day and night she called out before the Lord to hear her cries, and in His timing, the Lord listened, and she bore Samuel (whose name means "God hears"). Yet Hannah had promised the Lord that, if He would give her a son, then she would in turn give her son to the Lord (I Samuel 1:11). Surely, holding her precious, long-awaited baby in her arms, Hannah could have had second thoughts. However, Hannah recognized that it was the Lord who had given her this child, and that Samuel belonged first and foremost to the Lord. So in the proper timing, she brought the young boy to the temple in Jerusalem, for service in the temple. She testified, "For this child I prayed, and the LORD has granted me my petition that I made to him. ²⁸ Therefore I have lent him to the LORD. As long as he lives, he is lent to the LORD" (I Samuel 1:27-28). Perhaps ironically, Hannah promised to "lend" her child to the Lord, when in reality, she recognized that the Lord has lent this child to her care! And indeed, while Hannah did not get to experience daily life with her precious child, she had the amazing joy and privilege of watching him grow up in service to the Lord, and the Lord use him mightily in ways she could never have imagined herself. In turn, the Lord blessed Hannah's trust and faithfulness, multiplying the joy and laughter within her household by granting Hannah three more sons and two daughters (I Samuel 2:21).

> *"And she said, 'Oh, my lord! As you live, my lord, I am the woman who was standing here in your presence, praying to the LORD. For this child I prayed, and the Lord has granted me my petition that I made to him. Therefore I have lent him to the LORD. As long as he lives, he is lent to the LORD.' And he worshiped the LORD there."*
>
> - I Samuel 1:26-28

Church planters in the Hispanic context may well relate to barren Hannah when looking to plant their church and raise up leaders. They have poured out their souls in prayer before the Lord for their communities, and in His timing, the Lord has graciously heard and answered their prayers. While it may be tempting to hold on to leaders for fear of loss, they must see these leaders as the Lord's answering and lending them leaders who may go on to accomplish work outside of the church plant that the church planter could have never imagined. They must see the opportunity to send leaders and members out as the opportunity to lend them to the Lord, to accomplish His greater purposes for them and for the Hispanic church. Reproducing may feel costly, but it is a testament to the Lord's listening on behalf of the Latino community, His provision, and His plans!

Identifying Readiness for Reproduction

One potential challenge in reproducing within the Hispanic church context may come along simply with being able to recognize whether or not the church is sufficiently stable to send others out. Following the Church Planting Timeline, the Reproduction Stage will most likely not happen until a church plant has been in existence for at least ten years, at which point, reproduction should be ongoing. Of course, reproducing fruit means that a tree must be sufficiently mature and receiving enough nutrients to both feed the leaves, but also put forth a harvest of seeds. The Reproduction Stage therefore follows Church Formation, but Hispanic church planters must have different metrics for measuring and defining maturity, success, and readiness than perhaps those of majority-culture churches. In general (and as demonstrated through the case studies in this book), Hispanic churches tend to remain small. Thus it may be tempting to delay the process of reproduction until the church reaches larger membership; but the reality is that helping to create more, small Hispanic churches within many pockets of the Latino community will have a far greater reach and emphasis than attempting to grow one particular entity.

The questions surrounding readiness for reproduction must therefore focus on whether the church plant itself is healthy, whether members are being fed, whether it is producing good fruit in mature members and disciples. Similarly, the church must have the capacity to be in a good rhythm of caring for its community, members, and leadership without feeling overworked or in crisis mode. Sometimes, after years of focusing on internal church growth, this may mean the church planter first taking time for personal renewal, and leading the church and church leaders in corporate renewal, as they turn toward the task of reproduction together. Once the church is fulfilling these metrics, it is time to begin the task of praying, preparing, and working toward the exciting and ongoing task of reproduction.

Conclusion

As church planters faithfully work through the years it takes to plant, grow, and establish a church within the Hispanic community, it may sometimes feel that reproducing and multiplying are ideas in an undefined, unreachable future. Yet even the initial goal of church planting is never to reach one neighbor, one *vecindario*, one community, or even one city; these are the starting points, certainly, but the goal of planting churches in Latino communities is to work toward the gospel goal of proclaiming the good news "in Jerusalem and in all Judea and Samaria, and to the end of the earth." While reproduction may at times feel impossible, it should remain as the goal for the church planter as it is, in fact, God's vision to multiply His church.

Reproduction and multiplication give church planters the opportunity to send out those whom God has lent them for a time – to evangelize, train, and disciple into leaders – and encourage them as they too, begin the work of reaching new Latino (and other) communities for the gospel. It gives church planters and their members the chance to celebrate and bear witness to God's goodness in His faithful guiding and provision, while trusting that He will continue to provide for them and the new target areas. It provides the incredible opportunity to catch a glimpse of what God is doing in the larger picture of expanding His Kingdom throughout the Latino context and beyond, and to know that He will indeed accomplish His purposes for His church!

PART 3:

PRACTICAL MATTERS

"Carry no moneybag, no knapsack, no sandals, and greet no one on the road. ⁵ Whatever house you enter, first say, 'Peace be to this house!'" – Luke 10:4-5

"Do your best to come to me soon… Get Mark and bring him with you, for he is very useful to me for ministry… When you come, bring the cloak that I left with Carpus at Troas, also the books, and above all the parchments." – II Timothy 4:9-13

CHAPTER 12:

PRACTICAL STEPS FOR THE MOTHER CHURCH'S GROWTH

"For though I am free from all, I have made myself a servant to all, that I might win more of them. [20] To the Jews I became as a Jew, in order to win Jews. To those under the law I became as one under the law (though not being myself under the law) that I might win those under the law. [21] To those outside the law I became as one outside the law (not being outside the law of God but under the law of Christ) that I might win those outside the law. [22] To the weak I became weak, that I might win the weak. I have become all things to all people, that by all means I might save some. [23] I do it all for the sake of the gospel, that I may share with them in its blessings."
– I Corinthians 9:19-23

The apostle Paul, a Jew by birth, became quite familiar with ministry in different contexts, as the Lord called him to take the gospel not simply to his own people, but to gentiles and people of every socioeconomic status (from plebians to kings, and even Caesar!). Paul knew, perhaps better than anyone, that ministry within different contexts would require humility on his part, and adaptations to fit the culture, without compromising the faith. Becoming a servant, becoming weak, becoming "all things to all people" involves humility; it involves cost; it involves learning the culture of those whom one is trying to reach. But as it is for the sake of the gospel, in order to share the blessings of the gospel, it is indeed worth it!

Chapter 1 of this book, *Counting the Cost,* discussed the need for a mother church wishing to send out a church planter into the Latino community to first commit to its own growth in cultural awareness in order to better serve both the anticipated church planter, and the church plant. This chapter will seek to provide several suggested steps for growth, based on the experiences of many Hispanic planters and leaders.

Developing Cultural Awareness

At the elementary level, as they commit to growth, mother churches (or sending agencies or presbyteries) may begin to learn by connecting with other churches that have endeavored to plant Hispanic churches in order to glean from their experiences, both positive and negative. The real-life examples of Hispanic church plants given in Chapter 5 of this book are meant to be a useful starting point; however, befriending and talking with those who have firsthand experience is invaluable. Through friendship and conversation, mother church leaders will be able to ask questions, listen, and be challenged by stories that may not fit their experiential knowledge of majority-culture church planting. Such conversations will provide a good foundation for thinking contextually when it comes to Hispanic church planting.

Additionally, as mother church leadership seeks to gain cultural awareness, a tool such as the *Intercultural Development Inventory*[17] may prove quite useful. This resource (or perhaps similar evaluations and trainings) will help leadership and individuals gain more understanding about the ways that both they and the church in general tend to respond to cultural differences. It will also help them identify areas of blindness and places for growth. It cannot be stated strongly enough that this growth in cultural self-awareness is a vital step in the preparatory work of a sending church or Presbytery wishing to reach the Latino context.

These first steps of developing cultural awareness and revealing potential blind spots for both the mother church and church planter are crucial. Nevertheless, there are many more areas in which sending churches must grow in their knowledge in order to be prepared to call, send, and support a church planter within a minority context.

In the first place, mother churches must seek to gain awareness regarding the various methodological approaches to planting in the Hispanic context (as given in Chapter 3: *Creating a Plan*), as they again differ from majority-culture church planting methodologies. Understanding these methodologies will help the sending church to be able to come alongside the church planter in order to capitalize on the strengths of the particular methodology he (or the mother church) has chosen, and seek to avoid the weaknesses. If a mother church is responsible for laying the plan for and calling a church planter, knowing some of the basic approaches for Hispanic church planting will help the mother church's leadership to discern which strategy might best suit their particular situation and context.

As they consider approaches, sending churches should be aware of certain methodologies that demand more involvement on their part, and the various elements surrounding a given methodology. For example, incubator methodology involves the sharing of facilities, resources, and potentially even staff. The sending church must be aware of these demands and assess the plausibility of such an approach for their particular church, or whether it may be wise to consider a different methodology.

Another vital element for the sending church to consider is the specific demographics of the area. It is easy for a dominant culture to have preconceptions regarding the needs of the target Latino community. They may, for example, assume the need for a Spanish-speaking church plant simply because they have seen many Hispanics in a particular area. Yet depending on the specific population make-up, a Spanish-speaking church plant may or may not be the best option. If the area is primarily second- and third- generation Hispanics, who may speak Spanish, but live out their daily lives primarily in English, they may be better served through an English-dominant service, potentially challenging some preconceived ideas of ministry the mother church may have. A church, Presbytery, or sending agency can avoid making such assumptions by spending time researching the demographics of their desired target area (whether the leaders devote time to this themselves, or bring in other staff or summer interns to devote time to this research), in order to be strategic in their planning and avoid costly mistakes.

Cultural Awareness with Respect to Choosing a Church Planter

Growing in cultural awareness also means learning to recognize which pastors will be best suited to a particular context. An incorrect (and highly detrimental) assumption is that every Hispanic pastor is the same, and will be able to plant a Hispanic church in any given Hispanic context. Rather, there are several aspects that the mother church will need to consider in calling a church planter candidate for a new work. Taking the time to assess the skill set of the church planting candidate in relation to the needs of the target community will ultimately serve the mother church, church planter, and target demographic alike.

In the first place, it is necessary to understand that Hispanic leaders often fall into one of two categories. There are those who have come (often recently, but not always) to the United States, but remain culturally immersed in Latin America. Others have perhaps spent far more time assimilating to US culture, and operate under a different mentality. These two broad categories will be able to engage first-, second-, and third-generation Hispanics in very different ways. It is often the case that a pastor who is effective in engaging first-generation immigrants is significantly less effective in engaging second- and third-generation, and vice versa. Sending churches should be aware that certain areas will have an abundant mixture of first-, second-, and third-generation Hispanics, while others will have a dominance of one of these groups. Thus, the mother church should discern a candidate's ability to socially engage with one particular group or another, or discern whether the candidate may have the awareness and experience to work within the dynamics of the different generations.

Related to the broad idea of generational suitability is an awareness of a potential church planter's contextual suitability to the ethnic specificity of the target Latino community. This requires that the mother church both understand the ethnic make-up of the target demographic, as well as the pastoral candidate's familiarity and adaptability to that particular group. It deserves reiteration here that not all Hispanics are the same, coming from 21 different Spanish-speaking nations and a far greater number of cultural backgrounds. A mother church should seek to learn what people groups live in certain Hispanic areas of the city as they consider the desires and affinities of the church planter. For example, certain areas of the city may be largely Caribbean-Hispanic, while other parts are majority Central-American Hispanic. The contextual dynamics between these groups can have all sorts of dramatic disparities. Of course, some planters will do very well navigating and speaking to these differences, but assessing his ability here takes discretion and wisdom.

If the church or church planter is targeting a particular segment of the Latino community, he should – either by personal and/or ministerial experience – have social competence and intuition particular to that group. Just as an English-speaking traveler who has grown up in the Australian outback does not automatically relate to a fellow English-speaking traveler from the Bronx, so an immigrant from Buenos Aires does not necessarily relate to another from Tegucigalpa simply because of a shared language. Shared language is helpful, but mother churches must seek to understand the cultural complexities at play in their target demographic before assuming any one Hispanic pastor will have a natural affinity to that context. As in the case of any pastoral search, a sending church must use discretion and wisdom in extending a call to the right candidate, and in Hispanic church planting, this involves a commitment to learning some of the ethnic complexities of the target population.

A final consideration for mother churches as they seek to find the ideal candidate, is the need for understanding what it takes to plant a Reformed church within the Hispanic context. In general, Reformed doctrines, piety, and practices tend to be culturally and religiously foreign to Hispanics. Moreover, while a potential church planter may be quite trained in Reformed theology, he may struggle to articulate Reformed doctrines in a way that is both clear and winsome within the Hispanic context. This may be particularly true if he has received his training (and thus the primary ways of communicating that knowledge) within the majority-culture. The sending church must understand these challenges, and encourage the church planter to connect with other Reformed Hispanic pastors who have dealt with the same issues. Furthermore, both the mother church and church planter can benefit from recognizing the opportunity to accurately and faithfully teach basic tenants of the Christian faith as found in the Bible (namely, Reformed faith), without the need of overcomplicating terminology and creating unnecessary obstacles for the community. Awareness of this reality can help sending churches interview and identify candidates who are in tune to and sensitive to winsomely engaging the context with Reformed faith.

Conclusion

It takes time, dedication, and humility for a mother church to prepare itself well to become involved in planting a Hispanic church and searching for the right candidate to lead that work. Yet the payoff is being able to help transform new communities with the gospel in a way that is sensitive to the needs and stories of a different culture. In fact, committing to growth in cultural awareness and adaptability may help the mother church not only in planting and supporting the one Latino church it had originally envisioned, but may help it to have a greater missional focus in general, and increase its reach to the nations.

CHAPTER 13:

RECRUITING AND RAISING UP HISPANIC CHURCH PLANTERS

"I appeal to you for my child, Onesimus, whose father I became in my imprisonment. [11] (Formerly he was useless to you, but now he is indeed useful to you and to me.) [12] I am sending him back to you, sending my very heart. [13] I would have been glad to keep him with me, in order that he might serve me on your behalf during my imprisonment for the gospel, [14] but I preferred to do nothing without your consent in order that your goodness might not be by compulsion but of your own accord. [15] For this perhaps is why he was parted from you for a while, that you might have him back forever, [16] no longer as a bondservant but more than a bondservant, as a beloved brother— especially to me, but how much more to you, both in the flesh and in the Lord." – Philemon 1:10-16

Onesimus was the slave of Philemon, and had run away to Rome (for reasons unclear in Scripture, although possibly for having stolen money from his master). In Rome, in accordance with God's sovereign plan, he met Paul, heard the gospel, and was converted. Not only was he converted, but Paul took Onesimus under his wing as his child, training him in the ways of the faith, that this young believer might become quite instrumental for the Kingdom. Prior to his conversion and training "he was useless" to Philemon (even as Philemon's slave and worker); however, after Paul's investment of gospel truth in his life, Paul sent him back as "indeed useful" and as "a beloved brother" in the faith, both for Paul, but also for Philemon. It is interesting (and intentional) that Onesimus' name literally means "useful" or "profitable." While this was not the case prior to his conversion, Paul saw in this young believer the potential for a profitable new leader whom he would be able to train and send back to Philemon to assist Philemon and the church meeting at Philemon's house in Colossae. And although Onesimus had even become quite useful to Paul during his imprisonment, Paul was excited for the opportunity to return him to his home, changed, and equipped to bring transformation into his community.

One of the great challenges in seeking to plant a new Hispanic church is finding the right leader who is uniquely qualified for the given context. As of 2022, within the entire PCA denomination, there are only fifty-six Hispanic Teaching Elders. This means that, as the Hispanic church seeks to reproduce and multiply in new areas, a focus on raising up new leader to reach the Latino context is imperative. Indeed, the most successful church planters are home-grown! The saturation church planting needed to reach Hispanics requires a strong and vital pipeline of candidates. As discussed in Chapter 11: *The Reproduction Stage,* Hispanic church plants in particular must keep this goal at the forefront as they move through the stages of church planting. Nevertheless, with the right thoughtfulness and intentionality, both Hispanic as well as majority-culture churches can make a commitment to help develop new Hispanic leadership.

Elements of a Robust Leadership Development Pipeline

Indeed, a leadership development pipeline is one of the best investments that sending churches can make. Consider how successful soccer teams are well known for their youth academies: they identify children as young as 7 years old, and provide camps and clinics led by high quality coaches. This is not "daddy ball." Translated into church planting, it means doing like Paul did with Onesimus: finding these potential leaders and training them to send them back out into ministry. It means intentionally seeking for gifted leaders in the local church (despite their relative youth or inexperience); observing them; giving them meaningful leadership opportunities; training them; and, if they show gifts for church planting, taking them through pre-assessment, continuing to build them up, and eventually launching them as new church planters. The rest of this chapter will discuss in greater detail the different stages of such a leadership development pipeline.

Recruiting

One of the first places for a church to look for church planting recruits is within its own backyard. Churches with eyes for the harvest and that seek to be obedient to evangelize all ethne, will prayerfully identify and disciple future pastors and leaders in their own evangelistic net. While identifying future Hispanic leaders is certainly a calling of each Hispanic church plant, it should go without saying that a pastor need not be Hispanic or speak Spanish to be able to identify and disciple prospects who may plant churches in the Latino context and/or among Spanish-speakers. In fact, every pastor, regardless of ethnicity or background, should be discipling the nations indiscriminately and seeking to create leaders among any and all who may exhibit potential. At the same time, Teaching Elders who do have the advantage of speaking

Spanish should place high priority on identifying future Spanish-speaking pastors and church planters who might otherwise be overlooked. Additionally, rather than passively observe gifted second-generation bilingual members slide comfortably into Anglo churches or predominately English-speaking contexts, pastors should prayerfully explore and challenge these individuals to use their unique cultural and linguistic competencies in a Spanish-speaking (or bilingual) setting, or Hispanic context.

It is also helpful to observe that not every church planter looking to plant a Hispanic work must necessarily be Hispanic. There have been cases in which bilingual and bicultural Anglo men have successfully planted Hispanic churches (see the case study of New City East Lake in Chapter 5; another example would be Rev. Brad Taylor, who planted Iglesia Hispana Briarwood, in Birmingham, AL). While there are certainly precautions in finding candidates with the right heart, churches looking to develop leadership should be alert for Hispanic recruits, but also men of other ethnicities who exhibit the heart, cultural awareness, and language skills to reach the Latino context.

Pastors and churches must be constantly looking for new recruits whom they can come alongside and encourage in the work of preparing for ministry within their context. As they identify these potential leaders, invest in their lives through discipleship, and see a true potential, desire, and heart for pastoral ministry, the next step is to help these individuals gain the appropriate training necessary to send them back out.

Training

Depending on the backgrounds and language skills of the potential leaders in question, the options for training will differ. Churches mentoring potential Hispanic church planters who are English-proficient may point them to one of the many excellent Reformed seminary options that are consistently providing training for new Reformed pastors throughout the United States. They might also benefit from programs offered through schools such as LAMP Theological Seminary, Miami International Theological Seminary (MINTS), etc. Alternatively, those who are not proficient in English, or who are bilingual have the option to choose an alternative route for theological and pastoral training, such as LAMP Theological Seminary Español, MINTS (also with Spanish-language options), or Clase Internacional de Teología Aplicada (CITA). While such training is quite useful, it is necessary to remember that even an M. Div. degree (or its equivalent) from one of these institutions does not qualify or equip one for church planting, and the work of preparing leaders does not stop here. Rather, all of the competencies, cultural sensitivities and methodologies as described in this book must be the content of ongoing training in required seminars, and all available in Spanish.

Assessing

Another useful tool for helping to train and equip Hispanic leaders is to both prepare them and assess their readiness through a formal church planting assessment. Although the PCA's Mission to North America (MNA) currently has a church planter assessment center that offers regular assessing for English-speaking church planting candidates, such a resource is not yet available in Spanish (although there are ongoing projects to create such opportunities). While an English-proficient potential church planter may benefit from attending the MNA's assessment (or a similar such assessment as offered by other denominations), the desire would be to eventually create an assessment center (or centers) available in Spanish, that will also assess a pastor's cultural awareness as he prepares to potentially engage new contexts. Such an assessment center would help not simply assess and prepare future church planters, but would be contextualized to help ascertain their fitness for church planting in the Hispanic-American context. Churches might work together with one another, and with current Hispanic leaders within the church to create such opportunities for better preparing future Hispanic church planters. To that end, Appendix E provides a comprehensive list of categories and related questions to help assist in evaluating candidates.

Investing: Cohorts

Cohorts are another way of investing in and preparing Hispanic leaders for the work of church planting. The structure and systems of the PCA (or other similarly governed denominations) are formal, and can be quite foreboding even for the unprepared Anglo, with parliamentary procedure often feeling more challenging than reading hieroglyphics. For pastoral candidates who are only proficient in Spanish, apprehending the systems in the *Book of Church Order* (BCO), such as requirements for licensure, ordination, church membership, and so forth, prove even more daunting. Cohorts provide an opportunity to come alongside future church planters and offer personal explanation for different proceedings, while taking the time to encourage them in their endeavors as well.

It is interesting that even the apostle Paul had an advocate who helped encourage him as he began his apostolic ministry. Paul needed Barnabas (the "son of encouragement," cf. Acts 4:36) to come alongside him, to fetch him from Tarsus, and help him begin ministry in Antioch (cf. Acts 11:25-26ff). Cohorts can do the same for qualified leaders: helping explain procedures as they enter ministry, and serving as "sons of encouragement" for future Hispanic leaders. There are many who already advocate in this way for majority-culture church planters (and again, English-proficient Hispanic church planters might benefit from participation in these cohorts), but churches must pray for and work towards similar cohorts for supporting and encouraging Spanish-speaking pastors and church planters within the Hispanic context.

> *"So Barnabas went to Tarsus to look for Saul, and when he had found him, he brought him to Antioch. For a whole year they met with the church and taught a great many people. And in Antioch the disciples were first called Christians."*
>
> - Acts 11:25-26

Investing: Mentoring and Residencies

Aside from cohorts, another way of coming alongside, developing, and encouraging Hispanic church planters is through mentorship. Church planting even within the majority-culture context is a specialized and difficult undertaking, which is best served by deliberate oversight and accountability to an experienced church planter. Within the Latino context, the need for such intentional oversight and encouragement is even greater. Churches seeking to raise up and equip Hispanic leaders need to examine the practices employed in English, and revise and tailor them to fit the Hispanic-American church planting context, using the cultural sensibilities and sensitivities described in this book. Experienced Hispanic and Spanish-speaking church planting pastors have a unique opportunity to serve rising leaders in this way, while other mentors may also be trained and prepared to serve in this way in Spanish.

When mentorship is not an option, another way to help develop Hispanic church planters is by investing in a church planter residency. A residency will allow a church planter to learn, get to know his target area, network, and select the site before he is formally released for church planting responsibilities. It provides an excellent time for growth and development before stepping into the official role of church planter.

Conclusion

There are many ways to identify and develop future leaders for the work of Hispanic church planting, and many potential opportunities that still need growth and development. Yet the important takeaway is that recruiting and training future Hispanic church planters and pastors is essential for the growth of the Latino church in the United States. Churches and pastors alike must recognize the need and prayerfully seek for both new leaders and training opportunities as they come alongside these men and help prepare them to be useful in the Lord's work of ministry to the Hispanic people and beyond.

CHAPTER 14:

PRACTICAL WAYS TO SUPPORT THE CHURCH PLANTER

> *"One day Elisha went on to Shunem, where a wealthy woman lived, who urged him to eat some food. So whenever he passed that way, he would turn in there to eat food. 9 And she said to her husband, 'Behold now, I know that this is a holy man of God who is continually passing our way. 10 Let us make a small room on the roof with walls and put there for him a bed, a table, a chair, and a lamp, so that whenever he comes to us, he can go in there.'"* – II Kings 4:8-10

The woman of Shunem in the book of II Kings gives an interesting picture of what supporting a minister of the gospel might look like. The woman, whose exact name is never given, saw a presumably hungry and perhaps lonely-looking man passing through her region one day. In her hospitality, she invited him to come and be fed at her table. It seems that her invitation was loving and needed, because, from that point on, Elisha made it a habit to stop and eat with her. While the woman may not have known Elisha's full identity at his first invitation to her table, over the course of time, as she provided for him in this practical way, feeding both his body and his soul, she understood that this man whom she had been so faithfully entertaining was "a holy man of God." Through these interactions and a growing relationship, the woman was able to recognize a further way to care for and bless the prophet. A wealthy woman, she encouraged her husband to help her use their resources to provide for Elisha additionally with a comfortable room where he might not simply eat, but also have lodging when he came through Shunem. She was then able to offer a place of rest, repose, and rejuvenation for a hard-working, weary prophet busy about the Lord's work. Thus, the Lord used this woman, the gift of wealth He had given her, her faithful attention to details, and the Lord's calling in her life, to bless Elisha's life and ministry in practical and encouraging ways.

Practical Ways for the Mother Church to Support the Church Planter

Mother churches have the same opportunity for blessing Hispanic church planters in practical ways as they commit to sending them out and supporting them in the work of church planting. Like the woman of Shunem with Elisha, it will look like spending time with the individuals, getting to know them and their needs, and providing through the abundance and blessings that the Lord has given to the sending church. While Chapter 3 of this book spoke to the need for mother churches to commit to support, this chapter will look at some of the practical ways sending churches may care for the men and their families whom they are sending into the Latino community, both physically and spiritually. Not all of these suggested methods are currently in existence for Hispanic church planters; the desire is that some of these ideas would spark sending churches, presbyteries, and even a denomination to work together to create such opportunities for supporting these individuals, their families, and their church plants. Like the work of the prophets in the time of Israel, the road for the church planter in the Hispanic context will be long and often lonely; thus, these commitments for support must be ongoing, such that the church planter may find rest, repose, and rejuvenation as needed over the years of church planting.

Prayer

First and foremost, the importance of prayer in supporting Hispanic church planters cannot be stated too strongly or reiterated too much. This book has already dealt at several points with the need to surround the ministry of Hispanic church planting with prayer, but it bears mentioning again that the most important thing a mother church can do for the work is commit to fervent, regular, and ongoing prayer, with and for the church planter. Necessarily, such a commitment looks like spending time with the church planter and getting to know his needs and struggles, as well as those of the target community, to be able to pray for him in specific ways. While it must involve the leadership of the church, it may (and should) also go further to involve members of the congregation as well. In speaking of the responsibilities of the church working together to care for one another, Paul instructs the members of the church at Thessalonica to "pray without ceasing;" such must be the mindset of the sending church as well in caring for the church planter (cf. I Thessalonians 5:17).

Moreover, the mother church can encourage the church planter to meet regularly to pray with others who are doing the same work. Although there may not be many other Hispanic church planters working within the same city or even region, modern technology permits pastors from across the United States and the world to connect with and encourage one another. Doing the research for such opportunities, or even encouraging the church planter to look for these methods is another way the mother church can participate in ensuring the work of Hispanic church planter is prayer-focused.

Personal and Family Support

Outside of prayer, the mother church should commit to encouraging the church planter routinely through regular interactions with his provisional Session. These meetings, while also dealing with the business aspects of ministry, are a time for the elders to speak lovingly with the church planter about his successes and failures, and encourage him in the work. The church (or provisional Session) must ensure these meetings are happening on a regular basis, not only to give the Session a chance to gauge what is going well and what aspects of ministry may need some adjustments, but also to build loving, caring relationship with the church planter, and to care for his emotional and spiritual needs as he engages in church planting. Even though (and especially because) Hispanic church planting looks different from that of majority-culture church planting, the provisional Session must commit to caring for the Hispanic church planter in this way for the long-term, ensuring that he is not left on his own after the first several months or even years of the process.

Related to the ongoing need for the provisional Session to meet with the church planter is the need for the mother church to care for the mental, emotional, and spiritual health of both the church planter and his wife. Church planting is challenging, and can sometimes even feel depressing, particularly in the Hispanic context, as there are many goals for finances, reaching a certain number of people, etc., and these goals come with many ups and downs. Elders of the sending church (both Teaching and Ruling Elders), along with women with shepherding hearts, should make a point of intentionally spending time with the church planting couple and learning the joys and challenges of church planting, such that they may care for and encourage them appropriately. Taking the time to commit to these relationships allows the mother church to ask hard questions (regarding sin struggles, depression, the couple's relationship), and assess how they can best continue to care for the church planter and his wife, and help them to flourish in the life of ministry. It also will help the church understand other ways they can care practically for the church planter and his family, whether that looks like supporting them through counseling, providing the church-planting couple with date-nights (and childcare, if applicable), or helping them be able to take a much-needed vacation.

Visionary Support Methods

Another way in which mother churches, sending agencies, and denominational agencies might commit to care for their church planters could be through facilitating cohorts of other Hispanic church planters. As mentioned in the previous chapter regarding the training up of new leaders, Spanish-speaking cohorts do not currently exist within the PCA denomination. However, a mother church might work with other sending churches or presbyteries to create one. A cohort could be as simple as setting up the space, funds, and accountability necessary for three or so Hispanic pastors who are all planting churches to meet together regularly to pray for one another, and share struggles and ideas. While church planters are unlikely to do this on their own due to their busy schedules or their personalities of independence, the chance to walk through church planting in the Latino context alongside others who are doing the same is invaluable. Mother churches could support their Hispanic church planters well by not simply providing such opportunities, but making it a part of their expectations for the church planter to participate: for his own benefit, and therefore for the benefit of his family and church plant as well.

On a grander scale than establishing cohorts, ideally mother churches, sending agencies, or denominational agencies could work to establish and offer "free" (or heavily subsidized) conferences for church planters and their wives to attend annually or even biannually. While these events exist for English-proficient pastors within the PCA and other denominations, there is a need for conferences that reach Spanish-speakers and that are contextualized to Hispanic church planting. Such conferences could offer training for planters, encouragement in piety, and much-needed fellowship with fellow planters and church planter wives from around the country. Certainly organizing conferences like this is a visionary item, and will take time, prayer, and effort. Yet mother churches, established Hispanic churches, and presbyteries who are determined to care well for the Hispanic church and church planters might begin praying towards this end, seeking to contact others who may be like-minded, and organizing efforts to create these opportunities.

Care for Wives

It is essential, when committing to support a church planter, that a sending church's plan for support also includes caring for his wife (if he is married). During the difficult season of church planting, the church planter's wife will necessarily be involved (whether formally or informally), and will also experience the joys and trials of church planting. Yet she will do so without the benefit of regular meetings with other pastors, mentors, and oversight that her husband has. In addition to possibly taking on extra household and financial responsibilities in the early years of church planting to support her husband as he is working, she often leads several ministries (without pay, and typically without any sort of training).

In addition, being an ethnic minority can further the sense of isolation and stress, especially if the wife is serving in a country outside of her country of origin. Linguistic differences will pose barriers to deep, relational connections; however, even if she is among fellow Spanish-speakers, or is English-proficient, she may be navigating cultural differences of Hispanics from different countries. Meanwhile, the reality is, whether she desires a spotlight or not, congregations will watch the church planter's wife carefully, and have certain expectations of her that may be a source of anxiety.

It is critical, therefore, that mother churches are committed to caring for and encouraging these church planting wives, and reminding them of the hope of the gospel when they grow weary or experience hurt in the journey. Having ways to be refreshed – mentally, physically, emotionally, and spiritually – will help these women to develop resilience in the church planting process, and not simply survive, but thrive. Finding ways to come alongside her, hear her, and encourage her will further allow her to encourage her husband, and find joy in the work of ministry.

In practical ways, it should go without saying that the mother church should ensure that caring women within the congregation are reaching out to, praying for, and befriending the church planter's wife, allowing her to have an outlet outside of the church planting community. Even in the presence of potential linguistic and cultural barriers, working to establish relationships will prove beneficial to both parties, as they learn one another's stories and share the commonality of sisterhood in Christ. Furthermore, sending churches might designate funds to cover expenses for activities that renew her spiritually and emotionally, such as workshops, retreats, conferences with her husband, and even childcare so she can spend time with her husband or make new friends. They might also help to connect her (potentially virtually) with other likeminded church planting wives, who can pray together and encourage one another even from a distance. For those who are primarily Spanish-speakers, investing in English classes and giving them opportunities to learn English or improve their fluency is also a practical, loving way of caring for these wives.

Additionally, the PCA offers ministries like *Parakaleo* that come alongside women in church planting, especially wives. These ministries can help women process challenges from a gospel perspective, connect them with others, and break through the feelings of isolation in church planting. Planning and budgeting for wives to participate in such support ministries clearly communicates that the mother church values women as co-laborers in ministry. If a mother church is not committed to actively and intentionally supporting the church planter's wife, they are also not caring well for the church planter, or his new work, as she plays a pivotal (though often behind-the-scenes) role.

Supporting other Key Leaders

As the church planter begins to work within his community and the church plant begins to take shape, the mother church has the opportunity to provide support and resources to other key leaders within the church plant as well. While it is typically (and rightly) the case that the church planter and his family receive most of the attention and resources, if they have the capacity, mother churches may also help provide for some of these rising lay-leaders as well. Certainly this would look like encouragement through prayer support, meals, and developing relationships to offer encouragement, although it could go further than this to provide needed trainings and resources as well. As these individuals are lay-people, and (like the church planter) also involved in a new work, they can benefit immensely from being connected to and hearing stories of others lay-leaders involved in church planting. As a sending church connects to these lay-leaders and encourages them, it will necessarily also support the church planter, by expanding his capacity to train and encourage his leaders as they reach the community.

Conclusion

The ways in which a mother church may commit to supporting Hispanic church planters are numerous and essential for his profitableness in the work. Without adequate, intentional support, the church planter and his family are at high risk for burnout in the long road of church planting. Like the Shunamite woman, sending churches must get to know the church planter and his unique needs, and seek to bring encouragement and refreshment as they are able. Prayerfully, mother churches will grow in this commitment, expanding ways of supporting these individuals and their families, and thus helping to expand God's Kingdom into and beyond the Latino context.

CHAPTER 15:

PRACTICAL CONSIDERATIONS REGARDING THE ORDINATION OF SPANISH-DOMINANT PASTORS

"Paul replied, 'I am a Jew, from Tarsus in Cilicia, a citizen of no obscure city. I beg you, permit me to speak to the people.' ⁴⁰And when he had given him permission, Paul, standing on the steps, motioned with his hand to the people. And when there was a great hush, he addressed them in the Hebrew language,* saying:

22 'Brothers and fathers, hear the defense that I now make before you.'

²And when they heard that he was addressing them in the Hebrew language,* they became even more quiet..." – Acts 21:39-22:2

*or Hebrew dialect, probably Aramaic

The apostle Paul was a Roman citizen, highly educated, and probably proficient at least in Greek and Hebrew, though (due to his education and citizenship) potentially also Latin. These languages were, in part, an indication of his high status as both Roman citizen and Pharisee; nevertheless, converted and changed through the grace of Jesus, Paul used his language skills for the redemptive purpose of sharing the gospel with multiple people groups. As Paul was under arrest and making a defense to the tribune in Jerusalem (Acts 21:37-22:2ff), he shifted from speaking with the tribune in Greek, to addressing the people in the Hebrew dialect (most likely Aramaic). The response of the people at hearing Paul speak to them in their own, heart language is astounding and noteworthy: they fell into complete silence, able to understand his testimony without translation, completely contextualized to speak directly to their souls.

The lesson from these verses, while subtle, is also powerful. People will pay attention most to the gospel message as it speaks to their context and their souls through their heart language. Thus it is imperative to discuss what it looks like to break through the language barriers that come in working within a majority-culture denomination in order help ordain equipped, Spanish-speaking pastors to the essential work of pastoring within their own language and context to best reach fellow Hispanics and Spanish-speakers. (Note that there are many bilingual and even some primarily English-speaking Hispanic pastors for whom the language barrier does not exist. Majority-culture churches must resist the urge to assume a language barrier for all Hispanic pastors simply based on race.) This chapter will speak to what this ordination process looks like, the challenges it presents, and how to overcome these challenges, specifically within the PCA denomination. Although the chapter speaks particularly to the technical issues and protocols regarding the ordination of men in the PCA, some of the considerations and principles may prove useful for similarly structured denominations as well.

Ordination of Spanish-Speaking Candidates

While it can certainly present challenges, the langue barrier for ordination in the PCA is not insurmountable. Several Spanish-speaking Latino pastors have been ordained and others are seeking ordination. As Hispanic church planting in the denomination has been growing, so has the need to be able to ordain pastoral candidates whose preferred language is not English. There are a growing number of individuals who are sound in the faith and committed to working in the denomination, but lack the English language skills to help them in completing the examination process successfully, as the procedures currently stand. From coming under care, to taking exams and appearing before the Credentialing Committee, to presenting themselves before the full Presbytery, these candidates face difficulties.

There is a great need, therefore, to be able to help candidates who are not sufficiently proficient in English be able to become ordained and serve in the full capacity of Teaching Elder within the PCA. Thankfully, at this point, the process is not unprecedented. In such situations, the South Florida Presbytery has taken the lead in demonstrating a high level of flexibility and commitment to their Spanish-speaking candidates and communities. From the Care Committee to Credentialing Committee, to the Presbytery, South Florida has a good number of fully bilingual, native Hispanics as well as Anglo-Saxons who can communicate in Spanish. These Teaching Elders are able to help other Spanish-speaking candidates complete their ordination requirements in their native language. Other presbyteries that do not already have fluent Spanish-speakers may need to enlist the help of other Spanish-speaking pastors from outside their Presbytery in order to help ordain qualified candidates.

In thinking through how this process could look, it will depend on the level of English that the candidate may possess (refer back to the Language Continuum presented in Chapter 8 of this book). Spanish-only candidates (or those with very little English skills) will necessarily need provision to conduct all their examinations in Spanish, while bilingual candidates who fall on the righthand side of the continuum (feeling more comfortable in Spanish, but able to communicate in English) may have more fluidity in how they complete the exams. The following will look at some real-life examples from both of these categories to help presbyteries think through how they can creatively help their Spanish-speaking candidates become ordained.

Spanish-only (or mostly Spanish) Candidates

In 2008, a mostly-Spanish speaking Colombian-born church planter in Coral Gables, Florida, was successfully ordained through the South Florida Presbytery. The Presbytery allowed him to go through the majority of the ordination process using his native language, with the help of a bilingual, Anglo Teaching Elder, who worked closely with the candidate for two years to help prepare him for the examinations. While the church planter had sufficient English skills to complete his written exams in English, the Presbytery permitted him to complete his oral examinations on the floor in Spanish by using a translator. After this pastor's ordination, as the number of Spanish-speakers within the Presbytery grew, the South Florida Presbytery approved the motion that a committee in the language of the candidate would be permitted to examine candidates, thus eliminating the need for a translator for credentialing exams. (Of note, it did take several attempts for the Presbytery to finally approve the motion – persistence is key!)

Another example through the South Florida Presbytery is that of a first-generation middle-aged Argentinian pastor and successful church planter in South Florida. After coming to Christ through a local PCA church, he felt a calling to ministry. Though a Spanish-only speaker, he was able to pursue a seminary degree fully in Spanish through Miami International Theological Seminary (MINTS: see Chapter 13, as well as the Resources page of this book for more details). Seeking ordination to be able to plant and serve within the PCA, the candidate was able to complete his care program with the help of other Spanish-speaking pastors within the Presbytery. When the time came for credentialing, the candidate was able to take advantage of the aforementioned motion and undergo both his written and oral exams in Spanish before Spanish-speaking members of the Credentialing Committee. On the floor, the Presbytery permitted him to answer questions in Spanish with an interpreter, and to preach in Spanish, with some of the Spanish-speaking pastors providing feedback and constructive criticism.

That the South Florida Presbytery already has a number of Spanish-speaking pastors has made it easier for Spanish-speaking pastoral candidates, like those in both these examples, to become ordained in a majority English-speaking denomination. While this could be a good goal for other presbyteries, it is not a current reality. Nevertheless, presbyteries could consider what it would look like to enlist the help of other bilingual and Spanish-speaking pastors from outside the Presbytery to come alongside these candidates as mentors and as translators, thus making provision for more, qualified pastoral candidates to become ordained and serve the Spanish-speaking context through the denomination.

Prefers-Spanish to Bilingual Candidates

While ordaining Spanish-only speakers (or those who fall closely towards the righthand side of the Language Continuum) presents challenges in many presbyteries, it is also necessary to consider how to help ordain candidates who may be considered bilingual, but still fall closer to the righthand side of the Continuum, having greater ease with Spanish. Such was the case, for example with at least three candidates who came from Puerto Rico to become ordained in the denomination and return to Puerto Rico to plant Spanish-speaking PCA churches there. While these individuals each had high levels of competency in English, when going through rigorous oral examinations, they still sometimes found it easier to communicate in Spanish, or needed to switch between English and Spanish to be able to explain their positions more accurately. Once again, the South Florida Presbytery was able to accommodate these needs through their number of Spanish-speaking members.

Once again, in these cases, the South Florida Presbytery was able to utilize the skills of its bilingual Teaching Elders to help on the Care and Credentialing Committees, and to provide real-time translation for English-only speakers and vice versa. These men were (and are) able to translate questions coming from the floor for those being examined, as needed, to ensure full understanding for the candidates, and to permit them to answer in English, Spanish, or both, as they felt comfortable.

It is important to note here that not every Spanish-speaking candidate for ordination within the PCA is starting at the beginning of ministry. Rather, some candidates have years of ministerial experience coming from other denominations, but have found and embraced the Reformed faith. Even though they may be fairly fluent in English, they may find it easier to preach in their mother tongue, since they are better acquainted with the Scriptures in Spanish. This was the case, for example, with one pastor who grew up in Spanish-speaking churches in Puerto Rico and in South Florida and is fully bilingual. Although he passed all his written and oral examinations in English, he chose to preach in Spanish as he was accustomed to doing from his upbringing in Spanish-speaking congregations. His sermon was evaluated by the Spanish-speaking pastors in the South Florida Presbytery.

The level of flexibility that the South Florida Presbytery has demonstrated, along with their non-threating, welcoming approach to Spanish-speaking candidates is one that other presbyteries must emulate if the PCA wishes to see growth of the denomination among the Spanish-speaking Latino population in the United States. It is, in fact, the sort of flexibility and creativity to which the gospel calls the church in order to love the nations, welcome the foreigners, and help pastors to serve their contexts as they have been called. While ordaining Spanish-speaking candidates may take more creativity and flexibility within other presbyteries that do not have many (or any) bilingual members, they must pray, think creatively, and assist the help of others in order to allow Spanish-speaking candidates to formally fill these much-needed positions.

Some presbyteries are doing just this. For example, in one case in south Texas, English-speaking Teaching Elders were able to mentor one bilingual (although righthand-leaning on the Language Continuum) candidate all the way through his studies for licensure and ordination. The encouragement is for Teaching Elders in the PCA to be alert for opportunities to mentor bilingual candidates (including righthand-leaning bilingual candidates) of other ethnicities who may in turn plant or pastor churches in languages other than English. Several monolingual PCA pastors have already done this effectively. Presbyteries must consider such avenues of service with a desire of spreading the name of Jesus to all peoples and languages not simply abroad, but here in the United States.

Spanish-Speaking Candidates without Credentials, or who Transfer Credentials

Outside of simply language barriers, there have also been situations in which Spanish-only, or Spanish-preferring candidates have come for ordination within the PCA either without formal seminary training, or through transfer of credentials from a Reformed Presbyterian denomination within their country of origin. In some of these former scenarios, it may be appropriate to invoke the extraordinary clause of the PCA's *Book of Church Order* (BCO) 21-4. The purpose would not be to lower the standard for ordination, but to ensure that a truly qualified candidate is not excluded.

It is necessary to remember that some of these candidates have been studying and pastoring for years in other contexts, and (perhaps with the aid of some mentoring like that suggested above in areas specific to the denomination, or as needed) may be quite qualified for ordination. This was the case of the south Texas pastoral candidate referenced in the preceding paragraph. While he had not studied formally at any seminary, through mentorship, years of experience, and his own dedication to independent study, he did exceedingly well in all of his examinations to become ordained.

The question regarding ordination of pastors from Reformed denominations outside of the United States is one of whether to examine these individuals as a transfer of credentials, or as new candidates seeking ordination. Again, these candidates typically come with substantial ministry experience and possess exemplary character. Here, several Presbyteries have demonstrated missional flexibility and have opted to give these candidates transfer examinations. For these examinations, there is still a question of how to approach the language barrier, if the candidate is not fully bilingual. In one such instance the candidate was allowed to take the written portion of the exams in Spanish. A bilingual Teaching Elder thoroughly reviewed the exam and reported his findings to the Committee of Credentials. During the oral exams, the candidate had access to a translator for any point where he might need help clarifying the question or formulating his response. In another Presbytery, the candidate was asked to answer the written exam in English, but was provided with a translator for all the oral examinations.

Other Presbyteries looking to ordain Reformed, Spanish-speaking pastors from denominations outside of the United States have insisted on giving the previously-ordained candidates the full ordination exam. The danger in this approach is that it devalues the knowledge and experience of the men coming for ordination, and the number of those who have submitted to and completed this process is negligible. They stand as losses in a system stacked against them, and speak to missed opportunities for the PCA. Their examples also point to a need for individual presbyteries, and the denomination as a whole, to prayerfully consider how they can best care for these qualified Spanish-speaking transfers, and help them to flourish within a new denomination, a new country, and among a people-group that desperately needs their care.

The Question of Presbytery Participation

Outside of simply ordaining Spanish-speaking candidates to pastoral ministry, Presbyters often have a further question of how Spanish-dominant pastors can become an active part of the Presbytery. In the first place, it again involves fellow Presbyters having a heart for their fellow brothers and workers in Christ, and seeking to engage with these men to the best of their ability, even if it feels uncomfortable or requires learning some Spanish! Other Presbyters might seek to love their fellow Spanish-speaking pastors by coming alongside of them and playing to the English skills they do have to help them participate. The other reality is that the English proficiency of these men nearly always improves over time, and so also their ability to participate in the work of the Presbytery. Patience, love, and recognition of equal status as men serving the Great Shepherd, make Spanish-speaking pastors feel welcome, and allow them to become necessary, contributing members of the Presbytery.

Conclusion

While some presbyteries within the PCA have worked to make the process of ordination for Spanish-speaking candidates smooth and simple, there is still much work to be done within the denomination as a whole. Presbyteries wishing to serve the Spanish-speaking and Latino context must prayerfully consider what it looks like to love their fellow workers in Christ as they help free them to the work of pastoral ministry within the Latino context and within the language the Lord has given them for service. Helping to ordain these men requires flexibility and creativity, but it will go far for furthering the Lord's work of building up the church in the growing Spanish-speaking community within the United States.

CHAPTER 16:

REALISTIC BUDGETS AND ADDITIONAL FUNDING STRATEGIES FOR HISPANIC CHURCH PLANTING

"Let the elders who rule well be considered worthy of double honor, especially those who labor in preaching and teaching. ¹⁸ For the Scripture says, 'You shall not muzzle an ox when it treads out the grain,' and, 'The laborer deserves his wages.'" – I Timothy 5:17-18

The work of a pastor or church planter is a high calling. Scripture is clear when it comes to provision for pastors: the church is to honor their work without being stingy. As Paul writes to Timothy in his first letter, showing "double honor" for a pastor or church planter (i.e., "those who labor in preaching and teaching") looks like caring for him well, even financially. Such provision ensures that pastors are able to do the work of ministry effectively, without being restricted by concerns for how they will provide for themselves or their families. While the manner of caring for both the church planter and his church plant will vary depending on the demographic and which church planting methodology is in place, it is imperative that sending churches and the church planter work together to build a budget that will realistically be able to support and care for both the church planter and also the work of ministry.

Planting a Hispanic church, as this book has shown, is complex. Therefore, churches and church planters must come to the discussion of the of funding and budgeting with a willingness to learn to become innovative, creative, and flexible. This chapter will look at some practical strategies for designing realistic budgets within various contexts, as well as some additional ideas for funding and offsetting costs that are not typically used in majority-culture PCA churches.

In the PCA, the church planter's call package must be approved by the local Presbytery. Yet the reality is that the majority of PCA churches are located in upper and upper-middle class neighborhoods. This presents a real challenge to presbyteries who are then charged to approve the salary of a church planter trying to reach those in a lower socioeconomic stratum of American society, since the goal is for the church plant to eventually be financially self-sustaining. While the PCA Retirement and Benefits publishes call package guidelines, these guidelines have limited value for those seeking to plant a church aimed at a different demographic. Understandably, the cost of living varies widely from state to state, and even in cities within the same state. The attempt here to bring clarity to this difficult issue, is just that: an attempt to help the church planter to set up a budget that allows him not to have to carry undue financial burdens, and that the church plant will one day be able to support through internal giving.

Budget Considerations

Necessarily, designing a budget for the church plant will look different depending on which methodology the church planter is following. For example, independent methodology will require additional expenses for renting space and materials that integrated methodology will not need, and incubator methodology should not need, at least in the first years. Yet regardless of methodology, the first consideration in crafting a realistic budget must be the needs and package of the church planter himself. National metrics show that for a family of four to subsist in the top fifty cities in the United States, the household income must exceed $54,000.[18] Interestingly, Presbyterian salary studies have demonstrated similar data, requiring a minimum compensation for a pastor/assistant pastor of a church of less than 100 people to be no less than $55,000.[19]

Yet mother churches often wrestle with what is fair compensation for a Hispanic church planter. The often-used Return on Investment (ROI) metric, which churches borrow from the business world, lies at the root of the question. A mother church may project the amount of money the Hispanic congregation will likely contribute to the overall financial stability of the church and wonder if it would be wise to pay the Hispanic pastor less. The irony is that they do not ask that question regarding the compensation of full-time staff who work in administration or with children and youth. Part of counting the cost (see Chapter 1) means that, if God calls a church to reach people from different socioeconomic and ethnic backgrounds in order for their body to more fully reflect the diversity of the Kingdom of God, then they must be willing to do so sacrificially. Moreover, it is unequivocally true that if God calls a church planter (Hispanic, Spanish-speaking, or other) to reach the Latino context, his salary requirements should not be reduced (1 Tim 5:18).

Therefore, the financial data given above is important as it provides a picture of the investment needed in order to support a church planter in his journey of planting a Hispanic church. Data demonstrates that the first four years of the planter's journey in the Hispanic context most likely will not include any internal giving. Consequently, the planter and planters (i.e., mother church, Presbytery, et. al.) must account for these numbers.

By the fourth or fifth year of church planting (during the Worship Stage of the Church Planting Timeline), the church plant should begin generating some internal funds. This money must go towards the expenses of ministry first, rather than beginning to cover a portion of the church planter's salary. Understanding these metrics helps the church planter to be realistic, but also helps him to communicate to others about what statistics have demonstrated regarding financial needs within this context. While it is certainly true that God could do more with less, using these metrics to design and communicate a realistic budget helps others to be able to prepare to support the church planter and the church plant for the long-haul, clearly understanding what is needed and why. The following chart provides a visualization of what the needs versus anticipated internal giving might look like on a ten-year plan to financial self-sufficiency:

Timeline of Church Plant Budget vs. Funding Expectations											
Year	1	2	3	4	5	6	7	8	9	10	Total:
Salary	$55k	$55k	$55k	$55k	$60k	$60k	$60k	$65k	$65k	$65k	$660,000
Ministry	$6k	$6k	$9k	$18k	$25k	$30k	$40k	$45k	$45k	$45k	$269,000
Total:	$61k	$61k	$64k	$73k	$85k	$90k	$100k	$110k	$110k	$110k	$929,000
Internal Giving	---	---	---	$26k	$36k	$50k	$60k	$70k	$70k	$85k	$337,000

Of course, this chart does not speak to the specific needs of any one church plant, but rather offers a way of thinking realistically regarding budget needs, growth over the course of church planting, and expectations of growth in internal giving that help to calculate the total need for church planting. It is helpful to note that the ministry budget in the first few years of church planting is quite small, given that the majority of the work involves small-group and one-on-one meetings for networking, evangelism, and discipleship. As the church plant enters the Worship Stage of ministry, this budget will need to increase significantly in church plants following independent methodology, or those churches who will need to pay for their own worship space. There are a number of other variables as well, including the salary package for the church planter. While the given figure should not decrease, in some cases the number may need to increase to accommodate the cost of living in his particular zip code, or to provide adequately for a larger family, etc. Tools such as the MIT Living Wage calculator, which takes numerous financial factors into account, may help to come up with an appropriate, realistic number here.

Creative Funding Strategies

While these numbers can feel overwhelming both for the church planter and his sending churches or supporters, it does not serve the church planter or the church plant to try and reduce them simply to have a smaller fundraising goal. Rather, these numbers are where innovation, creativity, and flexibility must come into the discussion of funding and budgeting. Support raising need not consist simply in raising funds, but in helping reduce expenses in creative ways.

Mother churches and presbyteries can assist in this process of creative funding by asking themselves where the Lord has blessed them in unique ways that they can use for caring for the church planter. The church planter can help potential supporters to think likewise. For example, a church with low overhead expenses (mother church or other supporting church) – regardless of church planting methodology – may agree to host the planter's payroll and benefits for a time, significantly reducing the cost of procuring these benefits for himself. Other churches may find that they have unused resources (chairs, sound equipment, etc.,) that they could either donate to the church plant if needed, or sell in order to raise funds for the church planter. Depending on the context, perhaps a school attached to a church might agree to provide a part-time teaching job to cover a part of the $55,000 needed to support the church planter's family (as reflected in some of the case studies in Chapter 5). Or a Presbytery might find a grant or scholarship for a seminary student that would allow this student to work as a part-time collaborator with the ministry, without incurring further expenses to the church plant.

While some supporters or supporting churches may feel limited by financial resources, they may have the capacity to host outreach events for the church plant, such as VBS, Christmas events, etc., for which they already have people and resources, thus helping the church planter not need to dip into his own resources. Some churches may use preparation ministries (such as tutoring, soccer, music, and mercy ministries, etc.) as a segue into supporting a church planter through continuing to provide these activities at no extra cost (see Appendix A). Other churches or individuals may choose to donate bilingual Bibles, or pay for the church planter's coffee and meal expenses. Perhaps the church has an unused manse, or a member of a supporting church can provide a rental home at reduced cost. Sometimes, there are Presbytery or supporting church members who work in medical professions and are willing to donate yearly eye, dental, or other exams to defray medical costs. Someone may have a car to donate, or a church school may be able to provide a scholarship for the church planter's children, or free daycare that permits the church planter's wife to work. When prayerfully thinking outside of the box, the possibilities are endless. When approaching churches and individuals for support, the church planter may assist in this process by speaking to needs, and asking supporters to consider their gifts and resources outside of purely financial abilities.

Additional Funding Methodologies for Hispanic Church Planting

Aside from non-traditional support raising, a mother church and church planter may need to consider other methodologies for funding the church plant in order to allow it to thrive. There are at least six new funding models that a church planter could consider when planting a church among the immigrant community, each discussed in turn below.

Co-vocational Funding

While bi-vocational ministry was discussed as an additional methodology for church planting in Chapter 3, it is helpful to clarify that co-vocational ministry and funding is somewhat different. A bi-vocational pastor or planter has a full-time, secular job, while also being responsible for shepherding a church and pastoring the community. Many times, the burden of the full-time job leads the pastor to be less effective in ministry, thus signifying a higher potential for burnout.

Co-vocational ministry, on the other hand, is different in that the full-time employment is not disconnected from the church planter's work of ministry. Rather, it seeks to focus intentionally either on the parish, the people or on the vision. In the case of parish focus, the planter would seek to find employment within his target demographic, ensuring that the work provides opportunities to network within the community. Target-group focus looks like the church planter pursuing employment that connects him with the specific individuals he is trying to reach. For example, if he is desiring to reach first-generation immigrants, seeking to become a general contractor might gain the church planter access to such individuals who are working in manual labor. Vision focus could look like the church planter finding employment that allows him access to individuals (families, singles, young adults, business people, etc.) who share the same passions and goals of the church plant.

Whatever job he fills, working co-vocationally gives the church planter another means of offsetting the cost of church planting. Although it gives him connections into the community, it will also reduce the amount of time he is able to commit to the work of church planting itself, thus perhaps necessitating a larger ministry budget to enlist the help of others as the work grows.

Business as Mission/Entrepreneurial Funding

Another funding strategy, for church planters and sending churches that may be business-minded, is to look at some entrepreneurial approaches to funding and offsetting church plant costs. Such approaches are not uncommon outside of the United States, but are beginning to take root in some churches in the country as well. For example, a church in Minneapolis raised funds to start a grocery store that closes on Sundays to become the gathering space for the church. During the week, the store serves the dual purpose of not only providing for the needs of the community, but also providing the pastor/church planter (who manages the store) with income and a way to connect with his community. In another case, a church began by opening a needed laundromat in the middle of a community. The success of this laundromat allowed the church to start another laundromat which provided the capital necessary to hire a full-time pastor. In a third scenario, the pastor of a house church partnered with some of the women of the church who donated their time to make delicious tamales during one weekend each month for two years. At the end of this time, the church had money to buy a piece of land and build a facility that allowed the church to grow in the community.

A second layer to an entrepreneurial approach would be for a lay-person to run a business and commit the profits to the work of the church planting ministry. Such an application has the potential of providing a good deal of funding for the church plant, without overburdening the church planter himself. The business can become an opportunity to employ church members from other surrounding churches, along with those within the target community as a form of mission, and can continue to serve and fund the church even after particularization. For church members who are well-resourced, looking to serve the Hispanic population, and entrepreneurial, this may be an exciting and appealing option for supporting a church planter.

While an entrepreneurial approach to funding requires business-minded individuals and seed-money for the project, this strategy may be attractive for the right church planters or some potential supporters as it is a way not simply of caring for souls, but putting down roots in a city to make connections through tangibly meeting needs as well. Once again, with a creative mind for needs and business, the possibilities here are endless.

Funding via Trust Fund or Seed Funds for Exploration

Not every Hispanic church planter is called to work co-vocationally, or able to open a business. Other options for helping raise the needed funds for church planting would be through trust funds or seed funds for exploration within the target community. A church planter may do research and find that there are grants available for starting new church planting projects – some that may even fully fund the planter's first year or two as he is learning his demographic. While such funds exist, they will necessitate the planter being very diligent in fulfilling the complete list of requirements, and providing the requested updates and financial documentation both before and during the funding period, in order to continue receiving such funds. For those who are willing and able to do this sort of written documentation, looking into the availability of and qualification for these types of funding can be quite beneficial.

Funding a Part-time or Double-part-time Church Planter

In some cases, church planting in the Hispanic community does not have to start large, even if the desire is to grow over time. In these instances, large churches (or churches with available budgets) might hire a part-time church planter in charge of engaging the immigrant or Hispanic population in the community where the church is located. This approach permits the church to begin reaching out to the immigrant community while maintaining a smaller initial commitment as the work is in development.

Similarly, a church looking for part-time help might hire a "double-part-time" planter to work part-time within the Latino community, and part-time on the staff of the mother church to support its work as well. While either of these part-time strategies may have some appeal, a mother church should be cautious in taking this approach too hastily, as there is a risk of the church planter feeling stretched too thinly, and burning out. Moreover, he may not have adequate time to devote to the Hispanic church, and it may struggle to get off the ground. Churches must prayerfully consider whether or not this may be the best approach to helping fund a Hispanic church planter. (On the positives and negatives of this approach, see also the discussion of Bi-vocational methodology in Chapter 3.)

Funding as a Presbytery Director of Hispanic Engagement

Presbyteries that have sufficient resources and cover a region with a large Hispanic presence might consider helping deflect costs by hiring a Hispanic church planter to work also as a Director of Hispanic Engagement within the Presbytery itself. Such an approach provides the potential for a capable pastor to start not just one church, but to begin planting seeds for gospel communities in Hispanic areas throughout the city or region. This greenhouse approach could lead to the establishment of healthy, house-sized churches able to fund a fulltime city pastor who cares for and helps raise leaders in each of the small communities throughout the city, while maintaining the connection with all of them. (See also the discussion of House Church Methodology in Chapter 3 for some of the positives and negatives to this sort of approach.)

Funding via a Reverse Tier Model

A mother church seeking to fund a church planter could also consider a reverse tier model, which provides less money at the beginning, and increases support as the group grows. This approach can add value to growth and movement, permitting more resources to be available as the ministry gains traction and requires additional funding to continue. For example, a church could initially call a planter to the field and begin funding him as an apprentice until he is able to gain some momentum in ministry. At this point, he might be promoted to a planter-in-training, with the appropriate salary increase to reflect the position change. As ministry continues to grow, he would eventually be called as a planter, receiving full pastoral salary compensation, and with funding for the church lasting for another 3 to 5 years. This reverse approach to funding carries with it some advantages, and it may be effective for new or young pastors who have limited experience in ministry and would benefit from a transitional, learning-based approach to ministry. It may also benefit gifted and experienced church planters, who may see growth in their churches, without having adequate resources to care for the entire congregation. In these cases, reverse-tier funding can help the planter add the necessary staff and resources to his team to ensure that his reach does not plateau, but can continue to grow.

Certainly, each of these additional funding strategies can be fluid, and some churches or church planters may use a synthesis of various models. The key is thinking creatively, playing to the needs of the church planter and his demographic, as well as his unique giftings and callings, and the resources the Lord has provided his community and partners. In all of this, if the Lord has indeed called the church planter to plant within the Hispanic community, He will provide the resources for the plant to take place, however that may look.

Conclusion

The discussion of money and funding for church planting, especially in a traditionally low-income target context, can feel overwhelming, and the temptation may be to cut budgets unrealistically to make them feel more achievable. Yet the truth is that Lord provides for His people, and provides abundantly; churches must reflect this attitude as they seek to send out workers into the Hispanic community and allow them to flourish. Whether the funding comes through stock investments and checks from generous churches and donors, or whether the Lord permits church planters and supporters to gather support through different means and methods, fundraising requires great trust in the Lord for His tangible provision. At the same time, watching the Lord provide for His work through His people is one of the greatest and most amazing privileges of church planting. It may not always look like the church planter had envisioned or hoped, but seeing the Lord's endless provision in His perfect timing and His perfect ways will only work to confirm the work to which the planter has been called.

CONCLUSION

"For this reason I bow my knees before the Father, [15] from whom every family in heaven and on earth is named, [16] that according to the riches of his glory he may grant you to be strengthened with power through his Spirit in your inner being, [17] so that Christ may dwell in your hearts through faith—that you, being rooted and grounded in love, [18] may have strength to comprehend with all the saints what is the breadth and length and height and depth, [19] and to know the love of Christ that surpasses knowledge, that you may be filled with all the fullness of God.

[20] Now to him who is able to do far more abundantly than all that we ask or think, according to the power at work within us, [21] to him be glory in the church and in Christ Jesus throughout all generations, forever and ever. Amen." – Ephesians 3:14-21

Church planting is hard work. Church planting in the Hispanic context comes with even greater complexities, as this book has sought to demonstrate. Yet none of these complexities are too great for the One who has called all nations to Himself, and who is raising up a generation of Hispanic leaders within the United States to reap a harvest among the rapidly-growing Hispanic-American population. The task of church planting among Hispanics is urgent, but that urgency must go hand-in-hand with thoughtfulness. It is "for this reason," as Paul writes in Ephesians, that the church must bow their knees before the Father, interceding on behalf of Hispanic church planters that "according to the riches of his glory he may grant [them] to be strengthened with power through his Spirit in [their] inner being[s]," that they may not only know the love of Christ that surpasses knowledge, but bring that love and the fullness of God into a context that so desperately needs to hear this truth.

The church must pray for wisdom in seeking to reach this growing body of Latinos from different cultures, backgrounds, and generations, and act in faith to raise up and send out gospel leaders. It is the prayerful desire that this book has helped to break down some of the misconceptions regarding church planting in the Hispanic context, and that this will in turn help to prevent more pain and heartbreak from further failed attempts to church plant within the Hispanic community. Prayerfully, the lessons, examples, and practical wisdom of those who have come before in this book will help motivate more churches and church planters to join the movement and establish a clear path for those called to reach the Hispanic harvest in the United States.

May the American church truly see the need for thoughtful, contextualized Hispanic ministry in the United States, and seek earnestly to provide every means necessary to allow it to flourish, bringing a diversity of believers into the fold.

May the Hispanic pastor be encouraged that his labor is not in vain. Even as he toils in the long road of church planting, may he entrust all the work "to him who is able to do far more abundantly than all that we ask or think, according to the power at work within us;" may he see the Lord's hand at work in his daily life and ministry. As he looks back and sees Hispanic communities being transformed for Christ, person by person, may he give to God all "glory in the church and in Christ Jesus throughout all generations, forever and ever." May he see the work of God in and through his life, and lift his eyes to the great Savior and Shepherd, and say "Amen!"

APPENDICES:

APPENDIX A

	Preparation Ministry Ideas
	Mother churches can begin the work of tilling the ground for a Hispanic church plant and testing their own willingness to participate in such a ministry through beginning outreach into the intended Hispanic community prior to even calling a church planter. These activities can then become incorporated into the initial work of the church planter in gathering and training a launch team. Preparation ministries typically fall into five categories, and ideas are given below:
English as a Second Language (ESL)	• ESL classes • SSL (Spanish as Second Language) ministry for church members (led by ESL students)
Educational Ministries	• Tutoring • After-school care • Online education (*"plaza comunitaria"* site) • Open a charter school for under-resourced students
Soccer Ministries	• After-school soccer • Summer soccer camps • Soccer opportunities for children of ESL students • Church soccer team • Form a local soccer club
Music Ministries	• After-school music programs • Summer music program
Mercy Ministries	• Open a food pantry • Provide affordable health care • Clothing closets • Provide back-to-school supplies • Community development

APPENDIX B

Tools for the Demographic Study
The following provide some places to begin a demographic study of the target location:

- City/county planning commissions
- School boards and districts
- Public utilities and telephone companies
- University sociology departments
- Police and Fire departments
- Marketing reports
- Newspapers, magazines, their marketing / research department

- Chamber of Commerce
- Secular media
- Public libraries
- Ethnic associations and media
- Internet:
    - www.ethnicharvest.org
    - www.TheARDA.com
    - www.barna.org
    - www.census.gov

APPENDIX C

Networking Ideas

The best networking happens when the church planter (and his team) finds and joins existing special-interest groups. Although it is possible for the church planter to start his own groups, this requires significantly more time and energy. When it comes to planning networking, it is important to bear in mind the quantitative and qualitative research, along with the church planter's interests, in order to determine which ideas may best serve the demographic. The following list provides some ideas for a church planter to get started in networking:

- Join a Chamber(s) of Commerce
- Participate in town hall meetings
- Join a sports league (player or team)
- Take classes in the community
- Volunteer at a Food Coop
- Volunteer at Health Clinics
- Volunteer at a center for cultural affairs, etc.
- Join Toast Masters
- Join a soccer team supporter
- Join an art club
- Join (or form) your Homeowners Association (HOA)
- Volunteer for Habitat for Humanity
- Host a political/cultural/holiday celebration
- Host a block party with a cultural interest, or make up a reason for the party
- Host a Q/A tertulia on any hot topic, even a theological one.
- Participate in a local political campaign (one that does not identify party affiliation)
- Become an advocate for immigrants: there are myriads of opportunities
- Learn the culture through books, movies, college classes, language study for conversation pieces.
- Travel to the country of your target group. The ensuing conversations open doors
- Cultivate relationships with local political, fire and police leaders
- Find a competent informant, a trustworthy person who will explain local culture and customs
- Befriend the mayor, and restaurant owners in the target area.

Outreach Ideas

Different from networking, outreach programs are activities where a church planter (and his team) invite those from their circles of influence (contacts from networking!), or others from the community into their personal "space," whether that is their homes, or the church plant's meeting facility (if applicable). Depending on the size of the launch team and resources available, some church planters will be able to host more outreach events than others. Nevertheless, the goal of outreach is to deepen the relationships formed through networking, and continue building confianza.

Ideas for weekly outreach programs:	Special events to complement outreach programs:
<ul><li>ESL program</li><li>Tutoring program</li><li>After school program</li><li>Dance classes</li><li>Chess classes</li><li>Fitness classes</li><li>Soccer camps, etc.</li></ul>	<ul><li>Movies</li><li>Camping</li><li>Medical clinics</li><li>Citizenship classes</li><li>Food/ clothing distribution</li><li>Back to school supplies</li><li>Thanksgiving food</li><li>Little Angel (Christmas gifts)</li></ul>

Evangelism Ideas

Hospitality and evangelism go hand-in-hand. As confianza *within the community grows through networking and outreach, some of the following ideas can help to build the bridge between outreach and evangelism:*

- Youth camps (Sports, Music, etc.)
- Children camps (VBS, Backyard Bible Clubs, etc.)
- *"Encuentros"* (retreats)
- Overview Bible studies or topical studies of the gospel (especially with plenty of familiar biblical narratives)
- Any activity within the church planter's home-life that may open doors to more interaction and eventually, gospel-conversation (i.e., inviting neighbors to a quinceañera party, to a soccer game, to the movies, etc.)

APPENDIX D

Church Planting Proposal Outline

Every church plant proposal will look different, and should reflect the personality of the church planter, and his unique demographic. However, the following outline is designed to help the church planter think through some of the fundamental elements of his proposal, and a potential structure for providing flow to the proposal or presentation. Not every proposal needs to speak to each of these points in great depth; pictures, graphs, diagrams, and maps are also useful to convey information.

- Why plant this church?
    - Provide the salient details describing the urgent need:
        - Why is it crucial to reach the given target group?
        - What are the felt needs of the demographic?
    - Support with data — demographics.
    - Vividly describe the location of the target group.
- Why are you uniquely gifted to plant this church?
    - Explain who you are and why you feel called by God to plant this church in this location.
    - Describe what you plan to do upon arrival at the location.
- What kind of church will this be?
    - Give the core values.
    - Give and expand the mission and vision statements.
- What are the strategies for reaching the target group with the gospel?
    - Describe networking and evangelism strategies (The Strategic Plan).
- What will be the process for discipling believers?
    - Describe the intended process for making mature disciples.
- How long will it take?
    - Describe a realistic timeline for the project.
- How much will it cost?
    - Include a start-up budget and expected funding streams.
    - Define a funding strategy.
- How can others help?
    - Invite physical, financial, and prayer participation.

APPENDIX E

Assessment Center Categories and Questions

An assessment center should assess candidates for church planting in the following four categories (in Spanish, as necessary): 1) Cultural IQ Competencies; 2) Interpersonal and Relational Competencies; 3) Professional Competencies; 4) Character and Spiritual Competencies. The following questions for each category are how the candidates would ideally be assessed in each of the four areas:

Category:	Questions for assessing preparedness:
Cultural IQ Competencies* (*note that the Intercultural Development Inventory mentioned in Chapter 12 may prove useful in assessing this category)	• Where is the candidate most suitable on the cultural evolutionary continuum? • Does the candidate embody the aspirations of those he desires to lead? • Is the candidate incarnational, possessing the skill to be effective in a culture not of his first affinity? • Does the candidate understand "mainstream" culture and possess a collegial spirit in relation to it? • What is the candidate's language proficiency and its implications for his target? • What is the candidate's calling and dream? Does he understand his calling and can he clearly articulate it? • Does the candidate possess biblical impartiality when ministering to groups significantly different from him?
Interpersonal and Relational Competencies	• Does the candidate love people? Does he enjoy people and see the awesomeness in all image bearers? • Is the candidate outgoing? Does he make friends easily? Are people attracted to him? • Is the candidate humble and teachable? Does he accept mentoring? • Is the candidate a team player? Does he work with others, both in the mission/church, and in his support network? • Is the candidate humble? Is he willing to work with others to disciple second- and third-generation, if his English is limited? • Is the candidate married, and if so, is his wife called to church planting? Is there any obstacle in the marriage

Category:	Questions for assessing preparedness:
Interpersonal and Relational Competencies (con't)	that would preclude church planting? Is the couple hospitable, welcoming strangers into their lives and home in the way the Trinitarian God does? • Does the candidate have a covenantal family? Is he training up his children in the fear and admonition of the Lord? Is he conscientiously providing for his wife spiritually and in her areas of competence? • Is the couple able to do marriage counseling? Individually and/or collectively? • Is the candidate's family an asset to ministry?
Professional Competencies	• Is the candidate very sure of his calling and willing to make the extreme sacrifices that will be required of him? • Is the candidate a leader/entrepreneur or an administrator/maintenance man? • Is the candidate a preacher/teacher or even primarily a theologian, or is he an evangelist/gatherer/disciple-maker? He must give evidence of evangelistic fruitfulness and ability to gather. • Does the candidate preach in such a way that makes the hearer think, "I wish my unsaved friends were here"? • Is the candidate committed to Reformed theology/covenantal theology and comprehend its fitness and application to Hispanic and Roman Catholic culture? • Is the candidate knowledgeable and conversant in Roman Catholic distinctives and their negative impact on a biblical understanding of the grace, freedom, joy and assurance we have in Christ? • Is the candidate competent in leadership development? Does he have disciples who are now pastoring, teaching, and leading others? • What kind of leader is he? A lion (aggressive and forthright)? A fox (he may do an end run, but he gets it done)? A lamb (need not apply)? Is he exclusively a cacique, or has he developed a participatory style where he is not afraid to delegate? • Does he know his primary and secondary spiritual gifts? Does he know where he needs help in his leadership or organizational style?

Category:	Questions for assessing preparedness:
Personal and Spiritual Competencies	<ul><li>How would you gage the candidate's spiritual formation and maturity? What is his prayer life like? What are his study habits in the Word of God and other readings?</li><li>What is the nature of his physical health? What are his personal disciplines of caring for God's temple? Does he enjoy and contemplate the beauty of the Lord in His creation?</li><li>Is the candidate vulnerable, available, and sensitive to others and their interests and needs?</li><li>Is the candidate humble in the sense that he sees himself as sinner saved by grace, and that what he is, he is by the grace of God?</li><li>Is the candidate confident and assured of God's grace, love, acceptance and favor on him in Christ so that he can joyfully and contagiously communicate that assurance to others?</li><li>Is the candidate able to witness effectively to non-Christians who are morally superior to him?</li><li>Is the candidate committed to his citizenship in heaven and to his identity to the people of God and the one holy nation, or does his nationalistic pride teeter toward idolatry?</li><li>Is the candidate able to "take off" or "put on" culture like the Apostle Paul to become all things to all men in order to win the greatest number possible?</li></ul>

While such an assessment center in Spanish for rising church planters in the Hispanic context does not currently exist, it is exciting that conversations are happening around this need. It is the desire that these questions may help provide a sounding point for assessing candidates, and also a jumping off point for working together to develop this much-needed resource.

DEFINITIONS OF KEY TERMS

- **bi-vocational vs. co-vocational:** While these terms are sometimes used interchangeably, bi-vocational pastors typically have the desire to work as a full-time pastor, but are willing to serve bi-vocationally in order to be able to do the work of ministry; co-vocational pastors, on the other hand, see their two vocations working together indefinitely as part of the way the Lord has called them to ministry.
- *comunidad:* Literally, "community," but within the Hispanic context, the significance is more than simply a neighborhood and its surroundings, but a tightly-knit group of neighbors sharing life with one another.
- *confianza:* Literally, "confidence" or "trust"; yet in the Hispanic context, this word goes further to speak to a sense of mutual reciprocity in a relationship, in which both parties recognize a sense of deep and abiding trust and commitment to one another through the development of a long-term relationship (aka, *gente de confianza*).
- **connectionalism:** A word used within Evangelical circles to describe the need for pastors and churches to be connected with one another, and seek to make connections with other bodies for the glory of God and building up of the Church.
- **core group vs. launch team:** There is a technical difference between the terms "core group" and "launch team." Most majority-culture churches start with a ***core group***: a biblically and theologically trained group of volunteers who are committed to helping the church plant grow and thrive in a particular area. A committed core group is part of what enables majority-culture churches to launch worship quickly and effectively. On the other hand, ***launch team*** refers to the group of individuals that scratch planters form and train in order to help them be able to reach and disciple individuals prior to public launch. As most Hispanic church planters will, by default, employ a launch team over a core group, this book primarily uses this term, although it may also use core group from time-to-time, recognizing that there may be (rare) instances in which such terminology could fit the Hispanic church planting scenario.

escuela dominical: While the literal translation is "Sunday school," in the Hispanic community, the idea specifically refers to church instruction for children on Sundays or during the worship service, and does not speak to further adult classes or instruction.

Hispanic vs. Latino: Historically, "Hispanic" refers to people from Spanish-speaking Latin-America, while "Latino" refers to those from any of the Latin-American countries, regardless of language. In spite of these different origins, these terms tend to be used interchangeably today to describe individuals with Latin-American ancestry in the United States. Studies have shown that U.S. Hispanics/Latinos are equally divided on preference for terminology, with a slightly higher preference for "Latino" as a racial identification. Therefore, this book will use the terms interchangeably, as they are used throughout the United States today.

machista: Literally, a "male chauvinist," or within the Hispanic community, typically referring to men who have the need to prove themselves as the *jefe* (boss) within a relationship and show excessive dominance (potentially with aggression), resulting in damage both to the relationship of the couple, but also to any children who may be involved.

reproduction vs. multiplication: A **reproducing** church is defined as one that has been directly involved in supporting, providing for, and opening a new, autonomous church work within the past year; a **multiplying** church takes this definition a step further by being involved in a greater number of church plants per year, while also being significantly active in raising up new church planters: preparing them, sending them, and financially supporting them.

sazón: Literally "seasoning" or "flavor," but can be used colloquially to speak of something or someone with a full personality or gravitas. Something with *sazón* is filled with just the right flavor and spice, either literally or culturally.

tienda: Literally a shop or a store, but tends to bear a more significant meaning within the Hispanic context of a community-based local shop or general store.

¿Vale la pena? Literally, "Is it worth it?", a common Spanish phrase used to determine whether the potential results of an action are worth the cost involved to get there.

vecindarios: More than simply a neighborhood, *vecindarios* represent the joining of many dwelling near one another into one, connected group. They may represent a large group of neighbors in the same building, neighborhood, or area of town.

RESOURCES

Cultural Awareness Resource:

Intercultural Development Inventory: <<https://idiinventory.com/>>.

Spanish-language resources for training leaders:

Books:

Bavink, Herman. *Nuestro Dios maravilloso: una teología sistemática*. Spanish Edition. Translated by Publicaciones Kerigma. Salem, Oregon: Publicaciones Kerigma, 2020.

Burkholder, Justin. *Sobre la roca: un modelo para iglesias que plantan iglesias*. Nashville: B&H Publishing Group, 2018.

Calvino, Juan. *Institución de la Religión Cristiana*. Spanish Edition. Translated by Juan Carlos Martín. Grand Rapids: Libros Desafío, 2012.

Coxe, Nehemiah. *Ancianos y diáconos bíblicos*. Spanish Edition. Pensacola: Chapel Library, 2017.

Frazee, Randy, and Robert Noland. *Creer – pensar, actuar, ser como Jesús*. Spanish Edition. Translated by Belmonte traductores. Grand Rapids: Zondervan, 2014.

Helm, David. *La predicación expositiva: cómo proclamar la Palabra de Dios hoy*. Spanish Edition. Translated by Jorge Eduardo Peña and Gustavo Morel. Wheaton: Crossway, 2014.

Hodge, Charles. *Teología Sistemática*. Spanish Edition. Translated by Santiago Escuain. Barcelona: Editorial Calidad en Literatura Evangélica, 2010.

Keller, Timothy. *Iglesia centrada*. Spanish Edition. Translated by Athala Jaramillo. Miami: Editorial Vida, 2012.

Matthews, Andrew W.G. *Núcleo de la Fuerza Cristiana: Guía de discipulado anual para conocer y vivir las doctrinas cristianas*. Spanish Edition. Translated by José Portillo. Independently Published, 2019.

Ramsay, Richard B. *Católicos y protestantes: ¿cuál es la diferencia?* Spanish Edition. Medley, Florida: Editorial Unilit, 2005.

Ramsay, Richard B. *¿Cuán Bueno Debo Ser? Aprendiendo a vivir por la gracia de Dios*. Spanish Edition. Barcelona: Editorial Calidad en Literatura Evangélica, 2009.

Rinne, Jeramie. *Los Ancianos de la Igelsia: cómo pastorear al pueblo de Dios como Jesús.* Spanish Edition. Translated by Daniel Puerto. Colombia: Poiema Publicaciones, 2015.

Strauch, Alexander. *Liderazgo bíblico de ancianos: Restaurando el liderazgo bíblico de las iglesias.* Spanish Edition. Translated by Spanish Translations Ministry: Dante N. Rosso, Director. Pensacola: Chapel Library, 2008.

Thune, Robert H., and Will Walker. *La vida centrada en el evangelio.* Spanish Edition. Wheaton: Crossway, 2021.

Van Dixhoorn, Chad. *La fe que confesamos: una guía de studio a la Confesión de Fe de Westminister.* Spanish Edition. Translated by Timoteo Sazo. East Peoria: Versa Press Inc., 2022.

Warfield, B.B. *La persona y la obra de Jesucristo.* Spanish Edition. Barcelona: Editorial Calidad en Literatura Evangélica.

Spanish Translation and Publishing Companies:

Poiema Publicaciones: <<https://poiema.co/>>

Children's Ministry International, Inc., Translations: <<https://www.childministry.com/cmi-translations>>.

Many of Tim Keller's works have been translated into Spanish and are available for purchase online through Amazon and other sellers.

Websites, Seminaries, and Institutes:

City to City (Redeemer Tim Keller) Discipleship in Spanish: <<https://www.citytocitylatam.com/>>.

Clase Internacional de Teología Aplicada CITA-EDU, Inc: <<https://citaedu.org/es/home-espanol-2/>>.

Seminario LAMP Español: <<http://seminariolamp.org/>>.

Thirdmill Institute in Spanish: <<http://thirdmill.org/>>.

Immigration Resources:

Bier, David J. "'Why Don't They Just Get in Line?' Barriers to Legal Immigration." Cato Institute. April 28, 2021. https://www.cato.org/testimony/why-dont-they-just-get-line-barriers-legal-immigration#documented-immigration.

Deymaz, Mark, M. Daniel Carroll R., and Matthew Soerens. "Illegal Immigrants in the Church? Christian thinkers weigh in on what churches should do about meeting the sojourner." *Christianity Today.* March 1, 2011.

Fikse, Susan. "Immigration: Reforming Hearts as well as Policy." *By Faith Magazine.* May 12th, 2014.

Metro Atlanta Presbytery Immigration Overture. Metro Atlanta Presbytery, PCA. 2018.

Nazario, Sonia. *Enrique's Journey: The Story of a Boy's Dangerous Odyssey to Reunite with His Mother.* New York: Random House, 2014.

Payne, J.D. *Strangers Next Door: Immigration, Migration, and Mission.* Downers Grove: InterVarsity Press, 2012.

For further reading and study:

Chan, Sam. *Evangelism in a Skeptical World: How to Make the Unbelievable News about Jesus More Believable.* Grand Rapids: Zondervan, 2018.

Chan, Sam. *How to Talk about Jesus (Without Being That Guy): Personal Evangelism in a Skeptical World.* Grand Rapids: Zondervan, 2020.

Gonzalez, Juan. *Harvest of Empire: A History of Latinos in America.* Revised Edition. New York: Penguin Books, 2011.

Martinez, Juan Francisco. *Walking with the People: Latino Ministry in the United States.* Eugene: Wipf & Stock, 2016.

Moran, David L. "Manual for Church Planting Among Hispanic Americans." Distributed by Mission to North America, 2003.

Pérez, Rich. *Mi Casa Uptown: Learning to Love Again.* Nashville: B&H Publishing Group, 2017.

Rodriguez, Daniel A. *A Future for the Latino Church: Models for Multilingual, Multigenerational Hispanic Congregations.* Downers Grove: IVP Academic, 2011.

Sánchez, Daniel R. *Hispanic Realities Impacting America: Implications for Evangelism & Missions.* Fort Worth: Church Starting Network, 2006.

Smed, John. *Prayer Revolution: Rebuilding Church and City Through Prayer.* Chicago: Moody, 2020.

Taylor, Braden E. "A Handbook for Planting Hispanic American Churches in the Southeastern United States." Doctoral thesis, Reformed Theological Seminary, Charlotte, 2021.

NOTES

[1] Daniel E. Martínez and Kelsey E. Gonzalez, "'Latino' or 'Hispanic'? The Sociodemographic Correlates of Panethnic Label Preferences among U.S. Latinos/Hispanics," *Sociological Perspectives*, Vol. 64, no. 3 (June 2021): 365–386.

[2] Aristotle (384 BC – 322 BC), *The Nicomachean Ethics*.

[3] Nelson Searcy, "Church Planting Focus – Launch Team versus Core Group," *ChurchLeaderInsights.com* (March 14, 2012), https://churchleaderinsights.com/church-planting-focus-launch-team-versus-core-group/.

[4] G. K. Beale and Mitchell Kim, *God Dwells Among Us: A Biblical Theology of the Temple* (Downer's Grove: Intervarsity Press, 2021), 81-82.

[5] Rich Pérez, *Mi Casa Uptown: Learning to Love Again* (Nashville: B&H Publishing Group, 2017), 165.

[6] Timothy Keller, "The Decline and Renewal of the American Church: Part 3 – The Path to Renewal," *Gospel in Life* (Spring 2022), https://quarterly.gospelinlife.com/american-church-the-path-to-renewal/.

[7] John Piper, *Let the Nations Be Glad*, 3rd ed. (Grand Rapids: Baker Academic, 2010), 15.

[8] M. Campesino, and G.E. Schwartz, "Latinas/os: implications of culture in conceptualization and measurement." *ANS Advanced Nursing Science* 29 no.1 (Jan-Mar 2006): 69-81.

[9] B. Schneider, S. Martinez, and A. Ownes, "Barriers to Educational Opportunities for Hispanics in the United States" in *National Research Counsel (US) Panel on Hispanics in the United States*, edited by M. Tienda and F. Mitchell, *Hispanics and the Future of America* (Washington, DC: National Academic Press, 2006), https://www.ncbi.nlm.nih.gov/books/NBK19909/.

[10] Aaron Earls, "New Hispanic Churches Often Do More With Less," *Lifeway Research* (July 24, 2019), https://research.lifeway.com/2019/07/24/new-hispanic-churches-often-do-more-with-less/.

[11] The Barna Group, "New Study Shows Trends in Tithing and Donating," released in *Leaders & Pastors* (April 14, 2008), https://www.barna.com/research/new-study-shows-trends-in-tithing-and-donating/.

[12] Peggy Halpern, "Refugee Economic Self-Sufficiency: An Exploratory Study of Approaches Used in Office of Refugee Resettlement Programs," *U.S. Department of Health and Human Services: Office of the Assistant Secretary for Planning and Evaluation* (November, 2008), https://www.aspe.hhs.gov/sites/default/files/migrated_legacy_files/42911/report.pdf.

[13] Steve Shadrach, *Fully Funding Your Ministry: 5 Keys to Personal Support Raising* (Ebook, Fayetteville: Center for Mission Mobilization Press), https://supportraisingsolutions.org/wp-content/uploads/2013/06/SRS_5Keys_eBook.pdf???.

[14] Roberto Suro, Sergio Bendixen, B. Lindsay Lowell, and Dulce C. Benavides, *Billions in Motion: Latino Immigrants, Remittances and Banking* (Washington, D.C: Pew Hispanic Center, 2010), https://www.pewresearch.org/wp-content/uploads/sites/5/reports/13.pdf.

[15] Meaghan Winter, "The Fastest-Growing Group of American Evangelicals," *The Atlantic* (July 26, 2021), https://www.theatlantic.com/culture/archive/2021/07/latinos-will-determine-future-american-evangelicalism/619551/.

[16] Lifeway Research, "Becoming Five Multiplication Study," sponsored by *Exponential.org* (February 2019), http://research.lifeway.com/wp-content/uploads/2019/03/2019 ExponentialReport.pdf.

[17] Intercultural Development Inventory, https://idiinventory.com/.

[18] Dr. Amy K. Glasmeier, "Living Wage Calculator," *Massachusetts Institute of Technology* (2022), https://livingwage.mit.edu/.

[19] "Standing Rules: Appendix 1," from the PCA *Book of Church Order* (November 2021).

Hernando Sáenz and his wife Debbie are uniquely gifted for Hispanic ministry in the USA. Hernando is an ordained pastor in the PCA. He and Debbie live in Atlanta, GA, and have four children and six grandchildren. Hernando was born in Bogotá, Colombia and lived there until he was 15 years old. In 1979 his family immigrated to Miami, Florida where he lived until 1982. From 1982 to 1986, he served overseas in the United States Air Force. He met his wife Debbie, a native Floridian, upon his return to Florida in 1986.

Hernando and Debbie were born again under the ministry of PCA pastor Rev. Al LaCour and married in 1990 in Immanuel PCA church in Miami.

In 1992, Hernando and Debbie started attending Christ Covenant PCA Church in Broward County, Florida where Hernando began his mentorship under the ministry of Rev. Brian Kelso. He was ordained as a Deacon and served as chairman of the Diaconate until his ordination as a Ruling Elder. In 1995, Hernando accepted a position on the church staff to oversee all the church ministries. From 1998 until 2001 he served as the youth pastor.

In 2001, Hernando was licensed to preach by the Presbytery of Southern Florida. Later that year he planted Iglesia Principe de Paz, in Broward County, Florida. In 2005, he earned an M.Div from LAMP Theological Seminary and was ordained by the Presbytery of Southern Florida.

The Sáenz family moved to Atlanta, Georgia in June 2006 to plant Grace International Church: a multicultural and bilingual church. Grace International Church merged with Christos Community Church, a bilingual PCA mission church, when Hernando joined the staff of Mission to North America in January 2011 as Hispanic Ministries Coordinator. The vision of MNA Hispanic Ministries is to fulfill the Great Commission by starting a movement of PCA churches committed to reaching Hispanics in the United States with the gospel. In fulfillment of this vision, the passion is to see new churches planted, new leaders developed, and existing churches equipped for thriving ministry.

Debbie Sáenz was born in Miami, Florida, and has loved art since childhood. She is talented in many styles and subjects, including mixed-media, abstracts, and representational. She works in both acrylics and oils, although she prefers painting in oil. Debbie enjoys allowing her art to reflect her faith, as she creates art to bear witness to our creative, artistic God. Her art may be found at debbiesaenz.com.

Made in the USA
Columbia, SC
07 October 2022